Library of
Davidson College

**Policy Studies in America
and Elsewhere**

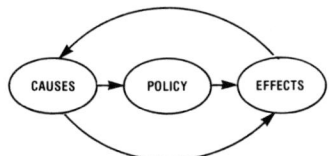

Policy Studies Organization Series

1. *Policy Studies in America and Elsewhere*
    by Stuart S. Nagel
2. *Policy Studies and the Social Sciences*
    by Stuart S. Nagel
3. *Methodologies for Analyzing Public Policies*
    by Thomas Cook and Frank Scioli
4. *Analyzing Poverty Policy*
    by Dorothy James
5. *Crime and Criminal Justice: Issues in Public Policy Analysis*
    by John A. Gardiner and Michael A. Mulkey
6. *Perspectives on Urban Policy*
    by Robert L. Lineberry and Louis H. Masotti
7. *Complex Policy Systems: Problems of Theory*
    by Phillip M. Gregg

Policy Studies in America and Elsewhere

Edited by
Stuart S. Nagel
University of Illinois

Lexington Books
D.C. Heath and Company
Lexington, Massachusetts
Toronto   London

Library of Congress Cataloging in Publication Data

Main entry under title:

Policy studies in America and elsewhere.

"Based on symposia coordinated by the Policy Studies Organization."

1. Policy sciences. I. Nagel, Stuart S., 1934- II. Policy Studies Organization.
H62.P59   309.2'12   75-2292
ISBN 0-669-99549-5

Copyright © 1975 by D.C. Heath and Company

All rights reserved. No part of this publication may be reproduced or transmitted in any form or by any means, electronic or mechanical, including photocopy, recording, or any information storage or retrieval system, without permission in writing from the publisher.

Published simultaneously in Canada.

Printed in the United States of America

International Standard Book Number: 0-669-99549-5

Library of Congress Catalog Card Number: 75-2292

Dedicated to the application

of political science

to important policy problems

Contents

	Introduction	xi
Part I	**General Approaches**	1
Chapter 1	**General Policy Science** *Yehezkel Dror*	3
	The Challenge	4
	Institutional Growth	6
	Developments outside the United States	12
Chapter 2	**Empirical Research Methods** *Thomas Cook, Frank Scioli, Barbara Salmore,* and *Stephen Salmore*	17
	Policy Analysis in Political Science: Trends and Issues in Empirical Research	17
	Resources for Public Policy Analysis	21
	The Comparative Study of Public Policy	24
Chapter 3	**Theory of Public Policy** *Vincent Ostrom* and *Philip Sabetti*	37
	Basic Issues and References	37
	Basic Facilities and Institutions	39
	European Contributions	41
Chapter 4	**Comparative Public Policy** *Richard Rose*	51
	Why Comparative Policy Studies?	51
	Resources for Policy Studies in Britain	54
	Concepts for Comparison	61
Chapter 5	**Administering Public Policy** *H. George Frederickson, Michael D. Reagan,* and *Alfred Diamant*	69
	Basic Issues and References	69
	Bureaucracy and Administration in Western Europe: A Case of Not-So-Benign Neglect	73

Part II	**Specific Policy Problems**	81
Chapter 6	**Environmental Policy** *Dean Mann, Geoffrey Wandesforde-Smith,* and *Lennart Lundqvist*	83
	Basic Issues and References	83
	Basic Facilities and Institutions	89
	Comparative Research on Environmental Policy	93
Chapter 7	**Free Speech and Civil Liberties Policy** *Samuel Krislov*	101
	Basic Issues and References	101
	Basic Facilities and Institutions	104
Chapter 8	**Economic Regulation Policy** *James E. Anderson*	109
	Recent Issues and Developments	109
	Sources for the Study of Economic Regulatory Policies	114
Chapter 9	**Electoral Policy** *William Crotty*	119
	Basic Issues and References	119
	Basic Facilities and Institutions	125
	Comparative Electoral Policy	128
Chapter 10	**Foreign Policy** *Richard L. Merritt*	133
	Public Opinion and Foreign Policy	134
	Foreign Policy Leadership	145
	Appendix 10A: Peace Research—The Search for Focus	154
Chapter 11	**Crime and Criminal Justice Policy** *John A. Gardiner* and *John Conrad*	161
	Crime and Criminal Justice Policy Issues in the United States	161
	The European Perspective on Policy Issues in Crime Control	168
Chapter 12	**Educational Policy** *Samuel K. Gove, Frederick Wirt,* and *William Walker*	175
	Basic Issues and References	175

	Resources for the Study of Education Policy	178
	Comparative Educational Policy	184
Chapter 13	**Poverty and Welfare Policy** *Theodore Marmor* and *Hugh Heclo*	199
	Some Preliminary Observations	199
	Basic Facilities and Institutions	202
	Comparative Poverty and Welfare Policy	204
	Index of Names	211
	Index of Subjects	219
	About the Contributors	225
	About the Editor	231

Introduction

This is the first book in a series of policy studies volumes to be published by Lexington Books based on symposia coordinated by the Policy Studies Organization. Each of those symposia will either be devoted to a specific policy problem or to a general approach to analyzing policy problems. Both kinds of symposia will be dealt with mainly from a political science perspective which emphasizes the relevance of government involvement in order to resolve the policy problems discussed. This perspective is in conformity with the primary purpose of the Policy Studies Organization, which is to promote the application of political science to important policy problems.

In discussing the role of governmental attempts to resolve various social problems, the editors of the volumes and the authors of the specific chapters will deal with issues relating to what *causes* government policies to be what they are, and to what are the *effects* of alternative government policies. Those two viewpoints are closely interrelated in the sense that actual or perceived policy effects are significant causes of future policies. An understanding of policy causation is also essential to analyzing the effects of policies on subsequent policies and to being able to make realistically feasible policy recommendations.

This first volume is designed to provide a survey of the basic issues, references, and institutions relating to the more important policy problems with which political science has been associated. These problems include environmental protection, civil liberties, economic regulation, election reform, foreign relations, crime, and poverty. This volume is also designed to provide a survey of the basic issues, references, and institutions relating to various general approaches which cut across those policy problems. These approaches include the relevance of empirical research methods, political theory, cross-national comparisons, and public administration. The chapter authors generally indicate what research has been done on the issues both in the United States and elsewhere. They also describe the basic institutions in each field which include journals, sources of grants, university programs, non-academic research institutes, data sources, and interest groups.

Future 1975 volumes in this PSO Policy Studies Series will be devoted to such themes as *Policy Studies and the Social Sciences* (edited by Stuart Nagel), the *Methodology of Policy Studies* (edited by Thomas Cook and Frank Scioli), *Analyzing Poverty Policy* (edited by Dorothy James), *Electoral Reform* (edited by Edward Tufte), and *Crime and Criminal Justice* (edited by John Gardiner and Michael Mulkey). Volumes scheduled for 1976 will be devoted to such themes as *Foreign Policy Studies* (edited by Richard Merritt), *Policy Studies and Political Theory* (edited by Vincent

Ostrom and Phillip Gregg), *Urban Policy Problems* (edited by Louis Masotti and Robert Lineberry), *Economic Regulatory Policy* (edited by James Anderson), and *The Politics of Education* (edited by Samuel Gove and Frederick Wirt).

All this activity with regard to the application of political science to important policy problems would not have been so likely to occur ten years ago. At that time, political scientists (in publishing for the leading political science journals) were emphasizing the application of quantitative techniques to understanding the behavior and especially the decisional propensities of various political actors such as voters, legislators, judges, and administrators. They were also busy analyzing the role of groups in influencing those political actors. When not taking a decision-making or group perspective, they were often describing the legalistic or institutional structures of governmental entities in a more traditional perspective.

In the late 1960s, a shift in the interests of prominent political scientists became apparent. A landmark occurrence was the inaugural address of David Easton as president of the American Political Science Association. His address was entitled "The New Revolution in Political Science." The revolution that he referred to consisted of applying scientific methods to problems that have broad significance to both policymakers and also to scholars interested in the causes and effects of political matters. This development is sometimes referred to as the post-behavioral movement within political science to indicate that it combines the behavioral quantitative methodology of the post-World War II period extending into the 1960s with the non-scientific concern for policy relevance of the pre-World War II period. This development is also sometimes referred to as the policy studies movement.

There are various reasons for this new concern with being both politically relevant and scientific. New applicable methods have been developed by mathematicians and computer scientists. The Vietnam war, the civil rights movement, and other social problems have aroused political scientists as well as others. Contacts have increased between political scientists on the one hand and economists, sociologists, and psychologists on the other. A virtual saturation point had also been reached with regard to quantifying what many had considered redundant political trivia.

Indicators of the new public policy trend within political science include the increasing list of relevant articles, books, convention papers, courses, book series, job openings, foundation grants, and summer institutes in the public policy field. Recent annual surveys by the American Political Science Association of major political science departments show that policy studies is the most rapidly developing field within political science. One additional indicator is the establishment and the expansion of the Policy Studies Organization. Another indicator is the establishment of the new

PSO Policy Studies Series published by Lexington Books in conjunction with the Policy Studies Organization which this volume inaugurates.

The Policy Studies Organization was founded in 1971 at the annual meeting of the American Political Science Association to promote the application of political science to important policy problems. It is designed to have a cooperative relation with the APSA like the Society for the Study of Social Problems has with the American Sociological Association. Its more specific purposes include publishing the *Policy Studies Journal* (whose symposia issues provide the basis for the expanded books in the Policy Studies Series), the *Policy Studies Directory* (describing policy studies activities in political science departments), the *Yearbooks in Politics and Public Policy* (synthesizing policy studies papers from the annual APSA convention, regional political science meetings, and other sources), and the *Applied Policy Studies Directory* (describing the use of political science research and personnel in government agencies). The organization also provides an information clearinghouse of policy studies matters, encourages relevant panels at conventions and conferences, and seeks to improve communication between political scientists, governmental practitioners, and other policy-oriented social scientists.

The policy studies perspective of emphasizing the policy relevance of political science is not meant to replace traditional or behavioral political science. Rather it is meant to add a dimension to political science research, teaching, and other activities that has possibly been relatively lacking in the past. Many political scientists and others feel that political science has or should have something to contribute to policy-making and policy-applying. One would think the study of political science would have more relevance to the political policy-making that occurs among legislators, high level administrators, and appellate court judges than it does. However, an analysis of congressional hearings, administrative rule-making proceedings, and Supreme Court opinions has generally revealed very few references to political science research. Such an analysis though might reveal frequent references to the works of scholars like natural scientists, economists, and psychologists. It is hoped that this volume on *Policy Studies in America and Elsewhere* and this Policy Studies Series will help further to indicate and stimulate the relevance of political science to important policy problems.

Stuart S. Nagel

Part I
General Approaches

1

General Policy Science

Yehezkel Dror

The idea of "policy studies" is an old one, going back in contents, though not in terminology, to founders of social sciences such as Bentham and Von Stein and reaching quite high levels of sophistication in more modern writings, such as Pareto's. Even the concept "policy sciences"—which I prefer, without necessarily insisting on its use—goes back more than twenty years. The questions must be faced, what if anything is innovative about the modern interest in policy sciences, and can these new features provide a basis for hope that such an endeavor may be more successful now and in the foreseeable future than similar interests and attempts in the past.

My answer to these questions is a double one: first, the contemporary policy sciences endeavor has a stronger intellectual basis, enjoys more developed knowledge foundations, and is more broadly supported than parallel efforts in the past; second, the contemporary policy sciences endeavor has reached a degree of institutionalization which does provide a possible starting line for a real take-off phase. These two answers provide no assurance of success, but do support some hope for the future of policy sciences—both in their descriptive-explanatory and in their prescriptive dimensions.

Description-explanation and prescription constitute integrated aspects of policy sciences, with consequences for methodology, such as need for shared concept packages and models. At the same time, the differences between these dimensions are very important, the main addition of a policy studies approach to "normal" social sciences being the emphasis on prescription and the search for methodologies which permit transformation of descriptive-explanatory findings and of analyzed values into preferable prescriptions. To avoid miscommunication, care must be taken when using various concepts—such as "policy analysis"—to make clear whether one uses them as referring to description-explanation (e.g., "policy analysis" as an attempt to explain the production of policies, as used, among others, by Thomas Dye and Ira Sharkansky) or as referring to prescription (e.g., "policy analysis" as an attempt to improve complex and heuristic decision-making, as used, among others, by myself).

This chapter is devoted, in its first part, to an exploration of the policy sciences challenge from a political science perspective, so that the intellec-

---

This chapter has been rewritten and updated, on the basis of articles published in the *Policy Studies Journal* 1, 1 and 2 (1973).

tual needs may be better understood;[1] and, in the second part, to a description of ongoing institutional growth of policy sciences, so as to demonstrate the basis for an optimistic view of the possibilities to satisfy needs and meet successfully the policy sciences challenge.

I. The Challenge

The present politics of political science being as they are, the idea of promoting the application of political science to important policy problems seems to need little justification. Who today dares to oppose "relevance" and who would disagree with the statement that scientists must contribute to the reduction of human suffering and the resolution of social problems?

But matters are more complex than that. There is a big difference between political scientists, even prominent ones, making statements about important policy problems and "application of political science" to policy issues. Application of science requires more than advocacy of predetermined positions with the help of scientific terminology. Even a majority vote by political scientists in respect to a concrete policy issue —however perhaps important as an exercise of the democratic rights and duties of political scientists in their capacity as (hopefully) enlightened citizen—cannot be regarded as "application of political science to important policy problems."

The least that is required for application of political science to policy problems is an explicit methodology for identifying preferable policies on the basis of scientific knowledge, that is: a prescriptive methodology. Additional requisites for applying political science to policy problems include, among others, the following:

1. Capacity to handle value issues in a way which distinguished between fundamental value choice and instrumental consideration of intermediate goals. In respect to fundamental value choice, clarification of the choice dimensions is needed, such as: consistency, trade-offs, time-evaluation, and risk propensities ("lottery values").[2] More important and nearer to the core of political science, social mechanism for determining choice between irreducable fundamental value mixes must be redesigned and even nova-designed (i.e., designed anew), for instance in respect to citizen participation, and in respect to presentation and explanation of alternatives in the mass media of communication.

2. Adjustment of paradigms, methods, methodologies and techniques to the needs of policy improvement. This involves, for instance, changes in the standards of validity and reliability: in respect to policy, preferization in the sense of arriving at solutions better than would otherwise be the case is the main goal. Usually, because of lack of time and complexity of issues,

preferable solutions will fall short from the requirements of "scientific truth," even when constituting significant improvements in social reality. Another illustration of needed new methodologies is social experimentation. Identification of better policies often requires pilot-testing, that is: social experimentation in real settings. Developing of suitable methodologies, which also make social experimentation politically feasible and morally acceptable, is something quite new for political science (and all other social sciences).[3]

3. New institutional frameworks for working on real policy problems, for developing policy-relevant knowledge and for educating students for policy-relevant work. This involves interdisciplinary teams, access to real issues, clinical teaching methods, and academic recognition for policy consultative studies.

Most fundamental is the already mentioned need for a prescriptive methodology, that is a methodology for moving from fundamental values, on the one hand, and from empirical and theoretical knowledge and concepts, on the other hand, to preferable policy alternatives. To be frank, I think political science is rather weak in prescriptive methodology. Political science is much better equipped than other social sciences for handling value issues, because of the traditional interest in political philosophy. Political science is also better equipped than other social sciences in respect to much of the empirical and theoretical knowledge, because, after all, policy-making is fundamentally a political process. But prescriptive methodologies are much better developed in economics, planning theory, management sciences and systems analysis. True, those disciplines and approaches have largely failed in their efforts to handle complex policy issues, mainly because of their inability to handle politics and political institutions. Nevertheless, they are much better developed than political science in respect to prescriptive methodologies. Therefore, a main need for application of political science to important policy problems is for fusion of traditional political science approaches with the instrumental-normative contents of the decision disciplines into a prescriptive methodology capable of contributing to complex policy issues.[4]

When speaking about the application of political science to policy problems, it is essential to consider the time dimension. Adopting a short time perspective, the main mission is to help in identification of preferable solutions to presently pressing policy problems. This surely is legitimate and necessary. At the same time, allocation of most of our mental and intellectual resources to current problems because of our sensitivities to present human misery is surely a mistake of which we must beware. New and even more difficult problems are sure to emerge, early cognition of which may permit much more effective treatment. More important, as political scientists, we must be constantly aware of the dependency of polities on the characteristics of the policy-making system. This leads, I think, to a most important conclusion: Improvements of policies depend largely on reform of the policy-making system.[5] Here, again, political science has a distinct advantage over the other social sciences, because of its traditional concern with the effectiveness and improvement of political and administrative institutions. It would be a great loss if exclusive involvement in pressing current issues leads to loss of this advantage— especially as the chances for adoption of significantly better policies without real changes in the policy-making system seem low.

My additional conclusion is, therefore, that concern with the improvement of policy-making, as distinguished from the preferization of discrete policies, must be a main concern of application of political science to important policy problems, within an integrated policy studies approach.

Adopting the concept coined by Harold D. Lasswell about twenty years ago, I recommend the term *policy sciences* as a verbal symbol for the special knowledge concerned with the application of political science, together with other social sciences and decision sciences, to policy problems. But the term does not matter. What matters is acceptance of the mission and recognition of the need for suitable changes in paradigms, methods, and institutions.

Quite a number of new books, periodicals, conferences, university programs, and collections of like-minded scholars testify to growing interest in policy sciences, however called. Up till now, most of this activity took place in isolation from one another. This is a pity. The endeavor is intellectually so difficult, emotionally so frustrating, and institutionally so resisted as to make mutual learning, cooperation, and support between those accepting the challenge urgently necessary. This requires, inter alia, significant changes in parts of political science and much self-innovation by those of political scientists who accept the challenge of policy sciences as their main profession and vocation.[6]

The challenge of policy sciences and the chances of meeting them are, in part, reflected in institutional growth, some consideration of which will serve to complete our initial look at the subject.

II. Institutional Growth

Policy sciences is quite a broad field, the domain of which is still fluid and the boundaries of which are not easy to define. Systems analysis, applications of operations research and management sciences to policy issues, planning, systems engineering, evaluation studies, social indicators and social problem mapping, urban studies, futures studies, applied social sciences in their various manifestations, parts of public administration and organization theory, psychology of judgment and thinking, and, of course, parts of political science—all these and other disciplines and foci of research and teaching are closely related to policy sciences, overlapping with in it various degrees. With time, the unique characteristics of policy sciences will become clearer and its differentation from other areas of research and teaching will become more apparent. But at present, with policy sciences being in its incipient phases, it is very difficult to decide which institutional development should be labeled as "policy sciences" and which are too distant from the core paradigms of policy sciences to justify their consideration within the context of policy sciences.

At the present state of development of policy sciences no clear answer to this problem is possible or desirable. This chapter adopts a rather strict criterion for inclusion of institutional developments within the domain of policy sciences: only institutional innovations and events which both (a) explicitly use policy studies-related terms (such as "policy sciences," "policy analysis," "public policy studies," etc.) and (b) in substance focus on the study and improvement of complex policies and complex policy-making systems through an interdisciplinary approach, are considered within my discussion of "institutional growth of policy sciences."

This should be regarded as a preliminary and personal survey, which identifies only some of the relevant activities particularly in the United States, but also in some other countries. Indeed, a main conclusion of this discussion is that more systematic monitoring is necessary to identify main policy sciences-relevant institutional developments—an identification needed for establishing mutual cooperation and for building up the formal and informal colleges without which no new intellectual and scientific approach can hope for success.

My preliminary survey of relevant institutional developments mentions some activities under three headings, namely (a) research institutes; (b) university programs; and (c) publications. Then, after enumerating some other developments, I will make some observations on similar attempts abroad and their particular problems, winding up with some conclusions.

A. Research Institutes

I think there can be no doubt that policy sciences, and indeed all systematic applications of interdisciplinary knowledge to complex policy issues, has originated and is mainly developing in special policy research organization of the "think tank" type. The RAND Corporation, the New York Rand Institute, the Hudson Institute, the Urban Institute, and the Center for the Study of Democratic Institutions illustrate the more "pure type" think tanks. TEMPO, the Brookings Institution, the Institute for the Future, the Syracuse University Research Corporation Policy Institute, the Center for Policy Research, and the Battelle Seattle Research Center—these illustrate different variations of policy research institutes, less focused on systematic interdisciplinary policy research than the think tanks, but nevertheless intensely involved in policy sciences.[7]

Main contemporary developments in respect to policy research institutes vary from place to place. But the following trends seem to be quite pronounced and very significant for policy sciences:

1. All policy research organizations seem to move more and more into broad social problem areas. This trend is particularly obvious in the various policy research organizations which originally focused on defense problems (such as RAND and IDA), all of which devote increasing attention to social problems. This involves important changes in methodology, such as transformation of systems analysis into policy analysis (with much more attention to political variables) and social experimentation.

2. Despite some setbacks, policy research organizations seem to be again on the move, with more money becoming available as a result, among other factors, of a growing awareness that traditional university structures are not efficient vehicles for policy-oriented interdisciplinary research. There seems to be a trend to establish additional policy research organizations devoted to social problems: for instance, Stanford Research Institute established a new Center for the Study of Social Policy, and the National Institute of Education—while still suffering from great difficulties—may, in part, move in the direction of policy research, as originally intended. In other countries, interest in policy research organizations is growing, as illustrated by the decision of the Canadian government to establish an Institute for Research on Public Policy, the establishment of the *Wissenschaftszentrum Berlin* in the Federal Republic of Germany, and the establishment of a Policy Sciences Research Institute in Tokyo.

3. Very important from the point of view of policy sciences is the attempt of the RAND Corporation to go into advanced teaching: In 1970 the RAND Corporation established the Rand Graduate Institute in Analysis, which runs a three-year doctorate program. This program is distinguished by a close fusion between theoretic study and a clinical method, with students working as Rand staff members on real problems within regular Rand assignments. This is a very innovative experiment which may pioneer new forms of training in policy sciences which fit its particular characteristics.[8]

As a whole, policy research organizations continue to serve as main centers for the advancement of policy sciences and may fulfill expanding roles in advancing policy sciences knowledge, in applying it to concrete policy problems, and in providing unique training for policy scientists.

B. University Programs

The institutional advancement of policy sciences is not a zero-sum game, in which progress by one actor leads to retreat for another actor. The opposite is true: the difficulties of policy sciences make essential a redundancy of approaches and experiments, so as to increase the probabilities of some success and to compress the time needed for progress.

This assumption is borne out by the fact that advancement of policy sciences within special policy research institutes goes hand-in-hand with the emergence of a number of novel policy sciences-oriented university programs. Among these programs, the following can serve as good illustrations: the Harvard Graduate Program in Public Policy; the Doctoral Program in Policy Sciences at SUNY at Buffalo; the Graduate School of Public Affairs at the University of California, Berkeley; the Institute of Public Policy Studies at the University of Michigan; the Lyndon B. Johnson School of Public Affairs at the University of Texas; and the School of Urban and Public Affairs at Carnegie-Mellon University.

These and additional university programs differ in objectives, curricula and educational assumptions.[9] At the same time, in the aggregative, they demonstrate the institutional growth of policy sciences at universities.

Again, a number of trends are significant:

1. Despite many difficulties, there exists a strong trend to establish additional policy sciences programs and to introduce public policy studies both on the undergraduate and the graduate levels. Thus, for instance, Brown University is introducing undergraduate public policy subjects; SUNYAB is considering establishment of a Policy Sciences Consortium for teaching and research; and Duke University has established an Institute of Policy Sciences and Public Affairs. In other countries, too, university interests in policy sciences are on the growth. In September 1973 a special conference of public policy studies was organized by the British Political Studies Association and a similar conference is scheduled for April 1975 at the University of Birmingham; a similar conference with German policy scholars and practitioners, supported by the Volkswagen Stiftuny, will take place in Cologne in 1974. In other countries, too, progress occurs. Thus, attempts were made to introduce policy studies directions at the Universidade Federal de Minas Gerais in Belo Horizonte, Brazil; Bolivar University in Caracas, Venezuela, introduced a policy sciences program; and Tokyo University experimented in this direction, under the name "social engineering."

2. Despite significant quantitative progress, the qualitative problems of teaching policy sciences at universities are far from solved. Particularly hard to meet within universities are two basic requisites of policy sciences teaching, namely (a) an interdisciplinary approach; and (b) on-going work

on real problems, both for clinical teaching and for realistic research. Some programs which started with much enthusiasm are in serious trouble because of resistance by established departments and difficulties in recruiting good staff. Other programs lack a coherent curriculum. Especially in Europe, the barriers to policy studies at universities are very great indeed, for reasons to be discussed below. Because of such problems, success is not assured for all policy sciences teaching endeavors. A main danger is of disrepute of the new approach, as a result of the failure of some programs.

3. The more successful programs seem to have some symbiotic relationship with policy research organizations. Internship of students in policy research organizations, collection of cases and other teaching material from the experience of policy research organizations, and movement of teachers between universities and policy research organizations—these are among the main forms of mutually beneficial interrelations between policy sciences university programs, and policy research organizations. They may well portend a main feature of the future institutional characteristics of policy sciences.

C. Publications

Publications constitute a main form of existence and growth of a scientific endeavor. The rapid increase of the number of books dealing with public policy and its improvement constitutes, therefore, a meaningful symptom of the growth of policy sciences.

Relevant books appear under a variety of names and, nominally, within a large range of disciplines—from systems engineering to economics and futures studies to strategy.[10] What is common to these books and articles is (a) their concern with the study of public policy and the improvement of public policy as (b) part of a scientific activity which (c) clearly goes beyond any one of the traditional disciplines. The growing concern with public policies and their improvement within political science is also very pronounced.[11] Similar literature is also emerging in other countries and languages.[12]

Especially significant is the emergence of literature using explicitly the verbal symbol "policy sciences" or related terms. Noteworthy are the Markham Series in Public Policy Analysis and the Elsevier Policy Sciences Book Series. In 1970 the periodical *Policy Sciences* began publication and this provides a much needed professional forum. In 1973 the *Policy Studies Journal* was founded and in 1974 *Policy Analysis* joined the professional periodicals explicitly and exclusively devoted to policy studies. The number of papers dealing with policy sciences and published in periodicals identified with more established professions and disciplines is also growing. In addition to the general periodicals in political science (as well as other disciplines, such as operations research and planning), one should especially mention in this context new interdisciplinary journals, such as *Socio-Economic Planning*, *Technological Forecasting and Social Change*, and *Futures*. Similar trends can be discerned in other countries, such as with the periodical *Analyse und Prognose* and a newly planned journal in "Public Planning and Decisionmaking Sciences" in Germany.

If a variety of governmental publications, working documents, and research reports are added to the picture,[13] the growth in policy sciences literature is very pronounced and serves as a clear indicator of its institutional development.

To illustrate additional dimensions of relevant institutional activities, let me mention the following:

1. *Conferences*. In 1968 and 1969 special symposia on policy sciences were held at the Annual Conferences of the American Association for the Advancement of Science. Meetings devoted in effect to the concerns of policy sciences are included in an increasing range of professional conferences, such as the International Sociological Association, the Society for General Systems Research, TIMS—The Institute of Management Sciences, and various political science conferences.

2. *Foundation Activities*. United States foundations seem to show increased interest in policy sciences subjects. Thus, the Social Science Research Council continues with its activities on the study of public policy and on policy-relevant research, while the Russell Sage Foundation seems to increase significantly its interests in evaluation, social experimentation and policy analysis. The National Science Foundation and the Ford Foundation, too, are increasingly active in the field; the latter, for instance, providing support to policy-oriented university programs. In other countries, too, a similar interest can be discerned. For instance, the Rowntree Trust in England moved from direct social aid to financing of social policy analysis and the VolksWagen Stiftung in the Federal Republic of Germany includes policy studies within its program in public administration.

3. *Government Units*. An increasing number of government units engage explicitly in activities such as evaluation, planning, and policy analysis—all of which are policy sciences related. This is true in the United States as well as in other countries, such as England and Canada. For instance, the Central Policy Review Staff in the Cabinet Office,[14] and various policy review and analysis units in local government, illustrate this trend in England, as does the Scientific Council for Government Policy in the Netherlands. Similarly, OECD and some parts of the United Nations family show interest in policy sciences, both for improvement of their own activity and as a main form of aid to member-countries.

4. *Consultants*. To judge from the little available material, a growing

number of new private consultant groups also try to apply policy sciences approaches and ideas to issues. An interesting illustration is the WEMA Institute (which originated in the Federal Republic of Germany and is now active in a number of countries), which uses a socioeconomic systems analysis approach explicitly based on recent policy sciences concepts and strongly oriented towards political and bureaucratic policy variables.

III. Developments Outside the United States

During my exploration of some policy sciences institutional activities, various developments outside the United States were mentioned together with similar developments in the United States. To avoid the somewhat misleading impression that policy sciences institutionalization in the United States and in other countries follows similar lines, let me point out some of the main differences in relevant contexts, which result in somewhat different problems and developments:[15]

1. In the United States there is a stronger tradition than in most other countries of practice- and policy-oriented activities at universities and of movement of senior persons between university positions and professional positions in government.

2. In quite a number of countries, ideological doctrines play a larger role than in the United States—hindering the open-minded and clinical approaches needed for policy sciences. This is a characteristic changing in some U.S. intellectual groups, thus reducing their capacity to engage in useful policy studies.

3. Policy research organizations of the think tank type are a United States invention, in part as a result of the above mentioned and the next factors, in part because of other cultural and socio-political reasons and, in part, perhaps a lucky accident. In any case, the establishment of the RAND Corporation twenty-six years ago was a main critical step which provided an early institutional basis for policy sciences in the United States, which still is unequalled outside the United States.

4. Policy sciences research depends on access to governmental information, including quite sensitive ones. Despite complaints about secrecy in the United States, such information is relatively much more available there than in most other countries. Thus, in England, strict provisions of the Official Secrets Act combine with conventions and cultural norms to impose a cloak of secrecy on governmental processes quite absent in the United States.[16]

5. To illustrate the richness and subtlety of cross-national and cross-cultural distinctions relevant for policy studies, let me mention the fact that in quite a number of languages there exists no verbal distinction between

"politics" and "policy," with the result that often the latter is hard to identify as a specific subject for action and study. For instance, in French, German, and Spanish, as well as most of the Slavic languages, the "politics"/"policy" distinction is hard to express because of the absence of different verbal symbols for these concepts.

Despite these and additional local characteristics, it seems fair to regard the development of policy sciences institutions as an international phenomenon. Differences between countries are significant, but the basic concern is similar. United States experiences and efforts do pioneer policy sciences and influence its advancement everywhere, but work in other countries makes important contributions which can be expected to increase. For instance, writings on policy studies in Germany are superior in considering the societal limitations on feasible policy sciences-based improvements in policy-making and in questioning philosophical assumptions. And English writings are superior in considering the relations between policy-making and planning.

In conclusion, it seems that our partial survey of some policy sciences-related institutional activities clearly shows that the institutional growth of policy sciences proceeds at a fast rate. This growth takes place under a variety of names and proceeds along a number of dimensions. But all names and dimensions share a main characteristic, namely intense efforts to apply systematic knowledge—including political science—to policy issues.

The fast rate of growth of policy sciences-related institutions carries with it both a promise and a danger: It may constitute an infrastructure conducive to building up a useful policy-oriented body of knowledge and to applying that knowledge to real and significant social problems. But it also constitutes a danger of trying to do in a hurry what we as yet do not know how to do well. Unless policy sciences knowledge keeps up with the institutional growth and can provide a useful content for the institutional activities, the institutional growth by itself will do more harm than good by arousing hopes which will turn into disappointment and, even, anti-intellectualism. Therefore, the rapid (and not always well-considered) growth of policy sciences institutions makes even more necessary a crash program to meet the challenge of building up the scientific foundations of policy sciences, including policy-oriented political science. At the same time, the institutional growth provides many opportunities for doing so —and therefore should be closely monitored, guided and utilized.

Notes

1. For more extensive treatments, see Harold D. Lasswell, *Design*

for Policy Sciences (New York: American Elsevier, and Amsterdam: Elsevier, 1971); Yehezkel Dror, *Design for Policy Sciences* (New York: American Elsevier, and Amsterdam: Elsevier, 1971); and Yehezkel Dror, *Ventures in Policy Sciences* (New York: American Elsevier, and Amsterdam: Elsevier, 1971).

2. On value analysis, see Yehezkel Dror, "Scientific Aid to Value Judgment," in *Modern Science and Moral Values*, Proceedings of the Second International Conference on the Unity of Sciences, Tokyo, November 18-21, 1973 (New York: The International Cultural Foundation, 1973), pp. 257-264.

3. On methodologies for policy studies, see Yehezkel Dror, "Some Features of a Meta-Model for Policy Studies," 3 *Policy Studies Journal* 247 (Spring 1975).

4. See Lasswell, *Design for Policy Sciences*, Part I.

5. In other words, a main need is for what I call meta-policy-studies, that is, studies on the making of policies on how to make policies. For an extensive treatment of this subject, see Yehezkel Dror, *Public Policymaking Reexamined* (New York: Intertext, 1968, and Aylesbury, Bucks: Leonard Hill, 1973).

6. Lest the incorrect impression prevails that political science is more in need of changes to fit the requirements of policy studies than other disciplines, let me emphasize that other areas of "normal" sciences too need reprocessing and innovation in order to contribute to policy studies—all this without impairing the continuous growth of different disciplines along their own lines. See, for instance, Yehezkel Dror, "From Management Science to Policy Sciences," in Michael J. White et al. (eds.), *Management and Policy Science in American Government: Problems and Prospects* (Lexington, Mass: Lexington Books, D. C. Heath and Company, forthcoming).

At the same time, let me emphasize my view that political scientists who want to move into policy studies as a serious intellectual endeavor must engage in significant self-change. For instance, they must learn the main literature in areas such as systems analysis, prediction, simulation, uncertainty handling, planning, and decision sciences. Suitable opportunities for interested political scientists to study these subjects in a time-effective way are urgently needed, for instance through organization of intense summer training workshops. For a detailed discussion of one such workshop designed for use with political scientists and other social scientists as well as (with suitable adjustments) senior decisionmakers, see Yehezkel Dror, "Intense Policy Analysis Workshop for Professionals and Decisionmakers" (tentative title), in preparation for *Policy Analysis*.

7. A good survey of think tanks is provided in Paul Dickson, *Think Tanks* (New York: Atheneum, 1971).

8. See *The Rand Graduate Institute–Bulletin 1974-75* (Santa Monica, Calif., The RAND Corporation, 1974).

9. For a somewhat outdated survey, see *Policy Sciences* 1, 4 (December 1970), and 2, 1 (March 1973). A short recent discussion is provided in William L. Dunn, "The Implied Policy Analyst: An Examination of Eight Schools of Public Policy" (Santa Monica, Calif.: The RAND Corporation, P-5227, March 1974). See also Yehezkel Dror, *Design for Policy Sciences*, Chapter 14 and Yehezkel Dror "Universities, Training for Policy-making and Policy Research," *Proceedings of the Third Conference on the Unity of Sciences*, London, November 21-24, 1974 (forthcoming).

10. For detailed surveys of some of the relevant literature, see Yehezkel Dror, *Public Policymaking Reexamined*, pp. 327-356; and Yehezkel Dror, *Design for Policy Sciences*, pp. 143-149.

11. A good bibliographic list is provided in Ira Sharkansky (ed.), *Policy Analysis in Political Science* (Chicago: Markham, 1970), pp. 467-476. For critical discussions of political science literature dealing with policy-making, see Stuart H. Rakoff and Guenther F. Schaefer, "Politics, Policy, and Political Science: Theoretic Alternatives," *Politics and Society* 1, 1 (November 1970): 51-72.

12. For instance, German theoretic literature in the policy sciences direction is represented by the excellent book of Klaus Lompe, *Gesellschaftspolitik Und Planung* (Freiburg: Romback, 1971). German empiric research on policy-making is represented by the very thorough study of Hannes Friedrich, *Staatliche Verwaltung Und Wissenschaft* (Frankfurt/Main: Europaeische Verlagsanstalt, 1970).

13. For a Canadian government report which illustrates this trend and which explicitly refers to policy sciences, see Economic Council of Canada, *Eighth Annual Review: Design for Decision-Making–An Application to Human Resources Policies* (Ottawa, September 1971). Interesting and typical of growing interest and recognition are also the items on "policy sciences" and "policy analysis" in *Science Policy–A Working Glossary*, Committee Print, Subcommittee on Science, Research and Development, U.S. House of Representatives (Washington, D.C.: U.S. Government Printing Office, 1972).

14. Usually, very little material is available on governmental policy studies units. Two recent articles on the British Central Policy Review Staff constitute an exception, though they cannot disclose all one would like to know. See William Plowden, "The Role and Limits of a Central Planning Staff in Government: A Note on the Central Policy Review Staff," *Public*

Administration Bulletin, No. 16 (June 1974): 22-26; and Christopher Pollitt, "The Central Policy Review Staff 1970-74," *Public Administration*, Winter 1974, pp. 375-392. A different perspective is provided in Hugh Heclo and Aaron Wildavsky, *The Private Government of Public Money* (Berkeley and Los Angeles: University of California Press, 1974), chapters 6 and 7, *passim*.

15. For a more detailed examination, see Yehezkel Dror, "Policy Sciences: Some Global Perspectives," *Policy Sciences* 5, 1 (1974): 83-87.

16. The episode of Richard Crossman's diaries well illustrates the problem. Crossman prepared a two-volume diary to be published by Jonathan Cape and Hamish Hamilton. As he explains in the introduction (published in *The Sunday London Times*, November 17, 1974), the diaries try to apply Crossman's political science knowledge to his experiences as a cabinet minister—with important findings on top-level decision-making. Clearly, this is essential for the progress of policy studies. But, soon after he died and just before publication of the first volume—the British government refused to clear the diaries for publication. Problems of governmental secrecy will be examined within a comparative perspective in forthcoming writings and collections by Itzhak Galnoor.

2

Empirical Research Methods

Thomas Cook, Frank Scioli, Barbara Salmore, and *Stephen Salmore*

I. Policy Analysis in Political Science; Trends and Issues in Empirical Research

In the past decade political scientists have evinced considerable interest in investigating the correlates of public policy. Political scientists are now quite familiar with the vast number of studies utilizing multivariate correlational analysis to investigate the factors influencing policy formulation by state and local decision making bodies.[1] Employing a variant of Easton's model of the political system, researchers have concentrated on assessing the relationship of systemic variables (political and socioeconomic factors) to policy outputs.

The central question of this research has focused upon the relative contribution of political vs. environmental factors in explaining the variability of policy outputs across diverse governmental jurisdictions. Up to 1963, the tendency had been to view political variables as having a direct effect upon the policy making process.[2] That is, the policy enacted within a governmental jurisdiction was perceived as a direct function of the political characteristics (i.e., party competition, voter turnout, apportionment, form of government, etc.) of that jurisdiction. Beginning in 1963, with the publication of a study by Richard Dawson and James Robinson examining welfare policy, a number of political scientists have questioned the centrality of political variables in explaining policy outputs.[3] The work of Dye, Hofferbert, Jacob, and others suggested that the relationship between political variables and policy outputs may, in large part, be a function of the socioeconomic characteristics (i.e., income, urbanization, industrialization, etc.) of an area.[4] Moreover, this body of research argued that socioeconomic variables may influence public policy independent of political characteristics. The debate continues to the present time in recent studies such as those by Clarke, Sharkansky, and Hofferbert, etc.[5] Clarke argued, for example, that political variables are important when the outputs are of a more "political" nature; such as referenda outcomes.

Sections I and II of this chapter were authored by Thomas Cook and Frank Scioli. Section III was authored by Barbara Salmore and Stephen Salmore.

Although the findings may differ, the research cited above has generally treated political and socioeconomic factors as independent variables influencing dependent variables in the form of public policy outputs. The majority of these investigations have used financial expenditures by state and local governments in areas such as education, highways, welfare, etc. as the dependent variable in their assessment of factors influencing public policy. The investigation by Thomas R. Dye, for example, employed a wide variety of expenditures and tax measures as indicants of public policy in the five areas of education, health and welfare, highways, taxation, and regulation of public morality.[6] In fact, except for the distinction between expenditures and the results of expenditure policies made by Sharkansky[7] and the non-monetary measures of public policy employed by Jack Walker,[8] most other research investigations have defined *policy outputs* as dollar expenditures.

This body of literature, while useful, evidences several limitations. First, the utilization of expenditure levels as surrogates for the delivery of social services is highly questionable. Since expenditures are a gross measure of output they do not fully reflect the wide amount of variation which may exist in the delivery (i.e., implementation) of social services. Factors such as program personnel, extent of need for the social services, receptivity to the social service, and the contextual characteristics of the target area may interact with expenditure levels to affect the outcome of the social policy.[9] The concept of policy output, therefore, is a multi-dimensional phenomenon, the complexity of which goes beyond a summated expenditure level indicator. In our judgment a more fruitful approach would be to operationalize the output measures in terms of the nature and extent of program services delivered within a given policy category (e.g., education, highways, health, etc.). This would allow controls for variations in the output from service delivery under diverse substantive policies. To assume, for example, that all Headstart centers deliver a constant amount of program service is not supported by empirical evidence. The same can be said for other policy areas in that dollar amounts need to be translated into measures of actual service delivery.

A second limitation concerns the treatment of a policy output as an isolated phenomenon. The use of multivariate regression analysis has thus far focused upon the relationship between a *set* of independent variables (i.e., political and socioeconomic) and a *single* output measure (e.g., expenditures for highways). A more systematic approach (à la Bertalanffy) would be to examine the *simultaneous* relationship between theoretically important *sets* of input measures and *sets* of output measures.[10] The use of canonical correlation and simultaneous equation techniques offer promising alternatives to the current mode of analysis. Recent work by econometricians using simultaneous equation models may provide a useful beginning point for political scientists.[11] The main point to note is that the researcher would not only focus on the correlation between a set of input measures and an output measure, but more importantly, analyze the *within set interaction* of both his input and output measures in assessing the between sets relationships.

A final, and from our perspective, a more important limitation concerns the analytical focus of this body of research. As was stated above, to date, this research has treated policy outputs (i.e., expenditures) as the primary dependent variable. What has been neglected, however, is the development of a rigorous analytical framework for the systematic evaluation of policy impacts relative to policy objectives. The basic question of policy impact analysis can be stated simply as follows: does a public policy achieve the desired objectives for which it was designed? Examination of this key question necessitates attention to the measurement of policy impacts.

Impact in this context refers specifically to the measurable changes in the social or physical environment that the policy program was designed to produce. As contrasted with isolating the social, economic, and political correlates of public policy expenditures (i.e., policy output analysis) attention is focused on examining the impact(s) of the policy decisions. This line of analysis would treat policy outputs as independent variables and the impacts of these policy decisions as dependent variables.[12] The result would be a much needed shift in research focus from the causes of public policy to the question of what public policy causes.

To date the bulk of rigorous assessments of the impact of a particular policy have been conducted by those in psychology, sociology, and economics.[13] Compared to attention accorded to the analysis of policy impacts in those disciplines, the research investigations on the topic by political scientists are scant indeed. This lack of attention to policy impact analysis is reflected not only in the number of studies conducted but in the methodologies utilized as well. With rare exception the investigations have been *ex post facto* analyses with little attention given to the advantages of experimental and quasi-experimental designs for conducting the analysis.[14]

Several political scientists have however evinced interest in addressing questions concerning the impact of public policies.[15] The majority of research investigations by political scientists on the impact of public policy are concerned largely with the impact of judicial decisions. In fact, one writer in the judicial politics field has argued that "the main post-behavioral or policy-behavioral development within public law has been the increased concern for studying the impact of Supreme Court decisions."[16] The edited collection by Becker, *The Impact of Supreme Court Decisions*,[17] Wasby's, *The Impact of the United States Supreme Court*,[18] Jacob's, *Debtors in*

Courts,[19] and recent works by Nagel[20] attest to the interest of public law scholars in questions of policy impact. In addition, a significant number of studies have been conducted by political scientists, who are not in the public law area, concerning reapportionment policy.[21] These studies focus largely on examining the impact of reapportionment policy on achieving its intended objective of redressing partisan imbalance in state legislatures and the consequences of these legislative adjustments for state public policy formulation.

Several studies are beginning to emerge which attempt evaluation of the performance of governmental services from the viewpoint of the individual citizen. Utilizing survey methodology these investigations focus on assessing citizen perceptions of the delivery of goods and services by national, state, and local governments.[22]

This does not exhaust the studies of policy impacts conducted by political scientists but represents the general substantive focus and methodological emphasis (aggregate and survey) of those in the discipline concerned with evaluating the impact of public policy. In addition, a recent series of funded conferences and convention panels on the topic of impact analysis has produced a spate of additional research reports and discussion papers.[23] These recent conferences suggest, perhaps more than anything else, the interest of greater numbers of political scientists in questions of policy impact analysis. It is evidence, too, of interest in not only the impact of judicial policy but of interest in assessing the impact of specific public policy programs in areas as diverse as environmental control policy, housing policy, and manpower training policy.

However, for a variety of reasons many researchers are reluctant to enter the arena of policy impact analysis, where social-action programs are to be evaluated. One group, for example, would refrain from working directly with policy makers in evaluating social programs because their views run counter to the philosophies of those in decision making situations. One author, for example, urges social scientists to refuse to make their skills available to federal agencies insisting that their moral and professional obligation is to serve movements opposing central authority and the elite structures in society.[24] Such a view presupposes (i.e., assumes) that social scientists do indeed have meaningful contributions to offer governmental decision makers if they should be so inclined. Agreement on this assumption is far from unanimous among political scientists some of whom made clear at a recent conference[25] that the political scientists should not be giving out advice to policy makers mainly because, given the current state of the development of scientific theory in the discipline, the advice could not be reliable. Such people feel that the efforts of scholars in political science would be better spent in areas more likely to produce general scientific knowledge.

A third group reluctant to engage in social program evaluation is concerned with the "disciplinary responsibilities or competencies of political scientists in policy impact research."[26] In endeavoring to evaluate a program in the area of environmental protection, for example, must the political scientist gain expertise in meteorology, physics, and chemistry? Does he then sacrifice his skills as a political scientist and become a bastardized environmentalist? There are two ways of avoiding such an occurrence. One is through engagement in interdisciplinary research teams. The other is for the political scientist to evaluate only that part of a program which is involved directly with the political process, that is, leave the measurement of air pollution reduction to the chemist, and concentrate on what the reduction means in terms of citizen reaction to politicians in office.

The resolution of these issues is far from accomplished at the present time and as a result has hindered the development of rigorous models for policy analysis. It is hoped that this essay will serve to stimulate efforts toward recognizing the relevant issues of policy analysis in political science. It is only after recognition of the issues that resolution can begin.

II. Resources for Public Policy Analysis

At the outset it should be noted that as a discipline Political Science has only recently begun to devote resources toward the systematic analysis of public policy.[27] When one further refines the area to the topic of "empirical research methods," there are few institutionalized vehicles for the exploration and dissemination of information pertaining to the development of a methodology appropriate for public policy analysis. In this section we will mention some of the existing facilities and resources that are currently available, restricting attention to the area of empirical research methods.

A. Research Centers

An excellent reference book for academic facilities is a publication of the Urban Institute (Washington, D.C., 1969) titled, *University Urban Research Centers*. This booklet lists over 120 institutes, research centers, and bureaus engaged in various types of policy analysis. A few of particular note are the Institute for Research on Poverty (University of Wisconsin); The Bureau of Applied Social Research (Columbia University); The Institute of Public Policy Studies (University of Michigan); The Institute of Government and Public Affairs (University of Illinois, Urbana); The Institute of Public Administration (Pennsylvania State), and the Center for Urban Affairs (Northwestern University).

In addition to the above centers are the various non-academic facilities engaged in various types of policy analysis. At the state level, for example, the Commonwealth of Pennsylvania and the State of Michigan have been engaged in the development of an in-house research capability in the area of program evaluation. While generally not accessible through professional journals these research reports (i.e., program audits) may be obtained by contacting the appropriate state offices (e.g., division of program audit).

Focusing on the local level, the Urban Institute in Washington, D.C., has engaged in a number of projects dealing specifically with the development of research methodology applicable to the evaluation of social action programs. The Institute has been in the forefront of the move towards advancing the application of experimental design methodology to program evaluation. The working papers dealing with income maintenance experiments and housing allowance experiments are particularly instructive.[28]

Although too numerous to discuss in detail, another valuable source of material and information are the various federal agencies engaged in policy analysis/program evaluation (OEO, HUD, HEW, etc.). Many of these agencies (e.g., HEW) have organized their R&D component for access via the National Technical Information Service (NTIS). NTIS is a department of Commerce Clearing House which HEW, among other agencies, uses as a repository for its documents.

B. Periodicals

Recently, for example, The National Institute for Mental Health sponsored the publication of a comprehensive annoted bibliography compiled by Carol Weiss (Director, Program Evaluation, Bureau of Applied Research, Columbia University) entitled, *Planning for Creative Change: Use of Program Evaluation* (Washington, D.C.: Government Printing Office, 1971). This publication is valuable not only for its division into areas such as conceptual and methodological issues; design, measurement, sampling, and analysis; and illustrative evaluation studies; it also provides a good summary of the included references. A review of this bibliography reveals that publications on this topic appear in a wide variety of journals from numerous academic disciplines.

To date, however, there are no journals in political science dealing specifically with empirical research methods applied to policy analysis problems. While occasionally an article focusing on empirical research methods appears in one of the major political science journals most of the studies appear in disparate sources. Some of the more frequently cited journals are: *Policy Sciences, Administrative Science Quarterly, Journal of Applied Behavioral Science, Journal of Social Issues, American

Psychologist, Welfare in Review, Review of Educational Research, The American Behavioral Scientist, American Economic Review, and *Psychological Bulletin.* A promising new journal devoted to social science methodology and quantitative research is *Social Science Research,* edited by James Coleman and Peter Rossi, and, of course, the *Policy Studies Journal,* coordinated by Stuart Nagel.

C. Funding

An excellent guide to Federal research grants appears in the October, 1971 newsletter of *Behavior Today* (CRM Publications: Bel Mar, California) titled, "Money and How to Get It." The publication details foundations, fellowships, and strategies for getting funds. New funding programs such as RANN (Research Applied to National Needs) in NSF are described in terms of funding priorities (substantive) and the application of social science methodology to the analysis of social problems. Furthermore, each issue of *Behavior Today* contains a section detailing recently funded projects, forthcoming needs, and sources of funding.

Another source of information concerning funding opportunities is the Smithsonian Science Information Exchange Inc. (SSIE, Washington, D.C.). SSIE provides abstracts on research projects which list principal investigators, funding agency, and provide project descriptions. In terms of specific types of substantive research, federal and state agencies periodically publish brochures and send out announcements regarding funding opportunities. Interested researchers can contact the R&D office within these agencies and be placed on a mailing list for such announcements. Also, the Congressional Research Service of the Library of Congress is a source of funding information. A recent publication, *Major Federal Assistance Programs Relating to Corrections*, February 1973, is an example of the type of research funding information available, in this case dealing with criminal justice funding. Another source of funding information can be found in the publication, *Annual Register of Grant Support 1973/74* (Orange, New Jersey: Academic Media, 1973). This latter publication details the specifics of research funding across a wide range of substantive policy areas.

D. Data Sources

Besides the obvious types of relevant data sources such as the Bureau of the Census tabulations (e.g., County and City Data Book) and the Inter-University Consortium for Political Research (University of Michigan) political and economic series, there is a paucity of data sources devoted to public policy analysis. The need for coordination of data generation relevant to policy analysis is evidenced by a recent grant of $800,000 to the Center for Research Libraries, Chicago, to establish a census laboratory and clearing house. There is a desperate need for development of data files pertaining to the operation of social programs. Any researcher, for example, contemplating the use of a time-series analytic model faces the prospect of generating his own data files. Apart from a few efforts like the Banks & Textor, *Cross Polity Time-Series Data* and other studies scattered about in parts unknown to the general scholarly community, there is virtually no central repository for this type of data. This void is particularly evident when one considers research at the sub-national level.

E. Conclusion

In this brief section we have tried to provide an overview of some of the resources available for empirical research in public policy. We readily acknowledge the possibility of oversights in our coverage of the topic.

III. The Comparative Study of Public Policy

In the last several years, two distinct but complementary trends in political science have contributed to an increasing interest in cross-national studies of public policy: the burgeoning literature on policy outputs in the American states,[29] and the call by some leading students of comparative politics for a renewed emphasis on the "output" and "feedback" loops in models of political systems.[30] The "behavioral revolution" in political science brought a welcome emphasis on such "inputs" as political culture, socialization, and the role of groups and political parties, but at the expense of what perhaps is most innately political—the policy decisions of governments, the effect on policy of different government structures, and the effectiveness of such policies. While political science journals still reflect the great upsurge in research dealing with the social, psychological and economic determinants of political behavior, and while the largest body of policy-relevant literature is still confined to studies of national or subnational governmental units in the United States, a number of cross-national studies have begun to appear. They tend to reflect the concerns of the two research trends described above: an emphasis on effect of political structure, and an assessment of the relative salience of social, economic and political variables for various policy outputs—the major element in comparative study of state policy outputs in the United States.

In the rest of this section, we will examine three major questions related to the comparative study of public policy: (1) substantive research areas; (2) methods of analysis and major data sources; and (3) problems of cross-national policy research. For reasons of definitional precision and parsimony, we define "policy" here as the outputs of authoritative actors of a *national* government, and we will only consider studies that look at such outputs directly and study them empirically. Such a decision has the effect of eliminating exclusively theoretical studies of policy-making,[31] comparative studies of subnational units,[32] single-country studies,[33] and studies of outputs to the wider regional or international system.[34] While these are all interesting topics, space does not permit treatment of them here.

A. Substantive Policy Research Areas

Most cross-national studies of public policy are confined to one policy domain. Possibly the two single broad-gauged exceptions are Alexander Groth's *Comparative Politics: A Distributive Approach*[35] and Frederic Pryor's *Public Expenditures in Capitalist and Communist Nations*.[36] Groth generally divides nations into what he calls ideal types of democracies and autocracies, although he then does distinguish between traditional and innovating autocracies, and stable and unstable, less and more inclusive, democracies. He then examines the policies characteristic of such systems in the areas of political participation, group life, taxation and budgets, other economic policies, education, culture, social welfare, social change, justice, bureaucracy and public service. Although the system typology is crude and the data somewhat ad hoc, Groth's book is a first attempt to range over a large number of policy areas. The chapters on participation and group life are particularly interesting in that they study the impact of government structure on these phenomena, rather than the reverse order so common in the political science literature. Pryor's study is much more methodologically sophisticated, but deals with only fourteen nations—seven market economies and seven centrally planned economies. Pryor studies expenditures for defense, welfare, education, administration, internal security, and research and development, and finds some differences between the two groups, but the distinctions decline over time.[37]

Probably the largest number of studies of a single policy area deal with a comparative analysis of social security or social welfare policies.[38] There are at least two reasons for this emphasis. First, such studies flow logically from the generally earlier work in this area in the American states, and second, comparative data of relatively high quality is readily available over time.[39] Thus, the studies tend to organize themselves around the five major social welfare programs defined by the International Labor Organization (pensions, health insurance, workman's compensation, unemployment insurance and family allowances), and like the state studies , tend to concentrate on the relative explanatory power of economic and political variables. Like the state studies, earlier research, mainly by sociologists and economists, generally concentrates on total expenditures, with findings indicating the overwhelming importance of temporal and economic factors.[40] Later work by political scientists, examining distribution of expenditures and financing burdens, finds that political factors are salient in these areas.[41]

The impact of government on economic development is another well-represented area, and the studies here are diverse. Using twenty-four of the judgmental political variables of the *Cross-Polity Survey*,[42] Tsantis finds that stable legislative and bureaucratic institutions, and high levels of associational group life are positively related to economic development in seventy-two developed and undeveloped nations.[43] The findings about interest articulation confirm an earlier study by Adelman and Morris of seventy-four non-Communist underdeveloped states.[44]

Two narrower studies dealing with economic development are concerned with the role of military governments in effecting economic change,[45] and a comparison of the economic performance over time of COMECON and OECD nations.[46] Nordlinger's demonstration that most contemporary military governments do not commit themselves to economic development (an argument against much of the "conventional wisdom") is rendered suspect by the fact that his data for the dependent variables precede in time the data for the independent variable. Bergson's study tries to show that the performance of socialist governments has either only matched or lagged behind that of capitalist systems in terms of economic gains, particularly productivity.

In a book dealing with the relation of defense expenditures to other public expenditures in the period since World War II, Russett concentrates largely on the United States, but includes some material on Canada, France and Britain.[47] He finds that Canada has been somewhat more successful than the United States in maintaining or increasing capital formation and public sector social investment during periods of increasing defense expenditures, and that France and Britain have successfully dealt with lower defense spending by increasing capital formation. Public sector social investment has generally suffered in the United States when defense expenditures increase. Russett's study stands alone as an innovative attempt to consider relations within the whole policy matrix. However, it should be noted that his major findings have been criticized on methodological grounds, and that reanalysis with slightly different but orthodox statistical techniques appears to modify the somewhat dismal conclusions regarding the relationship of "guns and butter" in the United States.[48]

Finally, we mention the studies in comparative foreign policy, which stand at the interface of comparative politics and international politics. Students of foreign policy face a somewhat unique problem in that so much of the "policy" content in this domain cannot be measured in the fiscal terms common to the previously reported cross-national research. Symbolic or verbal outputs such as threats, promises, accusations, denials and the like comprise a much larger and more important part of foreign as opposed to domestic policy. To deal with this problem, several researchers have defined a single foreign policy "event" as each discrete, publicly reported, action by an authoritative national actor which has an external target. Although some such event collections treat the internal political structure as a "black box," and deal mainly with international interactions, some focus on the impact of regime structure,[49] bureaucratic structure,[50] and leadership personality[51] on foreign policy. All of these variables, as well as size and economic development,[52] have been found to be important explanatory variables for various types of foreign policy.

B. Major Data Sources and Types of Analysis

Unfortunately, the researcher of cross-national policy finds no ready-made data banks such as students of, say, voting behavior, enjoy. Virtually all of the studies reported here utilize some type of "hard" or "soft" aggregate data which are operationalized as representing policy outputs, or the dependent variables, by the researcher. Much of the "hard" data, particularly that used in studies of economic development, is drawn from publications of the U.N. and its associated organizations, including the annual Demographic Yearbooks, Statistical Yearbooks, and Yearbooks of National Accounts. The International Labor Organization has many publications containing data on social welfare and labor-related questions. In addition to these sources, there is the plethora of statistical yearbooks and related publications of individual nations, and relevant cross-national data collections by specialized agencies of the American government, such as the Arms Control and Disarmament Agency, the Department of Health, Education and Welfare, and the State Department. Some useful budget and other materials can also be found in the annual *Statesman's Yearbook*. The "soft data" alternatives include the performance of various content analysis procedures (particularly by the compilers of events data)[53] and the construction of indices or scales based entirely or partially on judgmental criteria.[54] Such data collections are generally not yet available from such major archives as the Interuniversity Consortium for Political Research, and must be obtained from the individual researchers who collected the data. These lacunae no doubt slow the pace of further work in the comparative study of public policy.

C. Problems in Cross-National Policy Research

This topic is deserving of as thorough a treatment as Frey's important contribution on problems of cross-national survey research,[55] but space permits only a statement of the major problems.

We have already noted the problem of data *availability*. Whereas researchers dealing with microanalytic problems can construct survey instruments and use other techniques of some precision, the policy researcher must make do with data collected originally for quite unrelated purposes. It is the researcher and not the U.N. who decrees that GNP or energy production "equals" economic development. While such slippage between concept and indicator is common to all empirical research, the problem may be particularly severe in the case of policy analysis. Moreover, the *reliability* of such data is not always the best, even in nations with the most sophisticated data collection and analysis procedures.[56]

As important as, and related to, the question of availability and reliability is the question of *comparability*. While the publications of international organizations attempt to report cross-national data in comparable categories, footnotes noting exceptions to this rule are very frequent, and so is missing data. National budgets are particularly difficult to deal with in a comparative fashion. Not only do the budget categories vary, but so do the comprehensiveness of the reports of transactions and the explicitness of the information. Translating many different currencies into constant monetary units is also a problem. While one may be able to specify with some precision the amount in dollars that, say, the United States and the U.S.S.R. spent on housing or health programs in a given year, it is very difficult to determine exactly what these figures "mean" in view of the very different proportions of a citizen's budget these costs entail in the two nations.

The same problems of validity and reliability are associated as well with the "soft data" alternatives. The validity of coding categories and the reliability of coding procedures, particularly in a cross-national context, are crucial factors in determining the scholarly worth of such studies, or their use in applied science.

D. Summary

From the foregoing, it may be seen that the comparative study of public policy has both great prospects and difficult problems. However, in time, the problems would seem to be largely surmountable. Those researchers in the areas studied earliest, particularly social welfare and economic development, have progressed the furthest in defining the problems and exploring them in terms of more sophisticated theoretical frameworks and methodological techniques. Perhaps the most provocative questions, dealing with allocations of resources among competing publics, the distribution of the burden of financing public goods, and the relationship between various policy domains, have barely been explored. The cross-national study of public policy should have an interesting and rewarding future.

Notes

1. The literature in this area is voluminous. For representative efforts the reader should consult the following: Richard Dawson and James Robinson, "Interparty Competition, Economic Variables, and Welfare Policies in the American State," *Journal of Politics*, 25 (May 1963): 265-289; Thomas R. Dye, *Politics, Economics, and the Public Policy Outcomes in the American States* (Chicago: Rand McNally, 1966); Thomas R. Dye, "Income Inequality and American State Politics," *American Political Science Review*, 63 (March 1969): 157-62; Heinz Eulau and Robert Eyestone, "Policy Maps of City Councils and Policy Outcomes: A Developmental Analysis," *American Political Science Review* 62 (March 1968): 124-143; Brian Fry and Richard Winters, "The Politics of Redistribution," *American Political Science Review* 64 (June 1970): 508-522; Robert Lineberry and Edmund Fowler, "Reformism and Public Policies in American Cities," *American Political Science Review* 61 (September 1967): 701-716; and Ira Sharkansky, "Environment, Policy, Output and Impact: Problems of Theory and Method in the Analysis of Public Policy," in Ira Sharkansky (ed.), *Policy Analysis in Political Science* (Chicago: Markham Publishing Co., 1970), 61-79.

2. John H. Fenton, *People and Parties in Politics* (Glenview, Ill.: Scott, Foresman, 1966); Malcolm Jewell, *The State Legislative* (New York: Random House, 1962); V. O. Key, *Southern Politics in State and Nation* (New York: Knopf, 1951); Duane Lockard, *New England State Politics* (Princeton: Princeton Univ. Press, 1959).

3. Dawson and Robinson, op. cit.

4. Dye, *Politics, Economics, and the Public*, op. cit., Richard I. Hofferbert, "The Relations between Public Policy and Some Structural and Environmental Variables in the American States," *American Political Science Review* 60 (March 1966): 73-82; Herbert Jacob, "The Consequences of Malapportionment: A Note of Caution, *Social Forces* 43 (December 1964): 256-261.

5. James W. Clarke, "Environment, Process, and Policy: A Reconsideration," *American Political Science Review* (December 1969):

1172-1182; Ira Sharkansky and Richard I. Hofferbert, "Dimensions of State Politics, Economics, and Public Policy," *American Political Science Review* 63 (September 1965): 880-899.

6. Thomas R. Dye, *Politics, Economics, and the Public*, op. cit.

7. Ira Sharkansky, "Environment, Policy, Output, and Impact," op. cit.

8. Jack L. Walker, "The Diffusion of Innovations among the American States," *American Political Science Review* 63 (September 1969): 880-889.

9. For elaboration of this argument see: Herbert Hyman and Charles Wright, "Evaluating Social Programs," in Paul Lazarsfeld, et al. (eds.), *The Uses of Sociology* (New York: Basic Books, 1967), 741-782; Edward A. Suchman, *Evaluative Research* (New York: Russell Sage Foundation, 1967).

10. Ludwig Von Bertalanffy, *General System Theory* (New York: George Braziller, 1968).

11. Teh-Wei Hu and Bernard Booms, "A Simultaneous Equation Technique for Public Expenditure Decisions in Large Cities," *The Annals of Regional Science* 5, 2 (December 1971): 73-85; J. M. Henderson, "Local Government Expenditure: A Social Welfare Analysis," *Review of Economics and Statistics* (May 1968): 156-163; Teh-Wei Hu, "Canonical Correlation Analysis vs. the Simultaneous Equation Approach: An Empirical Example Evaluating Child Health and Welfare Programs," paper presented at the European Meetings of the Econometric Society, Budapest, Hungary, September 5-8, 1972.

12. For a more thorough development of this argument the reader might wish to consult Thomas J. Cook and Frank P. Scioli, Jr., "A Research Strategy for Analyzing the Impacts of Public Policy," *Administrative Science Quarterly* (September 1972).

13. Donald T. Campbell, "Factors Relevant to the Validity of Experiments in Social Settings," *Psychological Bulletin* 54 (1957): 297-312, "Reforms as Experiments," *American Psychologist* 24 (April 1969): 409-429; Donald T. Campbell and H. Lawrence Ross, "The Connecticut Crackdown on Speeding: Time Series Data on Quasi-Experimental Analysis," *Law and Society Review* (January 1968): 33-53; H. Lawrence Ross, Donald T. Campbell, and Gene V. Glass, "Determining the Social Effects of a Legal Reform: The British 'Breathalyser' Crackdown of 1967," *American Behavioral Scientist* 15 (March 1970): 110-113; Donald T. Campbell, "Methods for the Experimenting Society," paper presented at the American Psychological Association Convention, Washington, D.C., September, 1971; Donald H. Fisk, *The Indianapolis Police Fleet Plan: An*

Example of Program Evaluation for Local Government (Washington, D.C.: The Urban Institute, 1970).

14. For a few of the exceptions see the following: Report of an experimental analysis by Martin A. Levin, "Policy Evaluation and Recidivism," *Law and Society Review* 6 (August 1971): 17-46; for arguments on behalf of experimental design see Thomas J. Cook and Frank P. Scioli, Jr., "Policy Impact Analysis a Suggested Research Strategy," paper presented at Conference on the Measurement of Policy Impact, Tallahasee, Florida, May, 1971; and Thomas J. Cook and Frank P. Scioli, Jr., "An Experimental Design for the Analysis of Policy Impacts," paper presented at meeting of the American Political Science Association, Chicago, September, 1971; Further, a recent quasi-experimental investigation has been conducted by David Seidman, "The Reactivity of Non-Reactive Measures or the Great American Anti-Crime Crusade," unpublished paper, Yale University, January 1972; Thomas J. Cook and Frank P. Scioli, Jr., "Experimental Design in Policy Impact Analysis," *Social Science Quarterly* 54 (September 1973): 271-280.

15. For an extended discussion of this research literature see Frank P. Scioli, Jr., "Policy Impact Analysis in Political Science Association Meeting, April, 1972, Chicago, Illinois; and Thomas J. Cook and Frank P. Scioli, Jr., "Impact Analysis in Public Policy Research: Notes on Choosing A Research Strategy," in K. Dolbeare (ed.), *Public Policy Evaluation* (Beverly Hills, California: Sage Publications Inc., forthcoming).

16. Stuart Nagel, "Some New Concerns of Legal Process Research within Political Science," *Law and Society Review* 6 (August 1971): 10.

17. Theodore Becker (ed.), *The Impact of Supreme Court Decisions* (New York: Oxford University Press, 1969).

18. Stephen L. Wasby, *The Impact of the United States Supreme Court: Some Perspectives* (Homewood, Illinois: Dorsey Press, 1970).

19. Herbert Jacob, *Debtors in Court: The Consumption of Government Services* (Chicago: Rand McNally, 1969).

20. Stuart S. Nagel, *The Legal Process from A Behavioral Perspective* (Homewood, Illinois: Dorsey Press, 1969); *Rights of the Accused* (Beverly Hills, California: Sage Publications, 1972); and *Effects of Alternative Legal Policies,* forthcoming.

21. For a review of this literature see Samuel C. Patterson, "Political Representation and Public Policy," paper presented at Social Science Research Council Conference on the Impact of Public Policies, St. Thomas, Virgin Islands, December, 1971.

22. See for example: Herbert Jacob, "Contact with Government Agencies: A Preliminary Analysis of the Distribution of Government Ser-

vices," *Midwest Journal of Political Science* 16 (February 1972): 123-146; Jay Schmiedeskamp and George Katona, "Phase II: No Big Change in the Outlook for Consumer Demand," Consumer Perspectives (Ann Arbor, Michigan: Institute for Social Research, October 25, 1971); and Elinor Ostrom, et al. *Community Organization and The Provision of the Police Services* (Bloomington, Indiana: Studies in Political Theory and Policy Analysis, Political Science Department, University of Indiana, 1971).

23. Among the conferences: Thomas R. Dye, chairman, NSF Conference on the Measurement of Policy Impacts, Tallahasee, Florida, May, 1971; Amitai Etzioni, chairman, NSF Summer Institute in Policy Research, Center for Policy Research, Columbia University, June-July, 1971; Douglas Ashford, chairman, Rockefeller Workshop on the Study of Policy Change Cross-Culturally, Cornell University, October, 1971; Austin Ranney, chairman, Social Science Research Council Conference on the Impacts of Public Policy, St. Thomas, Virgin Islands, December, 1971. Among recent panels at professional association meetings: At the American Political Science Association Meeting, Chicago, September, 1971—"The Measurement of Policy Outcomes in the Administration of Social Services," "Methodologies for Evaluating Public Programs," "The Impact of Social Science on Society"; At the American Society for Public Administration Meeting, New York, March, 1972—"Program Evaluation," "Hearings in the Impact of Public Policy," "The Measurement of Policy Impacts," "Midwest Political Science Association Meeting, April, 1972, Chicago, Illinois.

24. Philip Green, "The Obligations of American Social Scientists," *The Annals* 394 (March 1971): 13-27.

25. Conference chaired by Thomas R. Dye. See his "The Measurement of Policy Impact—Conference Summary," in Dye (ed.), *The Measurement of Policy Impact* (Tallahassee, Florida: NSF Report, 1971), 1-8.

26. Ibid., p. 5.

27. Thomas J. Cook, Frank P. Scioli, Jr., "Policy Analysis in Political Science: Trends and Issues in Empirical Research," *Policy Studies Journal* 1 (Autumn 1972): pp. 6-11.

28. Guy H. Orcutt and Alice G. Orcutt, "Incentive and Disincentive Experimentation for Income Maintenance Policy Purposes," *American Economic Review* (September 1968): 754-772. Those interested in obtaining both reprints and working papers dealing with program analysis, The Income Maintenance Experiment, and The Household Allowance Experiment should contact the Urban Institute, 2100 M Street, N.W., Washington, D.C. 20037, requesting information concerning the above material.

29. For a summary of this literature, see Herbert Jacob and Michael Lipsky, "Outputs, Structure and Power. An Assessment of Changes in the

Study of State and Local Politics," *Journal of Politics* 30 (May 1968): 510-38; and Bryan R. Fry and Richard F. Winters, "The Politics of Redistribution," *American Political Science Review* 64 (June 1970): 508-22.

30. See, for example, Joseph LaPalombara, "Macrotheories and Microapplications in Comparative Politics: A Widening Chasm," *Comparative Politics* 1 (1968): 52-78; Roy C. Macridis, "Comparative Politics and the Study of Government," *Comparative Politics* 1 (1968): 79-90.

31. For example, Charles Lindblom, *The Policy-Making Process* (New York: Macmillan, 1965); Norman Frohlich et al., *Political Leadership and Collective Goods* (Princeton: Princeton University Press, 1971); Joyce Mitchell and William Mitchell, *Political Analysis and Public Policy* (Chicago: Rand McNally, 1969); Robert Holt and John Turner, *The Political Bases of Economic Development* (Princeton: Van Nostrand, 1966).

32. For example, Robert C. Fried, "Communism, Urban Budgets and Two Italies," *Journal of Politics* 33 (1971): 1008-51; James B. Hogan, "Social Structure and Public Policy: A Longitudinal Analysis of Mexico and Canada," *Comparative Politics* 4 (1972).

33. James M. Wilkie, *The Mexican Revolution: Federal Expenditure and Social Change Since 1910*, 2nd ed. (Berkeley: University of California Press, 1970).

34. Charles McClelland and Gary Hoggard, "Conflict Patterns in the Interactions of Nations," *International Politics and Foreign Policy*, rev. ed., ed. James N. Rosenau (New York: Free Press, 1969).

35. New York: Macmillan, 1971.

36. Homewood, Illinois: Richard D. Irwin, 1968.

37. Ibid., pp. 280-312.

38. Henry Aaron, "Social Security: International Comparisons," *Studies in the Economics of Income Maintenance*, ed. Otto Eckstein (Washington: Brookings, 1967); Phillips Cutright, "Political Structure, Economic Development and National Social Security Programs," *American Journal of Sociology* 70 (1965): 537-50; B. Guy Peters, "Economic and Political Effects on the Development of Social Expenditures in France, Sweden and the United Kingdom," *Midwest Journal of Political Science* 16 (1972): 225-38; Barbara G. Salmore, "Political Structure, Economic Development and Public Policy: The Case of National Social Security Programs," *New Dimensions in Comparative Politics*, ed. James N. Rosenau et al. (New York: Free Press, forthcoming). More historical treatments include Arnold J. Heidenheimer, "Trade Unions, Benefit Systems and Party Mobilization Styles," *Comparative Politics* 1 (1969): 313-42; and Gaston V. Rimlinger, Welfare Policy and Industrialization in Europe, America and Russia (New York: Wiley, 1971). See also

Heidenheimer, "The Politics of Public Education, Health and Welfare in the U.S. and Western Europe," paper presented at the Annual Meeting of the American Political Science Association, Washington, D.C., September 5-9, 1972.

39. International Labor Organization, *The Cost of Social Security* (Geneva: various years); U.S. Social Security Administration, *Social Security Programs Around the World* (Washington: U.S. Government Printing Office, various years).

40. Aaron, op. cit.; Cutright, op. cit.

41. Peters, op. cit.; Salmore, op. cit.

42. Arthur Banks and Robert Textor, *A Cross-Polity Survey* (Cambridge: MIT Press, 1963).

43. Andreas C. Tsantis, "Political Factors in Economic Development," *Comparative Politics* 2 (1969): 63-78.

44. Irma Adelman and Cynthia Taft Morris, *Society, Politics and Economic Development: A Quantitative Approach* (Baltimore: Johns Hopkins Press, 1967).

45. Eric A. Nordlinger, "Soldiers in Mufti: The Impact of Military Rule Upon Economic and Social Change in the Non-Western States," *American Political Science Review* 64 (1970): 1131-48.

46. Abram Bergson, "Development Under Two Systems: Comparative Productivity Growth Since 1950," *World Politics* 23 (July 1971): 579-617. A narrower and less quantitative study of effects on economic development of political factors is Keith R. Legg, "Regime Change and Public Policy in a Clientilist Polity: The Cases of Greece and Italy," paper presented at the Annual Meeting of the American Political Science Association, Washington, D.C., September 5-9, 1972.

47. Bruce Russett, *What Price Vigilance?* (New Haven: Yale, 1970).

48. Jerry Hollenhorst and Gary Ault, "An Alternative Answer to: Who Pays for Defense," *American Political Science Review* 65 (1971): 760-63. This critique is of an earlier article by Russett, "Who Pays for Defense?" *American Political Science Review* 63 (June 1969): 412-26, much of which is incorporated into chapters 5 and 6 of his later book. See fn. 47.

49. Barbara G. Salmore and Stephen A. Salmore, "Structure and Change in Regimes: Their Effect on Foreign Policy," paper presented at the Annual Meeting of the American Political Science Association, Washington, D.C., September 5-9, 1972; Jonathan Wilkinfeld, "Some Further Findings Regarding Domestic and Foreign Conflict Behavior," *Journal of Peace Research* 5 (1968): 56-59.

50. Charles F. Hermann, "Bureaucratic Structures, Nation-Group-

ings, and Foreign Policy Mapping," Columbus, Ohio State University Mershon Center, 1972 (mimeo).

51. Margaret G. Hermann, "How Leaders Process Information and the Effect on Foreign Policy," paper presented at the Annual Meeting of the American Political Science Association, Washington, D.C., September 1972.

52. Stephen A. Salmore and Charles F. Hermann, "The Effect of Size, Development and Accountability on Foreign Policy," *Peace Research Society Papers* 14 (1969).

53. See, for example, Barbara G. Salmore and Linda P. Brady, "A Codebook for the CREON Descriptive Deck," Columbus, Ohio State University Mershon Center, 1972 (mimeo). Among the frequently used sources for events data collection are the New York Times, Keesings Contemporary Archives, Facts on File, Deadline Data, and regional sources such as Asian Recorder and the Middle East Journal.

54. For example, see Cutrights SIPE measure of social insurance program experience, Cutright, op. cit.

55. Frederick Frey, "Cross-Cultural Survey Research in Political Science," *The Methodology of Comparative Research*, eds. Robert Holt and John Turner, (New York: Free Press, 1970), 173-294.

56. For discussions of such problems, see Erwin K. Scheuch, "Cross-National Comparisons Using Aggregate Data: Some Substantive and Methodological Problems," *Comparing Nations*, eds. Richard Merritt and Stein Rokkan, (New Haven: Yale, 1966); Charles L. Taylor and Michael Hudson, *World Handbook of Political and Social Indicators* (New Haven: Yale, 1972), 2nd ed.; Oskar Morganstern *On the Accuracy of Economic Observations*, rev. ed., (Princeton: Princeton University Press, 1963); Charles L. Taylor, ed., *Aggregate Data Analysis*, (Paris: Mouton and Co., 1968), 63-142.

3

Theory of Public Policy

Vincent Ostrom and
Philip Sabetti

I. Basic Issues and References

Harold Lasswell, more than any other political scientist, has emphasized the function of the policy sciences in developing and clarifying policy alternatives. What was not clear in his early discussions was the distinctive contribution that political scientists could make to the clarification of policy alternatives. However, a new tradition is emerging which recognizes that various types of institutional or decision-making arrangements tend to realize certain possibilities or manifest certain capabilities. Such arrangements will, thus, be "good" for some purposes. In turn, each type of institutional arrangements will be subject to conditions of institutional weakness or failure which arise under specifiable conditions. The attention paid to problems of institutional weaknesses and failures is especially important in specifying the theoretical limits for any type of organization such as market structure, bureaucratic organization or constitutional government.

Economists have explicitly examined problems of market weakness and market failure since the time of Adam Smith. More recently, this examination has focused on the theories of externalities, common-property resources and public goods (Buchanan 1968). The implications which follow from both market failure and the failure of voluntary associations have been developed by Mancur Olson in *The Logic of Collective Action* (1965).

When neither market structure nor voluntary association will enable individuals to produce public goods, manage common-pool resources or avoid the joint costs of negative externalities, the limited coercion capability of public organization is needed in order to prevent holdouts. Some coercive capability is necessary to bind each member of a benefiting community to discharge his proportionate share of the obligations in controlling externalities, managing common-property resources or providing public goods and services. Recourse to public organizational arrangements also requires a recognition of the conditions of institutional weakness and institutional failure which are associated with public organizations. Gordon Tullock in *The Politics of Bureaucracy* (1965) provides an explanation for the loss of information and control in large-scale public bureaucracies. This

---

Sections I and II of this chapter were authored by Vincent Ostrom. Section III was authored by Philip Sabetti.

explanation accounts for bureaucratic dysfunctions and goal displacements observed generally by students of organization theory and resolves the anomoly created by the disparity between Max Weber's conception of bureaucracy as an "ideal" type and his characterization of a "full-developed" bureaucracy. William A. Niskanen's *Bureaucracy and Representative Government* (1971) pursues a similar logic to infer substantial limitations upon institutions of representative government in exercising control over the fully integrated bureau occupying an exclusive monopoly position.

A recognition of some of these limitations has engendered a reconsideration of basic decision rules characteristic of democratic government. Kenneth J. Arrow's *Social Choice and Individual Value* (1951), Anthony Downs, *An Economic Theory of Democracy* (1957), Duncan Black's *The Theory of Committees and Elections* (1958) and William Riker's *The Theory of Political Coalitions* (1962) pursue various implications of the majority-vote rule and have stimulated an intellectual exchange that has reached substantial proportions. James M. Buchanan and Gordon Tullock in *The Calculus of Consent* (1962), in their concern with the selection of decision rules, reconsider the problem of constitutional choice in light of the economic criterion of Pareto optimality. John Rawls in *The Theory of Justice* (1971) propounds criteria of justice as fairness as being relevant to a constitutional choice of institutional arrangements in a democratic society.

These contributions to political theory challenge many basic assumptions and inferences inherent in modern political science. It is precisely such a challenge that enables scholars to array alternative sets of hypotheses and to test those hypotheses by reference to empirical evidence. Alternative conceptual frameworks and alternative explanations also enable policy analysts to array alternative solutions to policy problems. By viewing alternative policies bearing upon the restructuring of decision-making arrangements as alternative hypotheses, we have an opportunity to use reforms as critical experiments and to test those hypotheses in most similar situations (Campbell 1969). Empirical evidence can be used to discard the weaker theoretical explanation.

An explicit awareness of the theoretical issues at stake in the analysis of policy problems will contribute to an understanding of both the capabilities and limitations of different decision-making structures or institutional arrangements for organizing social relationships. When political scientists contribute to the development of such an understanding, they will make a distinctive contribution to a clarification of policy alternatives for choices as among alternative decision structures. The theory contributing to this understanding will provide a basis for predicting the probable consequences to result from using different decision-making arrangements for odering human relationships in different situations. We may then be in a position to clarify what difference structural variables will have upon strategic behavior.

II. Basic Facilities and Institutions

Political Theory as a field of inquiry has had a long tradition of scholarship concerned with naming and classifying theories accompanied by descriptive discourses *about* theory. If theory is to be relevant for policy research or policy analysis, a different approach is required where assumptions and postulates are stipulated and a structure of inferential reasoning is pursued. Such a structure of inferential reasoning establishes an association between specifiable conditions and the consequences which can be expected to follow. A theory indicating an association between conditions and consequences can serve as an explanation and can be used either for formulating hypotheses for empirical research or for predicting the outcomes of alternative courses of action in policy analysis.

In the course of the last decade or so important advances have been made in the explicit use of theory as a tool for deriving logical inferences about the choice of strategies under stipulated conditions and the outcomes which follow from such a choice of strategy. Pioneering work in this regard can be identified with Frank Knight, R.H. Coase, George S. Stigler, Theodore Schultz and colleagues at the University of Chicago, Herbert Simon and colleagues at Carnegie-Mellon University, William Baumol and colleagues at Princeton University, William Riker and colleagues at the University of Rochester, James Buchanan and Gordon Tullock at the University of Virginia (now Virginia Polytechnic Institute and State University), James S. Coleman at the Johns Hopkins University, John V. Krutilla, Allen Kneese and colleagues at Resources for the Future, Inc.

In 1963 a conference on non-market decision making was organized by James Buchanan and Gordon Tullock to bring together a number of individuals associated with these different traditions of work in economic and political theory. Occasional meetings followed and in 1967 the decision was taken to organize the Public Choice Society to provide an opportunity for scholars pursuing related works in economic, political and social choice theory to function as an interdisciplinary community of scholars. Professor Mancur Olson, Department of Economics, University of Maryland, College Park, Maryland, 20742, is the current president of the Public Choice Society.

Professor Gordon Tullock, Center for the Study of Public Choice, Virginia Polytechnic Institute and State University, Blacksburg, Virginia, 24061, is editor of the journal *Public Choice*. Subscriptions to *Public Choice* and membership in the Public Choice Society is $10.00 per year.

Public Choice has begun a monograph series also published at the Center for Study of Public Choice and edited by Gordon Tullock.

A variety of more recent programs concerned with theory and its application to problems of public choice or to public policy analysis are being developed at the University of California, Berkeley (Aaron Wildavsky, School of Public Affairs), University of California, Los Angeles (Werner Hirsch, Institute of Government and Public Affairs), Carnegie-Mellon University (Otto Davis, School of Urban and Public Affairs), University of Pennsylvania (Julius Margolis, Fels Institute), University of Southern Califronia (Jerome W. Milliman, Center for Urban Affairs), Cornell University (Dennis C. Mueller, Robert D. Tollison and Thomas D. Willett, Economics), Indiana University (Vincent Ostrom and Elinor Ostrom, Political Science), University of Michigan (John P. Crecine, Institute for Public Policy Study), University of North Carolina (Duncan MacRae, Political Science), University of Texas (Norman Frolich, Joseph A. Oppenheimer and Oren Young, Political Science), University of Virginia (Roland McKean, Economics), The Urban Institute (Worth Bateman, and Harold Hochman).

The most extensive work in the use of theory in applied policy analysis has been done over the longest period of time at Resources for the Future, Inc., 1755 Massachusetts Avenue, N.W., Washington, D.C. 20036. The UCLA Institute of Government and Public Affairs, under the direction of Werner Hirsch, has an extended list of publications in applied policy analysis which relies upon theory as an essential tool for the formation of research problems. The Urban Institute, 2100 M Street, N.W., Washington, D.C. 20037, is doing important work in the explicit application of theory to urban problems and to the development of indicators for measuring the output of public services. Lists of publications can be procured by to each of these research centers.

In addition to *Public Choice* and to the major journals in economics and political sciences, policy analysts will find the following journals to have useful articles on the application of theory to problems of public policy analysis:

Land Economics
University of Wisconsin
Mary Amend Lescohier, Editor

Journal of Law and Economics
The University of Chicago Law School
R. H. Coase, Editor

Journal of Legal Studies
The University of Chicago Law School
Richard A. Posner, Editor

Journal of Political Economy
Department of Economics and Graduate School of Business
University of Chicago
Robert J. Gordon and Harry Johnson, Editors

Public Policy
John F. Kennedy School of Government
Harvard University
James R. Kurth and Thomas D. Willett, Editors

It should be noted that this review of centers of activity and specialized facilities concerned with the development and use of theory for public policy analysis represents the selective information and bias of its author.

III. European Contributions

Professor Richard Rose has suggested that what in the United States passes for political science research, in Europe may appear under the guise of political economy, political sociology, and the political science*s* more generally [1972:16]. The American political scientist viewing the European scene may be inclined at first sight to regard the Department of Political Science at the University of Leiden, the *Fondation Nationale des Sciences Politiques* in Paris, the *Facoltà di Scienze Politiche "Cesare Alfieri"* in Florence as exceptions to a general lack of concern with political science. Indeed, remarks about the "backwardness" of European political science have often been made by European scholars who, awed by North American efforts, have tended to depreciate their own [Bobbio 1961; Leoni 1960a; Sartori 1970]. But as American political scientists question the theoretical apparatus underlying their scholarship [Diamant 1959; LaPalombara 1968; Lowi 1964, 1969; V. Ostrom 1974], they will discover that the apparent dearth of European political science is an optical illusion; and that there exists a wealth of scholarship to build upon the tradition of Michels, Mosca, Ostrogorski, and Tocqueville. In addition, European scholars themselves may pause to reevaluate their own efforts and question the "Americanization" of their political science.

This problem is further complicated by differences between English and some of the other European languages in the use of terms referring to "policy" and to "politics." "Policy" as used in English is not easily rendered into French, German, Italian, and Spanish. Leoni [1957:226] notes how Lerner and Lasswell's *The Policy Sciences in the United States* had to be translated into French as *Les Sciences de la politique aux Etats-Unis*; Treves [1962:3-26] relates some of the difficulties of rendering "policy makers" into Italian. In these European languages, then, one may speak of "public policy" as particular lines of conduct on the part of government officials in dealing with certain problems.

Europeans refer to the *politics* of revenues, of education, of civil rights, of water, and so on. While particular lines of conduct may require reference to diverse bodies of knowledge, some European scholars have confronted these problems in terms of a logic of collective action that may be applicable to disparate types of issues—namely, the conditions that affect the choice and implementation of particular "policies" through voluntary and public efforts. If American scholars are willing to translate their interests into the appropriate European terms, they will find an abundance of scholarship on the theory of public policy.

Mancur Olson's *The Logic of Collective Action*, for example, specifies the conditions under which voluntary associations will or will not enable individuals to produce public goods, manage commonpool resources or avoid the costs of negative externalities. In the nineteenth century Italian political economists, including Mosca, Pantaleoni, and Pareto, were grappling with similar problems. In his study of the *Risorgimento* in Lombardy, Greenfield [1934] has indicated the extent to which such "publicists" as Giandomenico Romagnosi and Carlo Cattaneo and others before them worked with engineers, economists, lawyers, and peasants (*agricoltori*) to establish associations dealing with the artificial distribution of water in the Po valley. In the review *Giornale degli Economisti* from 1870 to 1920 one can find a rich source of material on a variety of policy problems. James Buchanan deserves credit for bringing some of these works to the attention of an English-reading audience [1960:24-72]. The work of Nullo Baldini dealing with the Ravennese peasants also indicates the extent to which a social analyst had brought his specialized knowledge to bear on questions of voluntary cooperative actions [1966]. Today the success and failure of voluntary efforts are considered in such reviews as *Rivista della Cooperazione* (Rome), *Documentation coopérative* (Brussels), *Coopération* (Paris), *Economie coopérative* (Paris), *Rivista di economia agraria* (Rome), *Rivista del diritto finanziario e scienza delle finanze* (Milan) and *Archives internationales de sociologie de la coopération* (Paris).

An example of how changing market conditions and bureaucratic organization affect the nature and operation of large associations may be gleaned by looking at trade unions. In France, England, and Italy, the last few years have been characterized by an almost unbroken succession of strikes on the part of trade unions both for wage and benefit demands and for "internal democracy." The study *L'Ouvrier français en 1970*, carried out by the *Fondation Nationale des Sciences Politiques* [1971] and the 1972 workshop on labor rights sponsored by the Italian trade unions (CGIL, CISL, UIL) in Bologna illustrate the essential validity of the theoretical analysis sustained by Leoni [1960b, 1967], Michels [1915], Montemartini [1903], Mosca [1949, 1971], Pantaleoni [1903] and Pareto [1897].

Leoni and Pareto were concerned with the degree to which the Italian state was regulating market mechanisms and taking over many industries and turning them into large-scale public enterprises. This is by no means just an Italian phenomenon. A recent French study [Turot 1971] shows the extent to which British enterprises are publicly owned; in Austria today they supply one-third of the economic product and provide for nearly 30 percent of the employed population. Leoni's, Michels', and Pareto's analyses allow us to predict a number of dysfunctions associated both with the oligarchic nature of large-scale organizations and with their provision of public goods and services. In turn, one can accept or reject these analysts' theoretical inquiry in terms of some of the empirical findings associated with the work of Crozier [1964], some of the studies done by the *Instituto per la Scienza dell'Amministrazione Pubblica* [1965] and others [Leon 1971; Osculati 1972; Spreafico 1965].

The emergence of state monopolies and the governmental policy of "full employment" affect the bargaining power of labor. The fear that Montemartini, Mosca, and Pantaleoni expressed was that since labor unions would not face a risk of great unemployment they would be less restrained in demands to escalate wage and other benefits which might exceed increases in productivity. The increased cost of production would then be passed on to the consumer as an inflationary price increase. In turn, high wages would create incentives to displace human labor by machine. But the strategic position of the unions and the *public* ownership of enterprises would generate difficult conflicts where problems would be resolved by shifting burdens to taxpayers and to consumers in monopoly markets.

If the value of a theory is to be judged by its ability to indicate consequences that are likely to follow from particular structural arrangements, then the contribution made by European scholars is substantial. Where they may be challenged is the extent to which they failed to pursue the implications of their analyses for proposing alternative solutions to policy problems. The "paradoxical view of bureaucracy" discussed by Crozier [1964:176] need not be a paradox. The same could be said for Michels' "iron law of oligarchy" and Mosca's "theory of the ruling class." Both Michels and Mosca failed to appreciate the extent to which centralized parties and the rule of the few were elements of centralized constitutional arrangements and to conceptualize alternative arrangements that could have mitigated both the iron law of oligarchy and the theory of the ruling class. Tocqueville's discussion of "democratic despotism" [*Democracy in America*, II, bk. 4] remains the best analysis of the consequences of centralization.

A recognition of some of these limitations has brought scholars to reconsider different structural arrangements for democratic governments. As Europeans attempt to fashion new superstructures for the European Community, new attention is being given to many basic issues in political theory. The place of the individual in an institutional setting characterized by highly centralized political monopolies has been the concern of some European scholars. Diamant [1951] indicated how the *droit administratif* and the creation and operation of the Council of State in France sought to restrain the power of the bureaucracy. To Mosca's idea of "juridical defense" [1939:130-152; *cf*. Lowi 1969], Leoni pressed on to conceptualize a system of positive constitutional law that would allow the individual to make claims on public officials [1961, 1964, 1966]. The review *Le Fédéraliste* (Pavia) has provided an interesting forum for the discussion of the position of the individual both as producer and user of public services in the European Community [Albertini 1969; Hallstein 1969; Rossolillo 1969]. The political theory found in *The Federalist* papers has been utilized by some contributors of *Le Fédéraliste* to analyze some of the institutional weaknesses of the American political system today [Albertini and Rossolillo 1962; *cf*. V. Ostrom 1971]. De Jouvenel's efforts toward a political science that would allow us to predict what consequences are most likely to follow from particular institutional arrangements and policies have led to the creation of the *Futuribles* venture [1963 and 1965; 1965]. Rita Perez's study of Italian agricultural policy represents an attempt to view particular legislation in terms of promise and then analyze the extent to which that promise is carried out [1971].

The realization that different European countries are faced with similar problems has led to a number of activities. The CIRIEC (Centre of Research and Information on Public and Co-operative Economy), established first in Geneva in 1947 and then Liège, was set up to study various aspects of public policy. Now it has branches in a number of countries and journals, such as *Annales de l'économie collective* (Liège) and *Economia Pubblica* (Milan), publish articles that analyze various facets of public enterprises, national and regional planning, activities of municipal governments and the role of trade unions in economic development. The ninth international meeting of CIRIEC was held in Vienna from May 23 to May 25, 1972. The main speakers—Lord Kennet, Great Britain; Professor Henri Janne, Belgium; Professor Helmut Frisch, Austria—dealt with problems of public and cooperative economy. Within the member states of the European Economic Community, there has been a growing realization of the need to consider common problems concerned with the production and provision of essential public services in each country. As a result the European Center for Public Enterprise (CEEP) was established in Brussels and for the past few years has brought together a number of politicians, EEC officials, and social scientists. The publication of the papers presented at their gatherings [CEEP 1967] provides an essential datum for an understanding of how individuals associated with the management and operation of vital national public services view their tasks.

Another interesting development has been the creation of a European Consortium for Political Research. It gathered a number of North American and European scholars to discuss public policy problems at its first "European Policy Workshop," held at the University of Strathclyde, June 18-23, 1972. The convenor was Richard Rose. The papers presented dealt with policy content, policy making, and policy effects in Britain, France, West Germany, the Netherlands, and Sweden. During the course of the proceedings, a group of participants—Herman Aquina, Nijmegen; Nils Elvander, Uppsala; Andries Hoogerwerf, Nijmegen; Jan Kooiman, Leiden; Lennart Lundquist, Uppsala; Robert Putnam, Michigan; Richard Rose, Strathclyde—suggested a strategy for comparative "behavioral policy research" that would treat policy both as dependent and independent variables. They also indicated that one of the most promising areas of research is the possibility of a number of scholars in several countries studying similar policy problems (e.g., environmental policy, tax policy, science policy).

The establishment of a European Consortium of Political Research has also led to the creation of a *European Journal of Political Research*, whose principal objective is "to foster communication and collaboration among European political scientists and the dissemination of research findings and information about ongoing research across national and linguistic boundaries in Europe, and thus to support the Consortium's principal aims." The editor is Arend Lijphart, Department of Political Science, University of Leiden, The Netherlands.

References

AA.VV. *Nullo Baldini nella storia della cooperazione*. Milano: Giuffrè, 1966.
Albertini, M. "La Signification politique do projet de loi." *Le Fédéraliste* 11 (December 1969): 98-107.
———, and F. Rossolillo. "La décadence du fédéralisme aux Etats-Unis." *Le Fédéraliste* 4 (1962): 219-246.
[Archivio] Istituto per la Scienza dell'Amministrazione Pubblica, *La Burocrazia Centrale in Italia*. vols. III. Milano: Giuffrè, 1965.
Arrow, Kenneth J. *Social Choice and Individual Values*. Second Edition. New York: John Wiley and Sons, 1963.

Bish, Robert L. *The Public Economy of Metropolitan Areas*. Chicago: Markham Publishing Company, 1971.

Black, Duncan. *The Theory of Committees and Elections*. Cambridge, England: Cambridge University Press, 1963.

Bobbio, N. "Teoria e ricerca politica in Italia." *Il Politico* 26 (March 1961): 215-233.

Buchanan, James M. *The Demand and Supply of Public Goods*. Chicago: Rand McNally, 1968.

_____. "La Scienza delle finanze: the Italian Tradition in Fiscal Theory." In Buchanan, *Fiscal Theory and Political Economy*. Chapel Hill: The University of North Carolina Press, 1960, 24-74.

_____, and Gordon Tullock. *The Calculus of Consent, Logical Foundations of Constitutional Democracy*. Ann Arbor: University of Michigan Press, 1962.

Campbell, Donald T. "Reforms as Experiments." *American Psychologist* 24 (April 1969): 409-429.

CEEP [Centre Europeen de l'Entreprise Publique]. *Les Entreprises Publiques dans la Communaute Economique Europeenne*. Paris: Dumod, 1967.

Crozier, M. *The Bureaucratic Phenomenon*. Chicago: The University of Chicago Press, 1964.

Diamant, A. "The French Council of State: Comparative Observations on the Problem of Controlling the Bureaucracy of the Modern State." *Journal of Politics* 13 (November 1951): 562-588.

_____. "Is there a non-Western Political Process? Comments on Lucian W. Pye's 'the Non-Western Political Process'." *Journal of Politics* 21 (February 1959): 123-127.

Downs, Anthony. *An Economic Theory of Democracy*. New York: Harper and Row, 1957.

Fairweather, George W. *Methods for Experimental Social Innovation*. New York: John Wiley and Sons, 1967.

Fondation Nationale des Sciences Politiques. *L'Ouvrier Français en 1970*. Paris: Colin, 1971.

Greenfield, K. R. *Economics and Liberalism in the Risorgimento*. Baltimore: The Johns Hopkins Press, 1934.

Hallstein, W. "Discour tenue a Milan le 15 fevrier 1969." *Le Fédéraliste* 11 (December 1969): 108-112.

Hinich, Melvin J. and Peter Ordeshook. "Plurality Maximization vs. Vote Maximization: A Spatial Analysis with Variable Participation." *American Political Science Review* 64 (September 1970): 772-791.

Jouvenel, B. de. *Futuribles, Studies in Conjecture*. vols. II. Geneva: Droz, 1963 and 1965.

_____. "Political Science and Prevision." *American Political Science Review* 59 (March 1965): 29-38.

La Palombara, J. "Macrotheories and Microapplications in Comparative Politics: A Widening Chasm." *Comparative Politics* 1 (October 1968): 52-78.

Lasswell, Harold D. and Daniel Lerner. *The Policy Sciences*. Palo Alto: Stanford University Press, 1951.

Leon, P. "Riflessioni sull'impresa pubblica in Italia." *Economia Pubblica* 1 (October 1971): 3-10.

Leoni, B. "The Meaning of 'Political' in Political Decisions." *Political Studies* 5 (1957): 225-239.

_____. "Un bilancio lamentevole: il sottosviluppo della scienza politica in Italia." *Il Politico* 25 (1960): 31-41.

_____. "Considerazioni sullo schema di legge per la tutela della liberta' di concorrenza." *Il Diritto dell' economia* no. 2 (1960): 191-202.

_____. *Freedom and the Law*. Princeton, N.J.: Van Nostrand, 1961. For some comments on this work and on the other works of Leoni, see F. A. Hayek' "Bruno Leoni the Scholar." *Il Politico* 33 (March 1968): 21-25, and Mario Stoppino, "Potere e potere politico nel pensiero di Bruno Leoni." *Il Politico* 34 (March 1969): 46-70.

_____. "The Law as Claim of the Individual." *Archiv fur Rechts-und Sozialphilosphie* 52 (1964): 45-58.

_____. "Filosofia del Diritto."Appunti dal corso di lezioni, Falcoltà' di Giurisprudenza, Università di Pavia, 1965-1966. Redatti da Stefano Lenghi.

_____. "Sciopero e serrata oggi in Italia." *Il Politico* 32 (1967): 49-70.

Lindblom, Charles E. *The Intelligence of Democracy: Decision Making Through Mutual Adjustment*. New York: The Free Press, 1965.

Lowi, T. J. "American Business, Public Policy, Case Studies and Political Theory." *World Politics* 16 (July 1964): 677-715.

_____. *The End of Liberalism*. New York: W. W. Norton, 1969.

Meehan, Eugene J. *The Foundations of Political Analysis*. Homewood, Illinois: The Dorsey Press, 1971.

Michels, R. [1915], *Political Parties*. Glencoe, Illinois: Free Press, 1958 edition.

Montemartini, G. "La cooperazione di classe." *Giornale degli Economisti*. 26 (January 1903): 63-76.

Mosca, G. [1896]. *The Ruling Class*. trans. by H. D. Kahn. New York: McGraw-Hill, 1939.

_____. *Partiti e Sindacati nella Crisi del Regime Parlamentare*. Bari: Laterza, 1949.

_____. *Il Tramonto dello Stato Liberale*. A cura di Antonio Lombardo. Catania: Bonanno Editore, 1971.

Niskanen, William A., Jr. *Bureaucracy and Representative Government*. Chicago: Aldine-Atherton, 1971.

Olson, Mancur. *The Logic of Collective Action*. Cambridge, Massachusetts: Harvard University Press, 1965.

Osculati, F. "Gli investimenti delle imprese pubbliche nell'ultimo decennio." *Economia Pubblica* 2 (April 1972): 15-32.

Ostrom, V. *The Theory of a Compound Republic. A Reconstruction of the Logical Foundation of American Democracy as Presented in The Federalist*. Blacksburg, Virginia: Center for Study of Public Choice, 1971.

_____. [1973]. *The Intellectual Crisis in American Public Administration*. University, Alabama: The University of Alabama Press, 1974 edition.

Ostrom Vincent and Elinor Ostrom. "Public Choice: A Different Approach to the Study of Public Administration." *Public Administration Review* 31 (March/April 1971): 203-216.

Pantaleoni, M. "Alcune osservazioni sui sindacati e sulle leghe." *Giornale degli Economisti* 26 (March 1903): 236-265; 26 (April 1903): 346-378; 27 (December 1903): 560-581. Refer also to the works cited in Buchanan's article listed above.

Pareto, V. "L'étatisme en Italie." *Bibliotheque Universelle et Revue Suisse*, March-April 1897; reprinted in V. Pareto, *The Ruling Class in Italy Before 1900*. ed. by G. Prezzolini. New York: Vanni, 1950, 107-143.

Perez, R. *Aspetti Giuridici della pianificazione in agricultura*. Milano: Giuffrè, 1971.

Rawls, John. *A Theory of Justice*. Cambridge, Massachusetts: Harvard University Press, 1971.

Riker, William H. *The Theory of Political Coalitions*. New Haven: Yale University Press, 1962.

Rose, R. "Why Comparative Policy Studies?" *Policy Studies Journal* 1 (1972): 14-17.

Rossolillo, F. "Europa, 'terra senza giustizia'." *Il Federalista* 2 (1960): 203-218. *Il Federalista* later changed its name to *Le Fédéraliste*.

Sartori, G. "Per una definizione della scienza politica." In G. Sartori (ed.), *Antológia di Scienza Politica*. Bologna: Il Mulino, 1970, 11-30.

Spreafico, A. *L'amministrazione e il cittadino*. Milano: Edizioni di Comunità, 1965.

Suchman, E. A. *Evaluative Research: Principles and Practice in Public Service and Social Action Programs*. New York: Russell Sage, 1967.

Tocqueville, A. de. *Democracy in America*. vols. II. Phillips Bradley editor. New York: Vintage Books Edition, 1961.

Treves, R. "Sociologi e centri di potere in Italia." In AA.VV. *Sociologi e centri di potere in Italia*. Bari: Laterza & Figli, 1962, 3-26.

Tullock, Gordon. *Politics of Bureaucracy*. Washington, D.C.: The Public Affairs Press, 1965.

Turot, P. "Les entreprises publiques en Grande-Bretagne." *Notes et études documentaires*. Paris: La Documentation française, 1971.

Wagner, Richard E. *The Fiscal Organization of American Federalism*. Chicago: Markham, 1971.

Williamson, Oliver E. "Hierarchical Control and Optimum Firm Size." *Journal of Political Economy*. 75 (April 1967): 123-138.

4 Comparative Public Policy

Richard Rose

I. Why Comparative Policy Studies?

America is a big country, big enough to have problems sufficient to keep an army of policy scientists busy for decades to come. Any overviews of the comparative approach to policy studies first requires justification for this activity.

All knowledge involves implicit or explicit comparison. For example, the study of income distribution compares the range of individual incomes around a mean. The study of American public policy has been much advanced by comparisons of state expenditure patterns. The introduction of a time dimension into studies of state expenditure and state legislation illustrates the value of making comparisons across time. Such comparisons can also be made if t_1 = period of enunciating the intent of policy-makers, and t_2 = period in which the effects of a policy are (or ought to be) visible. Understanding can also be advanced by making comparisons across policy areas: for example, the decision to drop the atomic-bomb differed in procedure as well as effect from that involved, say, in decisions about social security benefits. Cross-national comparison simply adds another dimension to our intellectual perspective.

A basic reason for studying public policy comparatively is that the policy of a national government often stipulates uniformity throughout the country, or constrains variety. This is most obviously the case with decisions about collective goods such as war and peace. It is also true insofar as federal legislation is of pre-emptive importance (e.g., taxation) or compels state and local governments to meet minimum standards. Only by making comparisons across national boundaries is there the possibility of variation. Once this is achieved, there is a minimal obstacle to the unwarranted generalization of universals from single case studies. For example, one might study why some nations remained neutral in the First (or Second) World War, and others did not, or why the United States does not have a national health service and other nations do.

The above examples illustrate that in the first instance, variations likely to emerge from cross-national policy studies may be qualitative. Moreover, instead of explaining why a country adopts the policy it does, with a seeming inevitably, one can consider empirically why it did not choose an alternative policy. This has considerable utility in handling the 'non-decision' problem while preserving respect for canons of empirical research.

Broadening one's research outlook inevitably widens the range of cultural and ideological values relevant to understanding politics. The curious coalition of interests in American party politics is reflected nowhere else in the Western world—except perhaps in the Republic of Ireland. In most European nations Socialist (and sometimes Communist) parties propound policy alternatives, and sometimes enact them into law. In Scandinavia, agricultural interest groups have organized as separate parties, thus permitting a comparison of interest advancement through electoral channels, as against pressure group channels conventional elsewhere. The direction and content of the policy influence of the Catholic Church and Catholic parties is a matter about which Popes, bishops and lay Catholics might disagree. Given the Catholic hierarchy's concern for safeguarding faith and morals, one would expect Protestant (and perhaps, predominantly anti-clerical) cultures to have different social policies than Catholic countries. Those who write about ethnic influence upon American public policy preferences would find Europe an even richer laboratory for comparative study. Both cultural and ideological influences become potentially greater as one moves from Western Europe to Eastern Europe countries.

Anyone who has ever studied European as well as American government realizes that there are major differences among nations in the structure of legislatures, executives, judiciaries and in central-local government relations. The policy studies approach poses a simple yet fundamental question: in what way, if any, do these institutional differences affect choices between policy alternatives, the implementation of policies, or the effects of policies? Do the oft-coveted powers of a British Cabinet allow it to adopt far more radical policy reforms than the incrementalist (or obstructionist) pattern of Presidential-Congress relations? What are the 'trade offs' between responsiveness and nationwide uniformity as between the co-operative federalism of America, and the centralist tradition of France?

The hypotheses about similarities can be confirmed more satisfactorily by cross-national analysis than by corss-state or cross-regional analysis within a society. (Practical policy issues confronting the European Common Market are already forcing forward a concern with cross-regional, cross-national comparisons.) One familiar proposition about commonality concerns the influence of economic and social conditions upon levels of public policy expenditure and/or the contents of these policies. *If* one knows the context of national policies and the methods of deriving indicators, *then* there is scope for regression-type analysis. But this method, while useful in cross-sectional comparisons, is usually insufficient to understand the dynamic processes that make policies change, in impact and content, through time—as national living standards rise. The current international concern with the costs of growth is likely to inhibit analysts from making any simple unilinear extrapolations about the future from statistical analyses, or assuming that 'more' always means 'better'.

The variety of questions stimulated by a comparative approach to policy studies is both a strength and a weakness. It is a strength, inasmuch as it encourages people to think more and especially to think carefully about culture-bound assumptions in research within their own national context. It is also a strength because knowledge derived from a much wider class of cases and experiences is more likely to prove valid. Not least, variety is a strength because it enables scholars to understand more about a larger portion of the world. This is particularly the case when nations and not individuals are the units of analysis.

The very breadth of the field is also a weakness. Is there any sense in which scholars concerned with disputes about linguistic issues in Africa or Europe are doing the same sort of work as those studying the administration of the railways in France or England?

Comparative policy studies, like many other branches of political science, is a field requiring simultaneous expansion on many fronts. On the one hand, there is a substantial body of knowledge that must be acquired about how policies actually work outside America as well as inside America. This knowledge cannot be gleaned solely from statistical abstracts—nor can it be reliably presented by ignoring all sources of quantitative data. Political scientists bred in a professional atmosphere that is increasingly narrow, as a price of its professionalism, may find that many other social scientists have already collected much useful evidence. The fact that they are called social workers, educational sociologists, town planners, or health administrators does not make their writings any less important. Europeans may have an advantage. The weakness of professional political science is an asset in bringing them more into contact with studies in economics, public administration and other social sciences. The proximity of political scientists to policy-makers is specially likely to occur in smaller European democracies, ranging from Ireland to Finland.

The substance of issues, as well as national contexts, differ in so many ways that one cannot automatically expect that pooling findings will cumulate knowledge. Even within a narrow European context, there are substantial distances between a comparative student of pressure groups and, say, a student of social services. This distance will be greatly magnified if the scholars involved not only speak different 'home languages' but also, different 'work languages', i.e., conceptual frameworks.

Knowing what really goes on is important, but it is only half the story. The other question to ask is: What does it mean? One must have concepts to give generality to specific facts. Conceptual clarity is a *sine qua non* for formulating and testing hypotheses that can be tested in more than one national context. It is also important to articulate clearly one's model of governing, to ensure that similar parts of the policy process are being compared across national boundaries. In any language, a student of policy studies should particularly have a good nose for 'What politics is about'.

II. Resources for Policy Studies in Britain

There are many reasons why American scholars interested in comparative policy studies should turn to Britain, besides the obvious advantage of ease in learning the language. The institutions of British government have long been praised by textbook writers. This creates the expectation that the policy outputs of these institutions are also worthy of respect and possible emulation. Even left wing critics of British government will praise much that is done in Britain—if America is the basis for evaluation. The early establishment of welfare programs in Britain makes it possible to analyze the long-term dynamics of policies, through historical scholarship as well as through contemporary studies. Today, British government is big government, both in the scale of its activities and the size of its problems. Established policies are being examined critically, as rising expectations outstrip available resources. Moreover, in some fields, researchers report that outcomes are inconsistent with historic intentions and expectations, thus raising questions about whether *more* resources are needed for established policies or different policies are needed. As in America, both major political parties are actively seeking new formulae for coping with problems old and new.

A. *Specific Policy Fields*

The range of policy issues available for study is as wide (or wider) in Britain than in the United States. In the field of social welfare, health and education services are internationally prominent. Provision for the social security of dependents—from children's allowances through state assistance to the elderly—is on a massive scale too. Housing is a welfare service not restricted to the poor: nearly one-third of all families live in government-built and government-owned housing. For generations the government has exercised substantial planning powers; hence, the Department of the Environment is a relatively strong agency to confront new issues of overcrowding and pollution.

Americans, recently rather scornful of British difficulties in combining economic growth with full employment and price stability, may wish after dollar devaluation to look again at the British economy. The much lower rate of unemployment in Britain than America is immediately noteworthy.

The British philosophy of voluntary negotiation in industrial relations rather than using legislation, also differs significantly. Nationalized industries have been established for a quarter of a century and there is substantial experience of government intervention in private firms, by share buying, grants, loans and directives. The Ministry of Technology (now, the Department of Trade & Industry) has sought by positive intervention to 'restructure' British industry to stimulate growth. Planning machinery has expanded and contracted cyclically, in accord with economic fashions and experience. Regional economic plans and subsidies also provide ample data for study.

Examining law and order in Britain is likely to stimulate Americans to emphasize contrasts. The English have maintained their relative freedom from violence, notwithstanding a secular trend upwards in crime. Policemen still go unarmed. Legislation enforcing conventional morality has been modified or repealed in such fields as censorship and abortion. The broadcasting media are regulated much more than in America; political reporting, as well as 'permissive' entertainment are both controversial subjects. The press is increasingly able to report more 'inside' information from government, but Whitehall is still far from the leaky sieve of Washington. In race relations, the absence of a Bill of Rights along American lines and the absence of judicial review has kept the courts from a significant role in a field which is increasingly worrisome to British politicians. Armed conflict in Northern Ireland raises basic questions about whether Ulster is exceptional in generalizations about British politics—or an exception that proves more general rules.

In the past decade, Britain has become less significant than formerly in foreign policy and defence. The Foreign Office no longer commands the influence it once enjoyed, and defence forces have been run down too. Concurrently, Britain has negotiated entry into the European Common Market. This provides an unusual opportunity to study the impact of a major policy. Researchers will face the classic problem of figuring out what consequences were intended, and which were unanticipated. Common Market entry is also expected to write a new chapter in relations with the Old Dominions and the new Commonwealth. Britain continues to have active diplomatic relationships with many Third World countries without military concerns.

B. Publications

A researcher wishing to read his way into the subject could do worse than start with a standard history of Britain since 1832. Without historical perspective, current circumstances may be misunderstood. T.H.

Marshall's collection of essays, *Class, Citizenship and Social Development* (Anchor, 1965) provides both history and concepts. Descriptions and analyses of British government today usually draw upon policy issues for illustration, but do not set out systematically what government does. The volumes in the New Whitehall Series (Allen & Unwin) provide descriptions, department by department, of institutions and functions in a dry but thorough way. Uptodate and broad reviews can be found in W.A. Robson and B. Crick, editors, *The Future of the Social Services* (Penguin, 1970), Peter Townsend and Nicholas Bosanquet, editors, *Labour and Inequality* (Fabian Society, 1972), and Wilfred Becherman, editor, *The Labour Government's Economic Record, 1964-1970* (Duckworth, 1972). The political values in these publications are usually easy to note. For contrary perspectives, see research publications of the Bow Group and its quarterly, *Crossbow* (Bow publications, 240 High Holborn, London, WC1), and monographs published by the Institute for Economic Affairs (2 Lord North Street, Westminster, London, S.W.1.) In *Left or Right: the Bogus Dilemma* (Secker & Warburg, 1968), Samuel Brittan has argued that British parties no longer represent meaningfully coherent alternative combinations of policies. PEP (Political and Economic Planning) has through the years published more than 500 monographs on specific policy issues in its *Planning* series. These surveys may be supplemented on economic issues by Sam Brittan, *Steering the Economy* (Penguin, 1971) and, for the environment, by a journalistic study of Tony Aldous, *Battle for the Environment* (Fontana, 1972).

New Society, a weekly now in its tenth year, provides the most comprehensive guide to current public policy. In addition to articles on topical issues, often written by academic specialists, its book reviews and notes provide uptodate bibliography, and comments on research findings and research in progress. It also has a quarterly index. *New Society* is biased toward social policy as its classified advertisements make clear. Economics and foreign policy are well catered for by the serious British press. As far as journals are concerned more information is probably given about policy matters in *Public Administration* than any other political science journal, albeit the form of presentation is often descriptive rather than social scientific. Economic journals contain articles that explicitly or indirectly address major policy concerns. The articles in *Sociology* and the *British Journal of Sociology* tend to discuss society in terms of academic concepts, rather than policy concepts. Among newer journals, those of special relevance include *Urban Studies, Journal of Social Policy* and *Policy and Politics*, subtitled, "Studies of local government and its services." Both the Conservative and Labour parties usually publish detailed campaign guides before each general election. In addition to party polemics, these guides review a wide range of policy areas, topic by topic.

No Labour Party guide was published in 1970. The Campaign Guide, 1970 (Conservative Central Office) is a very detailed 752 page publication, with much factual material.

British government publications provide much information of interest to policy analysts, though public officials would be the first to admit that the range does not provide everything of interest. The most useful single volume is *Social Trends* (No. 2, 1971, HMSO). In addition to trend statistics, it also contains a selection of articles analysing data. The *Annual Abstract of Statistics* (No. 108, 1971, HMSO) is the nearest counterpart to Continental Statistical Yearbooks. It is weighted toward economic data. Both volumes provide bibliographical guides to other government statistical sources. Censuses are detailed, but published slowly. Students of voting should note that census data is published by parliamentary constituency boundaries (*Census 1966: UK General and Parliamentary Constituency Tables*, HMSO, 1969). The Treasury now publishes an annual forecast of public expenditure, with useful prose discussions of policy issues as well as financial data. (See e.g., *Public Expenditure 1969-70 to 1974-75*, HMSO, Cmnd.4578, 1971).

C. Academic Perspectives and Programs

American scholars have time and again demonstrated the feasibility of undertaking studies in Britain, often within the compass of a one-year stay. The difficulties of access that can inhibit research into central government decision-making (or avoidance of decisions) are not so formidable when one seeks to analyse decisions as part of a more complex social and political process. The consequences of policies must be public and observable. A government cannot classify a policy outcome as 'top secret'. To admit ignorance is to say something about the limits of its own powers. Gradually government departments are welcoming contacts with the world of research. Each department is supposed to appoint an academic liaison officer. Many departments have also formed research or planning units. (For details of departmental offices, see the annual *British Imperial Calendar and Civil Service List*, HMSO). The involvement of pressure groups in policy making provides a second, if indirect route into departmental activities. The involvement of academics, as consultants, lobbyists and occasionally, as administrators, provides another network of contacts with officialdom.

The most important feature of the policy process in Britain is that it is *not* centralized in 10 Downing Street. The seamless web can be entered at many points outside Whitehall. These are points where overseas researchers are rarely found. Moreover, administrators outside Westminster are likely to know more about most policies than do MPs. The first place to look for knowledge is local government: most social services of the welfare state are administered by local rather than central government. (Regional devolution in Scotland and Wales provides other centres of administration.) There is functional devolution too, to the nationalized industries, and to a wide range of administrative bodies and boards. Many professional bodies, such as doctors, lawyers, accountants and sanitary inspectors, are involved in consultations with government departments collectively on policy matters, as well as concerned with conditions of work and payment. Each policy area tends to have its own specialist network. If a person knows what kind of problem interests him, he should be able, with diligence, common sense and courtesy to cut into policy questions at a significant point of entry.

British academics have long been accustomed to think in 'problem' or 'policy' terms, though there is very little use of the terms 'policy studies' as a symbol. Good researchers publish studies that draw upon knowledge from a wide range of sources, and maintain contacts with a mixture of politicians, administrators, lobbyists, media men and specialists. They will 'talk politics' 'talk housing' or 'talk pensions', rather than 'talk political science', or 'talk social theory.' The origins of policy studies in Britain antedate the founding of social science faculties in Britain, and Charles Booth and the Rowntrees were studying the nature, causes and cure of poverty before the American Political Science Association was founded. The tradition is not *ipso facto* better or worse than that in which young American researchers are trained. It is merely different—and the differences are probably lessening.

A visiting American researcher with political science training must first of all learn to think in inter-disciplinary terms, in order to make contact with those most interested in his own problem area. In part this is because of the bias toward institutional, rather than analytic studies, in British Political Studies (Cf Richard Rose, editor, *Policy-Making in Britain,* Free Press: 1969). Depending upon his interest, the visitor may find kindred researchers in departments of politics, economics, econometrics, sociology, social administration, planning (i.e., housing and land use) or operations research. Law faculties have yet shown few signs of encouraging 'public interest' studies along American lines. Relatively few researchers concerned with public policy are sophisticated in statistics or the methodology of measurement. (For exceptions, see A. Shonfield and S. Shaw, editors, *Social Indicators and Social Policy*, Heinemann, 1972). In almost all fields, people have a sophisticated awareness of the substantive and procedural characteristics of policy issues, and their political context. A listing of funded research can be most easily obtained by consulting the *Newsletter* of the state-sponsored Social Science Research Council. (Like *The*

Times—or the American SSRC—this British body sees no need to make its nationality part of its title). The *Newsletter* contains short articles on research trends—including the efforts of government departments to aid or encourage research relevant to their interests. There is as yet nothing like the Schools of Public Policy that have been springing up in America in recent years from Harvard to Berkeley.

Any listing of University departments risks being invidious and obsolescent, given movements of personnel, and the fact that good work (and bad work) can be done in unlikely places. In econometric studies, there are numerous extremely able academics, many with international reputations. The Institute of Social and Economic Research at the University of York has a group of senior economists specially concerned with public expenditure studies and questions of public choice: Alan Peacock, Alan Williams and Jack Wiseman. The Social Administration department of the London School of Economics has the largest collection of people working on social policy, including Richard Titmuss and Brian Abel-Smith. In neither institution do political scientists draw greatly upon these assets. The Politics Department at Strathclyde has been showing the most initiative among Political Science departments, in advancing methodologically sophisticated and substantively significant studies of policy questions. It was also host to a Workshop on European Policy Studies in June, 1972, providing continental contacts in this field.

D. Research Institutes and Funding

London is rich in institutions that specialize in policy oriented research, under university or government sponsorship, or in an inbetween world. The Royal Institute of International Affairs is the oldest of these (Director: Andrew Shonfield. Chatham House, St. James's Square, SW1). The Royal Institute of Public Administration is almost as old. (Director: Raymond Nottage. Hamilton House, Mabledon Place, WC1). The Institute for Strategic Studies seeks to complement their work in the defence field (Director: F. Duchene. 18 Adam Street, WC2). The Institute of Commonwealth Studies seeks to co-ordinate the resources of the University of London in studies of the non-Western world (Director: W.H. Morris Jones, 27 Russell Square, WC1). The National Institute of Economic & Social Research concentrates primarily upon the collection and analysis of economic data (Director: G.D.N. Worswick, 2 Dean Trench Street, SW1). The Centre for Environmental Studies is concerned broadly with social problems; the importance of housing and planning issues in Britain is reflected in the thrust of its work. (Director: David Donnison, 5 Cambridge Terrace, NW1). For more than 30 years PEP has done contract research on a wide variety of social and economic problems. (Directors: J. Pinder & R. Davies, 12 Upper Belgrave Street, SW1). A new addition to this ensemble of organizations is the Centre for Social Policy Research, initiated by a Rowntree grant to provide a 'Chatham House' study centre specially concerned with welfare state problems. (Director: A.S. Isserlis, 7 Arundel Street, WD2). The Civil Service College, 11 Belgrave Road, SW1, founded in response to the Fulton Committee's request for reforms, has an interest in encouraging research. Dr. Henry Parris is director of studies for public administration; none of the directors has a new-style 'policy analysis' title. All of these organizations publish annual reports describing their publications and facilities.

Outside London, the chief research centres are in universities. A review of scholarly achievement will show that in Britain as in America the national capital has no monopoly claim as the home of good researchers. One might specially note outside London research centres in fields not heretofore mentioned. Mass media studies are concentrated at the Centre for Mass Communications Research, University of Leicester (Director: James D. Halloran) and the Centre for Television Research, University of Leeds (Director: Jay G. Blumler). The SSRC has sponsored an industrial relations research unit at the University of Warwick (Director: Prof. H.A. Clegg); there are also active industrial relations research groups at a number of other universities. An SSRC sponsored research unit concerned with race relations operates as the SSRC Research Unit on Ethnic Relations at the University of Bristol (Director: Prof. M. Banton). The government's race-oriented Community Relations Commission also has a research director, Dr. Alan Little (Russell Square House, Russell Square, London, WC1). The SSRC's annual *Postgraduate Studentships in the Social Sciences* (State House, High Holborn, London, WC1) gives an exhaustive listing of postgraduate fields of studies in United Kingdom universities. The SSRC maintains a Survey Research Unit (Director: Dr. Mark Abrams) and sponsors community survey units at Durham (Director: A. Townsend) and the University of Strathclyde, Glasgow (Director: J.A. Brand). The clearing house for research on Ulster is the Northern Ireland Community Relations Commission (Research Publications Officer: John Darby, Bedford House, 16/22 Bedford Street, Belfast BT2). Those not wishing to become involved in participant-observation of political violence can settle in an armchair with Richard Rose, "Ulster Politics: a Select Bibliography of Political Discord," *Political Studies* XX:2, 1972.

American foundation policy in funding support for research in Britain is best ascertained by direct communication. Post-graduate students are eligible to apply for scholarships to Britain under schemes operated by the Fulbright program, the Marshall Fellowships, the Rotary International, and the Cecil Rhodes Trust. (Only the latter is restricted to a single institution). The Fulbright program has earmarked an annual faculty award, and a Fulbright studentship for work in policy studies at the University of Strathclyde, for the next three years. (Details from the Committee on International Exchange of Persons, 2101 Constitution Avenue, N.W., Washington, D.C. 20418, U.S.A. or from the author, at Strathclyde). British foundations normally only make research grants to institutions, on behalf of affiliated scholars.

III. Concepts for Comparison[a]

Comparison requires conceptualization, for a statement about the similarity or differences in public policy in two countries presupposes some generalized idea, equating activities otherwise described in a specific and contextual fashion. Both comparative and nation-specific research will benefit if scholars are first of all clear about concepts. Otherwise, there is a risk that policy scientists will be able to communicate informally in a common language—colloquial American—yet exchange professional papers that employ so many differing and vague conceptual languages that the result in an intellectual Tower of Babel.

A. *The Policy Process Model in General*

The term *policy* is perhaps best considered a generic symbol, rather than a scientifically precise concept. Scholars have used the term with a very wide variety of meanings, some overlapping and some mutually exclusive. It can refer to a set of expectations and intentions, or to a series of actions and their consequences, or to all of these together. There is justification for defining politics as the study of policy, or *vice versa*. Etymologically, the same Greek root appears in three English words: policy, politics and police.[1]

In the opinion of this author, the most useful framework for organizing knowledge at present is a process model.[2] In our present state of ignorance the first advantage of a process model is that it is open. One can introduce additional steps or influences without violating logical assumptions. The argument against rational-deductive models is the same as Braybrooke and Lindblom's argument against the synoptic conception of problem solving: such models assume that in advance of research, one can scan a very wide field of knowledge and know what to put in and what to leave out.[3]

A second positive feature of a process model is that it emphasizes

---

[a]This section is based upon a lengthier paper, "Comparing Public Policy," *European Journal for Political Research* (Elsevier).

relationships between political phenomena, and not the mere cataloging of information, or proliferation of taxonomies. We are not simply interested in a list of influences (or regression weights) that might in some unspecified way affect a policy. Instead, we wish to know how influences relate to one another, with more emphasis on the logic of causality than can be obtained from a correlation matrix. While a process model is open, an additional stage can be introduced only if the researcher specifies where it fits into the process, how it is influenced by previous stages in the process, and how it influences subsequent stages.

A third advantage of a process model is that it is dynamic. In moving from the left to the right of the flow chart, one is explicitly or implicitly moving through time. Dynamic properties are of crucial importance, because policies are not advocated, adopted, implemented and evaluated at one moment of time, even though social scientists, in their eagerness to be relevant, may study policies before substantial consequences can be evaluated. Established policy areas of the welfare state are specially suited for dynamic analysis. There is much historical material at hand, including evidence of policy impact in the past, and government response to such evidence. Moreover, the maintenance of routine, as Sharkansky has emphasized, is of major concern to bureaucracies everywhere.[4] A dynamic model will also help identify conditions in which policies become 'deroutinized'.

While the parts of the policy process must be considered one at a time, demands are voiced, alternatives reviewed, existing policies implemented and evaluated concurrently. The order and emphasis given the parts can vary with the political context or with the analytic interest of the researcher. The following outline adopts, for purposes of clarity and familiarity, a liberal model of governance; popular demands are depicted as providing the stimulus for government response. At least five other models of governing can be discerned: an authority model, in which government initiates demands and the populace must respond; models of social control or social autonomy, in which non-governmental institutions interact with popular demands; and two models of court politics, in which parts of the 'black box' of government interact with each other without regard to popular demands or response.[5] Re-arranging the parts of the process effects the impact of government. For example, a government will be more effective in achieving policies that it initiates (e.g., military conscription) than policies originating in response to popular demands (e.g., improvements in health or education).

The following outline is meant to be comprehensive in scope, rather than exhaustive in detail. We must first see the framework as a whole, to ensure that we are not lost in a mass of detail.

B. Specific Parts of the Model

1. *The initial state.* The process logically commences with an inspection of society *prior to* the first visible signs of activity in the area of enquiry. Inasmuch as government is, directly or indirectly, active in so many aspects of social life, the start of the process is likely to be a point that the researcher decides must limit his time span rather than a historical status quo ante. The information required here is likely to be objective and sociological. Governmental statistics, whether or not integrated into a set of social accounts, are a standard source of such information. Moreover, their use avoids the researcher seeking to argue that a 'need' exists. Statistics record a condition that may or may not be thought to demonstrate need. For example, poverty existed for centuries in Western societies without this objective social condition stimulating a positive policy response.

2. *Placing a condition on the agenda of political controversy.* This represents a crucial transition from study of the social system generally to concentrating attention specifically within the political system. The rapid international rise of public policy debate about matters as diverse as environmental pollution and moral permissiveness shows that the barriers to entry to the agenda of controversy are fewer than students of mass political behavior might expect and also, less durable. Comparative analysis provides a means of identifying variations in policy agendas. Moreover, the rapid contemporary diffusion of concerns across international boundaries raises very interesting questions about the diffusion of ideas, whether among urban terrorists, plant ecologists, university undergraduates or civil servants in central government.

3. *The advancement of demands.* Organized political activity is required to advance or oppose demands for government action. Parties and pressure groups are both well researched fields in Europe. The role of parties in policy-making is, however, less advanced than other features of the party literature. For example, Stein Rokkan has explicitly called attention to the importance of "a vast network of interest organizations and other corporate bodies" in the policy process in Norway, but most Norwegian research continues to emphasize the links of parties backwards to social structure, rather than forward into government.[6]

4. *The form of government.* The literature of pressure groups emphasizes that group demands are affected by, as well as influencing, the character of government. In a centralized state, group demands must be directed at a single point; in a government with a plurality of decision-making points, lobbyists must direct their efforts to a multiplicity of points, or accept partial success at best. Alexander J. Groth has sought to explore

the significance of institutional forms by asking a much wider question: What differences in policy follow from differences between democratic, authoritarian and totalitarian regimes.[7]

5. *Reviewing resources and constraints.* The formulation of alternative policies or combinations of policies goes forward on the basis of resources available, and constraints upon choice.[8] To note this is not to suggest that there will be a consensus about potential means; judgments will inevitably differ according to aspirations. Partisan ideologues will likely be more optimistic than skilled administrators, and those who subscribe to one or another technocratic ideology may perceive prospects in yet another light. The crucial point is that all possibilities are not simultaneously considered; only a finite number are considered possible responses to a given demand. Systematic cross-national comparison of debates about a similar set of demands—e.g., the construction of inter-city motorways—would enable one to see to what extent alternatives were not adopted because beyond the resources or because outside the perception of policy-makers.

6. *Shifting from no-decision to decision.* A debate about policy can go on for a very long time. For example, the British government deliberated about the introduction of decimal coinage in 1816; the decision to go decimal was taken 150 years later. Deliberations about a tunnel or bridge across the English Channel have been going on since 1802; the policy is still at a state of no-decision. A government takes a decision for any of three basic reasons: there is a routine (e.g., an annual budget cycle); there is a crisis with a known deadline (e.g., a military ultimatum), or in which delay is daily very costly (e.g., a balance of payments crisis). The residual third category of events is 'non-routine' and 'non-crisis'. This is the field most requiring analysis.

7a. *The determinants of government choice.* Reference to choice rather than decision underscores the serial character of the policy process. Big and small choices arise all the time in deliberations prior to action, and in the implementation of a course of action formally recommended. A decision can be no more than an initial statement of intention, operationalized by subsequent choices.

7b. *The content of choice.* Any choice, however determined, can also by analyzed in terms of its formal character. A government may choose to enact a law or, alternatively, it may choose to meet demands with a symbolic response, e.g., a ministerial speech about the need for change, or an appeal to public opinion, with legislation, personnel and money as well as legal authority committed. In the case of a speech, the only material resource invested is the paper on which the text is duplicated.

8. *Implementing policies.* A government's response only has meaning by the implementation of intentions. Many contemporary political scien-

tists de-emphasize the study of policy implementation in much of the 'modern' literature. Books such as Crozier's *The Bureaucratic Phenomenon*[9] have concerned culture and attitudes within the bureaucracy, rather than examining what difference the French style of administration makes for the results of policy.

9. *The production of outputs*. The identification of policy outputs is a necessary but not sufficient condition for completing an analysis of the policy process. The output of government can often be identified by standard bureaucratic documents: records of expenditure, personnel employed, and routine records of services rendered or undertaken. There is no assurance that these records are comprehensive. They are likely to be more accurate, say, in education than in police administration. Problems of data comparability are very important in any effort to measure outputs. There are fewer international conventions about budgeting than there are for social statistics. Moreover, changes in the value of currencies now create substantial problems in comparisons based on that onetime standard, the US dollar. Even official European Community publications can present contradictory data appearing on opposite pages. In one table Britain can be shown to have had its GNP drop by 6.9 per cent in 1967-68 while in another it is shown to have a rise of 2.6 per cent. Similarly, Germany is shown to have its GNP rise by 21.7 per cent from 1969 to 1970 in one table, and by 5.2 per cent in another table.[10]

10. *Evaluating impact*. It is a pre-condition of evaluation that the researcher specifies what he is evaluating for. There is no assurance that policy-makers will explicitly state one (or more) objectives, or that the objective states will be amenable to reliable or valid measurement. One advantage of comparative study is that it provides a quasi-experimental situation if a policy adopted in one nation is not adopted in another. For example, the long established differences between American and European policies for higher education permit a test of their effects on intergenerational social mobility. Comparisons may also be made of the effect of nationalization upon an industry left in private ownership in another country. The power of government to achieve intended goals may also be the subject of enquiry. One might, for example, compare the extent of under or over achievement of government targets in economic growth, price stability, unemployment, or some mix of the three.

11. *Feedback*. A process model of policy-making places special importance upon the flow of information to those who initiate and maintain the process. The difficulties that social scientists face in evaluating policies must also be faced by governors and those who demand policies. If an objective is conceived of in terms of outputs (e.g., more schools) rather than outcomes (e.g., more learning) then all involved will be confused, as and when evidence is adduced to show that outputs need not lead to desired

outcomes. This problem does not arise, however, at the 'routinization' stage; there is sufficient information to guarantee that the policy continues, but nothing that causes differences of opinion to arise placing new demands on the public agenda. Because the market for policy information is imperfect,[11] there is scope for the comparative study of how information feeds back to policy-makers, and may be made available to the general public. One might also compare the extent to which the social science community itself amplifies feedback, or whether this is undertaken through such primitive market mechanisms as general elections.

12. *Deroutinizing a stable state.* The change of an existing policy which is more or less routinized involves very different political forces from the start of a new policy. Administrators and their clients act as interested parties. Since no policy, whatever its costs, is devoid of benefits, there is reason to expect that even seemingly 'unsuccessful' policies will have entrenched support. Reciprocally, any policy, however unpopular, is likely to impose costs on someone or some group. In those nations where welfare services are most advanced, one can also study whether a high level of services leads to an increase in satisfaction and a levelling off of demands, or does it accelerate demands in a 'revolution of rising expectations'?

The above description is intentionally brief; there is a limit to what one can learn in the abstract. However, precisely because there is *no* limit to the amount of information that *might be* relevant to comparative studies of public policy, it is incumbent upon anyone working in this field to devise a schema for concentrating attention on some things of *a priori* significance, if we are to avoid drowning in a sea of minutiae.

Notes

1. The relationship of the concepts is discussed in a comparative European and historical context by Brian Chapman, *Police State* (London: Macmillan 1970), pp. 11ff.

2. See Richard Rose, editor, *Policy-Making in Britain* (London: Macmillan, 1969), pp. x-xiv. The European Workshop on Policy Studies at Strathclyde found that a process model is in general use among European scholars as a means of organizing their own ideas.

3. See David Braybrooke and C.E. Lindblom, *A Strategy of Decision* (New York: Free Press, 1963).

4. Ira Sharkansky, *The Routines of Politics* (New York: Van Nostrand Reinhold, 1970).

5. See Richard Rose, "Models of Governing," *Comparative Politics* (forthcoming), Fig. 1.

6. Stein Rokkan, "Norway; Numerical Democracy and Corporate Pluralism," in Robert A. Dahl (ed.), *Political Oppositions in Western Democracies* (New Haven: Yale University Press, 1966), p. 106.

7. *Comparative Politics: A Distributive Approach*, Ch. 1.

8. The specification of a limited but open series of alternative policies is a major and significant emphasis in the studies of national crisis of political change, edited by Gabriel Almond, Scott Flanagan and Robert Mundt, *Crisis, Choice, Change* (Boston: Little, Brown, 1972).

9. (Chicago: University Press, 1964).

10. *Basic Statistics of the Community 1971* (Brussels: Statistical Office of the European Communities, 11th edition), pp. 22-23. The detailed captions of the tables make clear that they are measuring different things. But only contextual, not statistical knowledge will explain the disparities cited there.

11. See Richard Rose, "The Market for Policy Indicators," in Andrew Shonfield and Stella Shaw, *Social Indicators and Social Policy* (London: Heinemann, 1972).

5

Administering Public Policy

H. George Frederickson,
Michael Reagan,
and
Alfred Diamant

I. Basic Issues and References

A. General Relations between Policy and Administration

There has always been a close link between the general study of public policy and public administration as a field in political science. Many political scientists who regard themselves as specialists in public policy have tended to identify with public administration. This linkage is quite understandable because political scientists who study policy areas such as transportation, environment, economic regulations, crime, education, housing, tend to be at least as fundamentally concerned with the problem solving aspects of these policy areas as they are with their theoretical or conceptual characteristics. For this reason, among others, public administration has been regarded as one of the least theoretically developed fields in political science. For example, until recently to study the details of transportation policy making and implementation in a given city seemed to most political scientists to be the most mundane and trivial of intellectual activities, except for public administration types. Similarly, for the political scientist to give attention to educating persons for public service seemed somehow a lesser calling than to develop the science of politics and prepare persons to teach more political science.

For these and other reasons public administration began a gradual drawing away from political science. This withdrawal from political science continues, with separate masters degree programs and new schools of public administration or public affairs sprouting like weeds. These degree programs and schools are usually highly interdisciplinary, that is to say they are more than political science, and they are usually applied or problem oriented. And, they take seriously the need to prepare persons to be policy analysts and policy makers.

In response what has been for decades known as public administration within political science is increasingly being labeled policy study or policy

---

Section I of this chapter was authored by H. George Frederickson and Michael Reagan. Section II was authored by Alfred Diamant.

analysis. This development should be regarded by those political scientists who identify with public administration as a most satisfying affirmation that their interests and concerns are now acceptable in political science circles although through the use of more palatable symbols.

If these arguments have validity, then the issues that have long concerned public administrations should be the same concerns of political scientists in policy studies, and they are. To illustrate this fact one needs simply to turn to the classic volume read by almost every student of public administration since 1952, Harold Stein's *Public Administration and Policy Development: A Case Book* (New York: Harcourt, Brace and Company, 1952). The policy issues treated in the Stein *Case Book* very much resemble the contemporary concerns of public policy scholars. These studies reflect the times in which they were written, but they are excellent empirical political science, exhibiting all the tones of the policy process. For the past twenty years students of public administration have been nurtured on these policy cases and their modern counterparts produced by the Inter-University Case Program, at the Maxwell Graduate School of Citizenship and Public Affairs, Syracuse University. Although neither analytical nor theoretical, the ICP cases (now numbering over one hundred) beginning with the Stein *Case Book* are first-rate examples of the narrative-descriptive approach to understanding public policy. But they have been used more to teach prospective public administrators than to build a coherent body of knowledge of the policy process.

B. Basic Controversial Issues

Although public policy subjects are much different in 1972 than they were in 1952, the big issues in the study of policy science tend to be the same. For example, policy scientists continue to analyze *legislative-administrative relationships* from the perspective of the increasing power of the bureaucracy. One of the major issues for contemporary students of administrating public policy is the relative power of administrators versus the power of elected officials. The increasing dominance of public service professionals over certain fields of policy making has been most thoroughly and thoughtfully analyzed by Frederick C. Mosher in his *Democracy and The Public Service* (New York: Oxford University Press. 1968). What is most fascinating about this book is that is it done by an eminent political scientist from the perspective of public personnel administration, the subfield in public administration that is regarded by most political scientists as the dullest of the dull. Yet the Mosher book is the best available analysis of the policy powers of civil servants and how these powers relate to the policy processes of the executive and legislative branches of government.

Public policy specialists are rightly concerned with the remarkable *absorption of power by professionals in specialized fields* such as defense, agriculture, education and law enforcement, and the seeming inability of elected officials to exercise meaningful controls over these professional fiefdoms. There have been two major responses to this issue. The first is represented by Theodore Lowi in his book *The End of Liberalism* (New York: W. W. Norton 1969) in which he concludes that administrators need to be much more constrained by highly specific enabling legislation. In his "juridical democracy" public administrators become functionaries carrying out legislature mandates precisely. Lowi's policy process is legislative-judicial. The alternative response comes from the so-called "new public administration" best represented by two collections of essays by younger public administration and policy science specialists, Frank Marini's *Toward a New Public Administration* (San Francisco: Chandler Publishing Company, 1970) and Dwight Waldo's, *Public Administration in a Time of Turbulence* (San Francisco: Chandler Publishing Company, 1971). In these two volumes most of the authors argue not for a lesser role for experts and administrators in the policy making process but rather for a wider but more visible role. The appointed policy makers should exhibit greater willingness to accept responsibility for decisions and to be less secretive about the problems of making and implementing public policy.

The third major issue for contemporary students of the administrative aspects of public policy is the *relationship between administrators and citizens*. This concern is manifest in many ways in the study of public policy but primarily through the contemporary call for increased citizens participation, neighborhood government and political and administrative decentralization. These issues in modern American political science trace back as far as James W. Fesler's classic *Area and Administration* (University of Alabama: University of Alabama Press, 1949). The controversy over school decentralization and citizens participation in the late 1960's and early 1970's is clear evidence that educational policy making cannot be left entirely to the experts. A special issue of the *Public Administration Review* entitled "Curriculum Essays on Citizens, Politics and Administration in Urban Neighborhoods" (November, 1972), edited by H. George Frederickson, is perhaps the most complete contemporary consideration of these questions. In this issue of *PAR* citizen participation and neighborhood control are considered not only in the general sense but in the context of policy areas such as criminal justice, the delivery of health service, education and social services. Thus the role of the citizen in the policy process has been an abiding issue in public administration as it is among policy scientists.

The traditional view of most political scientists toward public administration has been that it is a theoretical wasteland, a field in search of a paradigm. The evidence indicates the contrary. If there is a political scientist fundamentally tied to public administration as well as the *rigorous and scientific study* of the policy process it would have to be Herbert Simon. His development of rational decision making models in *Administrative Behavior* (New York: McMillan Company, 1957), his co-authored work with Donald Smithburg, and Victor Thompson, *Public Administration* (New York: Alfred A. Knopf, 1950), and his *Models of Man: Social and Rational* (New York: John Wiley and Sons, 1957), and his *The New Science of Management Decision* (New York: Harper Row, 1960), all display a high level of analytic and systematic rigor.

Of course any paradigm invites a counter paradigm, in this case perhaps best illustrated by the "muddling through" approach of Charles F. Lindbolm's studies, *The Intelligence of Democracy: Decision Making Through Mutual Adjustments* (New York: The Free Press, 1965), and *The Policy Making Process* (Englewood Cliffs, New Jersey: Prentice-Hall, 1968). Students of public administration have long been acquainted with the "paradigmatic dialogue" between the rational models of policy making versus the inclemental models of the policy process (not to mention the judgmental or intuitive models of policy making). That these models have had an impact on the policy process could be no better illustrated than by the development of the so-called planning-programming-budgeting-systems approach to fiscal decision making. PPBS is clearly the rational model at work, most of the workmen being economists skilled in the analysis of policy benefits and costs. Whatever one's personal position may be on the controversy over PPBS, an exposure to the literature about it is a good way of getting into some major issues relating to the administrative role in policy making. Among the more interesting compendia are Fremont J. Lyden and Ernest G. Miller, *Planning, Programming, Budgeting* (Chicago: Markham, 1967).

Among the more notable developments in the management of public policy development in our time is the politically very sophisticated (by accident more than design) system of *intergovernmental grants-in-aid,* in which fiscal and programmatic dimensions are thoroughly intermingled. Such books as those by Martha Derthick, *The Influence of Federal Grants: Public Assistance in Massachusetts* (Cambridge: Harvard, 1970) and Gilbert Steiner, *Social Insecurity: The Politics of Welfare* (Chicago: Rand McNally, 1966) illustrate through case studies the complex interactions of political and administrative forces at both state and federal levels in the development and continuing delineation of policy through the grant-in-aid device. Just what impact the newly inaugurated revenue sharing program will have on the categorical grant system (which now runs to $30 billion annually) remains to be seen. For a review of the intergovernmental policy making system as a whole, with special referenda to the pros and cons of revenue sharing, see M.D. Reagan, *The New Federalism* (New York: Oxford, 1972) and for an excellent review of the role of the states in the system, see Deil S. Wright, "The States and Intergovernmental Relations," *Publius,* Vol. 1, No. 2 (Winter, 1972) pp. 7-68.

C. Basic Sources

Turning from specific issues to the question of what sources can one use to keep abreast of developments in the administration of public policy, the following are particularly useful: *The Public Interest, Public Administration Review, Public Policy,* and *Washington Monthly.*

Finally, here are some answers to the question: What recent books in addition to those mentioned are especially stimulating, innovating, and significant in the field of administrative dimensions to public policy development? Graham T. Allison's *Essence of Decision: Explaining the Cuban Missile Crisis* (Boston: Little, Brown, 1971) (a difficult but rewarding book, one that uses the notion of "conceptual lenses" in a way that constitutes a major analytic advance); Harold Seidman's *Politics, Position, and Power* (New York: Oxford, 1970) (one of the best things I've seen on how organizational arrangements interact with substantive policy); and Francis E. Rourke's *Bureaucracy, Politics, and Public Policy* (Boston: Little, Brown, 1969) (an excellent succinct statement on bureaucratic roles in policy development). These books plus those by Waldo and Marini would constitute a fine short course in administrative policy making.

II. Bureaucracy and Administration in Western Europe: A Case of Not-So-Benign Neglect[a]

In the quarter century since the end of the Second World War, the study of West European politics has proceeded along a carefully bifurcated path: in the United States attention has focused chiefly on parties, voting, opinion, and political culture, while in Europe the more traditional concerns with administrative structure and organization have continued to occupy the attention of scholars there. As a result, American research about Western Europe (and teaching, as well) has been oriented to politics narrowly defined to such an extent that it has practically driven out all consideration of administration and the role of the bureaucracy in the political process. All this can be easily documented.

---

[a] A longer version of this section, which includes sections on attitude studies, sociology of public organizations, administrative structures, and innovation, is available on request from the author.

Taking teaching first, even a cursory examination of the major texts on European politics will show that administration and bureaucracy are either lumped together under the category of "outputs" which generally receive pretty short shift following extensive treatment of "inputs," or if they are identified separately at all, the treatment is brief and thus inevitably superficial; one need only compare the length, detail, and care lavished on chapters dealing with public opinion or political culture with the once-over treatment of bureaucracy and administration. For an example of the former see Lewis J. Edinger, *Politics in Germany: Attitudes and Processes* (Boston: Little, Brown and Co., 1968); for the latter, John Ambler, *The Government and Politics of France* (Boston: Houghton-Mifflin Co., 1971) or Arnold J. Heidenheimer, *The Governments of Germany* (New York: Thomas Y. Crowell Co., 1971). All this must necessarily leave the average undergraduate student of Western European politics with the distinct impression that when it comes to power, influence, and significant roles in the political process, the public bureaucracy must surely play a very insignificant part, or it would have received more attention than it now gets.

The situation in research is not much better. Surely, an important indicator of general concern would be the number of dissertations completed, added, or changed during a recent year, for these dissertations are a reliable guide to the interests of the faculty who instruct, guide, and supervise these graduate students. Taking only the most recent crop of doctoral dissertations reported in *P.S.* (vol. V, no. 4, Fall, 1972, 513-574), one finds in the two categories of "Public Administration" and "Foreign and Comparative Government and Politics" only two completed dissertations, one of which is slightly marginal for Western Europe: *Italy and Yugoslavia: A Comparative Analysis of Policy-Making in Economic Planning* (Beverly J. Springer, University of Colorado), and the prize-winning dissertation by Ezra Suleiman, *Administration, Politics, and the Higher Civil Service in France* (Columbia University). To these two, three dissertation projects begun during 1971-1972 should be added: *ENA: The French Approach to the Selection and Training of an Administrative Elite* (Reynold A. Riemer, Johns Hopkins/SAIS), *Town and Country Planning in the Federal Republic of Germany* (Andreas Wesserle, Southern Illinois University), and *The Politics of Administrative Reform: Decentralization and Re-Centralization in Three European Systems* (James R. Alexander, University of Colorado). To be sure, there must be several others now in various stages of completion, but the modest size of this output must be appalling to anyone genuinely concerned with a systematic study of European politics. What a scanning of *P.S.* reveals is that bureaucracy and administration are phenomena well worth investigating in the United States, Africa, Asia, Latin America, the USSR, and China, but not in Western Europe. Why, one asks? Is it an inaccessible region populated by hostile natives? Is the climate unfavorable? Are data unavailable? Perhaps no great foundation has decided that it is a critical area requiring massive infusion of funds? With this last question we come perhaps closer to the core of the problem; but the politics of scientific research and the ACLS/SSRC/FAFP power struggles are—fortunately—beyond the scope of this survey, though they would probably tell us quite a bit about the relative neglect of Western Europe and its ultimate causes.

Rather than examining under separate headings American and European work on West European administration and bureaucracies, I would like to look at the literature as a whole, not because American scholars pursue work along the same lines as do Europeans—there remain considerable differences between the groups—but because in spite of these differences in approach, certain common themes and interests are easily discernible. This is evident most strongly in the development of policy studies on both sides of the Atlantic—a development which is reviewed elsewhere in this volume. Though there is a danger that in the rush to policy studies, or rather to the study of the "content" and the "outcomes" or "outputs" of policy, the well-established concerns with administrative structure, social background, recruitment and training of civil servants (especially the higher bureaucrats), organization theory and organizational analysis will again have to take a backseat. If this were to be the case, it would be doubly frustrating for administrative studies to have finally emerged from the shadow of the political culture/parties/interest groups/public opinion giant only to be swamped by the "nouvelle vague" of policy studies. Another reason why an American-European division would not be a fruitful way of looking at existing work and work in progress is the fact of increasing American-European collaboration in administrative and bureaucratic studies. What follows now in the remainder of this survey is an attempt to identify some of the more interesting thrusts in Western European administrative and bureaucratic studies; it is not meant to be a systematic survey and bibliography—an enterprise which would burst the bounds of the present format and assignment.

A. *Methodology*

American preoccupation with methodology and research technique is proverbial; so it is not surprising that American scholars of administration have addressed themselves to that issue in a variety of ways. It was only to be expected that the first issues of two journals should be devoted to these concerns. *The Journal of Comparative Administration* (now retitled *Administration and Society*) in its vol. 1, no. 1 (May 1969) examines the problems of the comparative analysis of administration from a variety of perspectives, ranging all the way from Fred W. Riggs macro-taxonomic efforts, "Bureaucratic Politics in Comparative Perspective" through Keith M. Henderson's somewhat breast-beating "Comparative Public Administration: An Identity Crisis," to Dwight Waldo's accustomed balanced and slightly hopeful/slightly cynical "Public Administration and Change: Terra Paene Incognita." In order to pay at least some respects to the new political science, the issue concludes with Blanche Blank's and the present author's research note "Measuring National Bureaucracies: The Interaction of Theory and Research." Modesty requires a report that the hoped-for interaction has yielded more hope than action. Of the several methodological essays adorning the first issues of *Comparative Politics* (October 1968), the one by Joseph LaPalombara "Macrotheory and Microapplications in Comparative Politics: A Widening Chasm" is particularly relevant for comparative administration. No student of administration seems to have ventured into the precincts of *Comparative Political Studies,* and if he did, he does not seem to have reached the inner sanctum of the printed format. However, apart from these opening exercises, the work reported by these two journals is relatively free of methodological preoccupations; whether this is a curse or a blessing will be left to individual readers to decide.

B. *Planning*

The administration of planning could well be the subject of a separate report. Thus little can be done here except to indicate that in addition to the country-series on planning edited by Betram Gross and published by Syracuse University Press which is easily accessible to American scholars, there exists a very nicely done British P.E.P. comparative planning study, Geoffrey Denton et al., *Economic Planning and Policies in Britain, France and Germany* (London: George Allen & Unwin, Ltd., 1968). Literature on German planning has been collected and annotated by the legislative research service of the Bundestag, *Planung in Politik und Verwaltung in der Bundesrepublik Deutschland* (Bonn: Deutscher Bundestag/Wissenschaftlicher Dienst, *Bibliographien,* no. 30, September 1972). In addition to the writings on French planning by some of the principal protagonists such as Pierre Massé's *Le Plan ou l'Anti-Hazard*, American students will welcome Steven Cohen's, *Modern Capitalist Planning* (Cambridge: Harvard University Press, 1969). The special problem the legislature faces in trying to cope with planning is illustrated in Lucien Nizard, "Reflexions sur les Raisons Réelles de l'Inaptitude Parlementaire à Influencer Effectivement le Processus de Planification," a paper presented to a colloquium of the French political science association in November 1970.

C. The Political Role of Elite Administrators

One of the central strands in administrative and bureaucratic studies of Western Europe has been the analysis of the political role of the top civil servants, both those in traditional government agencies as well as the managers of nationalized enterprises. By "political role" one can denote two distinct, yet related, phenomena. The first one is the increasing role elite administrators play in the preparation of political decision, even though not personally committed politically. The second refers to the increasing politicization of some of these top administrators, that is to say their personal involvement in politics as shown by the pursuit of mixed administrative political careers which includes roles in party politics as well as the holding of sub-cabinet or even cabinet postions, and participation in French *cabinets ministeriels,* the small personal staff of the minister who aid him directly in the policy-process. Though once chiefly made up of journalists and young politicians "on the make," the *cabinets* are now staffed by career civil servants who see these positions as stepping stones to high administrative and eventually political office.

Four general factors contribute to the increasing political role played by elite administrators: (1) the increasing scope of the modern state: (2) the increasing complexity of the problems facing the modern state: (3) the increasing amount and intensity of popular political participation; and (4) the decline of parliament. Two world wars and the growth of the welfare state have clearly expanded the scope of the modern state, especially since 1950; and even though there might seem to be some trend towards decentralization, not many doubt that this is at most a diversionary phenomenon that will not detract from the essentially centralizing forces—the same forces which seem to place power in the hands of the top bureaucrats.

The increasing complexity of the modern state, too, is beyond doubt, and as it increases, complex decisions will have to be made by those permanently installed in the top levels of government, both specialists and generalists. Even the democratizing demands of recent decades seem to play into the hands of the elite administrators, for the greater the number of those who want to participate in government decisions, the greater the need for organization—and the greater the need for organization specialists. It might even be that increased political competition increases the need for a "neutral shield" between competing parties and groups—a function which can best be performed by the top administrators.

Finally, top bureaucrats have increased their power at the expense of representative institutions and even at the expense of the political executive—ministers and cabinets. In France, for example, the adoption of presidential government has greatly enhanced the power and the political role of the so-called *grands corps,* the elite administrators: finance inspectorate, *polytechniciens,* members of the *conseil d'Etat,* etc.

These changes in the role and position of the top bureaucrats needs also to be seen in the political/social system context. The existence of ethnic and linguistic cleavages; the functioning of a prefectoral system; ministerial instability; political patronage, and many other ecological factors affect and shape the senior bureaucracy.

Work exploring these broad and complex issues is being carried on both in Western Europe and in the United States. Mattei Dogan, who frequently lectures in American universities and who is affiliated with the Centre National de la Recherche Scientifique (Paris), is engaged in bringing together and editing a series of essays dealing with the political role of top civil servants. (I am greatly indebted to Mattei Dogan for the ideas in this section.) Some of these have been presented publicly and merit special attention. Among these are James B. Christoph, "British Higher Civil Servants and the Politics of Consensualism," which was presented to the American Political Science Association in September 1972. Though recognizing that forces making for a greater political role are at work, he concludes that top civil servants will continue to share in political decisions, but to share *only*. Though well placed to influence policy outcomes, Christoph concludes, they are not likely "to transform it into sole proprietorship." Other aspects of this minister-civil servant relationship are being explored by Bruce Heady of Strathclyde University. Another fascinating example of top civil servant politicization is Belgium with its deep communal cleavages, a phenomenon which has been examined by Leo Moulin in "La Politisation de l'Administration Belgique."

Also devoted to this general problem of the political role of top bureaucrats are a series of papers presented to the 1970 Munich meeting of the International Political Science Association, all exploring aspects of the French situation which has witnessed a particularly rapid escalation of civil service politicization: Jean-Claude Thoenig, "L'Example Francais des Grands Corps"; Jacques Lautman, "Développement Économique, Priorité Accordée a la Continuité et Communauté des Tâches et des Personnes entre la Politique, la Fonction Publique et l'Industrie dans la France Actuelle"; Daniel Derivry, "Les Dirigeants des Entreprises Publiques"; Marie-Christine Kessler, "Membres du Conseil d'État et Vie Politique"; Jeanne Siwek-Pouydesseau, "L'Interpenetration entre Personnels Politique et Administratif en France"; and by the same author an unpublished paper "Les Cabinets Ministeriels en France."

One other work deserves mention. The growth and complexity of state activity had originally been visualized as forcing public bureaucracies into making a choice between "generalist" and "specialist" administrators. As so often happens, this turned out to be a false dichotomy; for the more specialists there were, the greater the need for generalists. In fact, the trend towards a greater political role of elite administrators has only accentuated the need for generalists. These issues are fully explored in the essays in F. F. Ridley (ed.), *Specialists and Generalists* (London: George Allen & Unwin, 1968).

D. *Periodicals*

Most political science journals, as well as those in sociology and history will carry occasional articles dealing with European administration. *Comparative Politics* and the *Journal of Comparative Administration* have already been mentioned. To these should be added, in the United States, *Public Administration Review* and *Administrative Science Quarterly*. The former, being published for a professional as well as an academic clientele, can devote only limited space to Western European affairs. The latter, though it once was more hospitable to the more conventional studies of European administration, has, in recent years, changed direction quite radically and probably does not constitute a major source for us. Of the European journals, *Public Administration* (London) is most easily accessible. An informal publication which carries rather more innovative reports is *PAC Bulletin*, the publication of the Public Administration Committee of the Joint University Council for Social and Public Administration (218 Sussex Gardens, London W2). *Revue Internationale des Sciences Administratives*, published in Brussels by the international public administration organization has world-wide coverage and tends towards the more "applied" administrative handbook-type articles. The two principal German quarterlies are *Öffentlich Verwaltung* and *Die Verwaltung*, while in France one should consult *Revue Administrative* as well as *Administration*, the latter being published by the higher civil service of the Ministry of the Interior and the prefectoral corps. In both countries the mainstream political science and sociology journals will also provide a medium for occasional essays.

After this recital, how can I sustain the charge of "not-so-benign" neglect, one might well ask. I am convinced that nothing I have said really affects my original judgment. To be sure, various national communities of European scholars continue to examine their own administrative system in ways in which they have always done, but there is very little cooperation between them. The recently-founded European Consortium for Political Research focuses principally on "politics" as defined pretty much by the Michigan Survey Research Center and the American Social Science Research Council. Only in 1973 will one of the Consortium workshops be devoted to problem of administration and bureaucracy—under the chairmanshop of F. F. Ridley (Liverpool). In addition to this failure of scholarly cooperation and assistance within Europe and of American support for Europeans (the Consortium is financed by the Ford Foundation), we continue to face an almost total absence of organized activity in the United States and by American scholars. The Comparative Administration Group, supported chiefly by the Ford Foundation, devoted almost all its energies during the 1960's to problems of bureaucracy in developing systems. But not a single benefactor, public or private, has indicated willingness to underwrite an effort like that of the Comparative Politics Committee under the chairmanship of Gabriel Almond. Though one of the Comparative Politics Committee volumes, edited by Joseph LaPalombara, was devoted to administrative studies, *Bureaucracy and Political Development* (Princeton: Princeton University Press, 1963), the bulk of the volumes was devoted to "politics" and that did, by definition, not include the sort of concerns I have examined here. Now that "public policy" is about to replace "voting behavior" as the reigning deity, can I be faulted for seeing only gloom and neglect with regard to administrative studies of Western Europe? If anyone has "glad tidings" of whatever savior might be just around the corner, I will happily stand corrected.

**Part II
Specific Policy Problems**

6

Environmental Policy

Dean Mann,
Geoffrey Wandesforde-Smith,
and
Lennart Lundqvist

I. Basic Issues and References

The very term "environmental policy" suggests the difficulty of defining this field of policy analysis. Inevitably, the researcher in this field confronts the problem of establishing boundaries between environmental policy and urban, welfare, health, international and virtually every other field of public policy. On neither technical, economic, or political criteria is it possible to make entirely satisfactory distinctions because of the interpenetration of environmental policy with other fields of policy analysis.

This difficulty is mitigated by the fact that very little research has been done by political scientists on environmental policy. Much of what constitutes the best literature on environmental policy has been produced by economists, lawyers, planners and activists in the environmental movement. Whether political scientists can improve on their policy analysis remains largely to be demonstrated.

A further complexity is added by the fact that political scientists have probably done more in the area of natural resources policy than in any other field of public policy except foreign and military policy. The focus has been on the management of and public investments in natural resources, especially water resources, but seldom with an environmental focus in the sense of concern for the ecological balance and quality of life issues that are explicitly involved in current concern for the environment. Thus, an excellent little study, *Natural Resources and the Political Struggle* by Norman Wengert (Garden City, New York; Doubleday and Company, 1955) suggests the earlier orientation toward issues of costs and benefits, conservation of scarce resources and public versus private development and the relative lack of concern for ecology, aesthetics, and recreation. Pollution, for example, is virtually ignored.

The focus of this initial essay is therefore on what political scientists have done on *environmental* policy, while briefly tracing—where relevant—the scholarly antecedents in the study of natural resources.

Institutional analysis has long been a strong suit for political scientists

---

Section I of this chapter was authored by Dean Mann. Section II was authored by Dean Mann and Geoffrey Wandesforde-Smith. Section III was authored by Lennart Lundqvist.

although one can't argue so strongly that the perceptions have been particularly acute or the recommendations especially relevant. In reviewing environmental policy analysis for the past decade it is clear that some of the best work has been done by people who may best be styled political economists. Most are in fact economists who recognize the institutional character of most environmental problems and limitations of economic analysis. The names of Allen Kneese, Myrick Freeman, Marc Roberts, Edwin Haefele and Robert Haveman come quickly to mind.

Among political scientists Lynton Caldwell has established himself as perhaps the leading figure in the discussion of public organization for environmental management. His *Environment: A Challenge to Modern Society* (Garden City, New York: Anchor Books, Doubleday and Company, Inc., 1971) represents both his philosophy with respect to environmental policy and his analysis of the political steps required to achieve a higher quality environment. It is reasonable, thoughtful, and sensitive to the manifold values involved. It is not a particularly *political* book in the sense that it seldom suggests the reality of the political conflict and the technological and economic character of the issues that make the issues often intractable. His institutional analysis tends strongly toward the rational, comprehensive model as the means of achieving a higher quality environment.

More closely related to the political economists is the work of two political scientists studying environmental problems: Vincent Ostrom and Matthew Holden. Ostrom's article "Water Resource Development: Some Problems in Economic and Political Analysis of Public Policy" (*Political Science and Public Policy,* Austin Ranney, ed., Chicago, Markham Publishing Company, 1968) states some assumptions of the political system, analyzes consequences of various institutional forms, and challenges the rational-comprehensive model of decision-making with his own model of decentralized decision-making by public entrepreneurs. This work has recently been expanded into a much fuller statement of this position for the National Water Commission. In his *Pollution Control as a Bargaining Process: An Essay on Regulatory Decision-Making* (Ithaca, New York: Water Resources Center, Cornell University, 1966), Holden raises important questions concerning the application of effluent charges or the utilization of systems analysis in dealing with pollution, concluding that elements of bargaining among continuing participants in the decision-making process would lead to substantial divergence from the results anticipated by those espousing those techniques as the solutions for environmental problems.

For a more empirical and descriptive look at the pollution control efforts in the United States, one should turn to the study by J. Clarence Davies of *The Politics of Pollution* (Indianapolis and New York: Bobbs-

Merrill, Inc., 1970). Written from an insider's viewpoint and stressing water and air pollution control, this book covers in a traditional way the participants and institutions in the pollution control policy process, but adds interesting and insightful chapters on standard-setting and compliance.

Congress takes it usual lumps as a policy-making institution from the only scholars who have seriously looked at Congress and its role in cleaning up the environment. Richard Cooley and Geoffrey Wandesforde-Smith have compiled in *Congress and the Environment* (Seattle and London; University of Washington Press, 1970) a set of case studies which describe the manner in which Congress has dealt with environmental issues. The authors conclude that Congress has dragged its feet, in considerable part because of its alleged archaic structure. In the opinion of this reader, the cases do not always support the critical tone of the authors unless one assumes that the only values worth achieving are wilderness and scenic rivers.

With new agencies proliferating in the environmental field, we should look for careful studies of the manner in which they carry on their business. Until those are forthcoming we shall have to examine the implications of some excellent treatments that have been given at least two of the most important resource agencies: the Forest Service and the Bureau of Land Management. Herbert Kaufman's *The Forest Ranger* (Baltimore: Johns Hopkins University Press, 1960) and Ashley Schiff's *Fire and Water: Scientific Heresy in the Forest Service* (Cambridge, Massachusetts: Harvard University Press, 1962) demonstrate the orthodoxy and virtual ideology that infuse the Forest Service, the means used to ensure the persistence of that orthodoxy and the perils associated with it. Philip Foss has recorded for us the battles over grazing district administration in his *Politics and Grass: The Administration of Grazing on the Public Domain* (Seattle: The University of Washington Press, 1960) and Robert Morgan examined the record of the Soil Conservation Service in *Governing Soil Conservation: Thirty Years of the New Decentralization* (Baltimore: Johns Hopkins Press, 1965).

Studies by political scientists of the administration of the environment at the state level are seldom to be found as yet. The most recent and comprehensive study is by Elizabeth Haskell—*Managing the Environment: Nine States Look for New Answers.* (Washington, D.C.: The Smithsonian Institution, 1971.) Haskell examines the responses of nine states in terms of public organization and policy change to accommodate the demands for higher quality environment. In the field of water resources, Daniel Hoggan, an engineer, surveyed *State Organization Patterns for Comprehensive Planning of Water Resources Development*, (Logan, Utah: Utah State University, June, 1969).

The courts and their utility in dealing with environmental problems have been examined to some extent by the lawyers but little by political scientists. Joseph Sax has done some of the work most relevant for political scientists, who are not concerned with the strictly legal institutional questions. His *Water Law, Planning and Policy: Cases and Materials* (Indianapolis: Bobbs-Merrill, 1968) and especially his *Defending the Environment* (New York, Alfred A. Knopf, 1971) display his sanguine view about the ability of the courts to counter skullduggery in the bureaucracy, although he is less convincing that the judicial route provides an avenue for altering the basic processes for decision-making with respect to environmental issues.

Turning now to examinations of specific policy sectors within environmental policy, one finds that water resources have been the most studied of all resources. The enduring questions of the past-costs and benefits, federal organization, river basin organization, state functions—have tended to dominate the analyses. Arthur Maass' *Muddy Waters* (Cambridge, Massachusetts: Harvard University Press, 1951) is a classic example of this *genre* and William H. Stewart's *The Tennessee-Tombigbee Waterway: A Case Study in the Politics of Water Transportation* (University, Alabama: The Bureau of Public Administration, The University of Alabama, 1971) is a more recent example that strangely almost entirely ignores the environmental issues that are clearly involved in the project proposal described in the book. The works of Charles McKinley, Henry Hart, Norman Wengert, Ernest Englebert, Hubert Marshall and Albert Lepawsky all deserve praise in this field of study. Unfortunately few have continued this good work with respect to the broader issues of water—both quantity and quality—and environmental concerns. Among recent political science writings, perhaps the study by Roscoe Martin, et al., of *River Basin Administration and the Delaware* (Syracuse, New York; Syracuse University Press, 1960) was an initial effort to deal with what was both a quantity and quality problem in the Delaware River system. This was followed by Edward J. Cleary's study of Orsanco, the compact covering the Ohio River basin. *The Orsanco Story: Water Quality Management in the Ohio Valley Under an Interstate Compact* (Baltimore, Johns Hopkins Press, 1967). Both revealed the favorable prospects for the interstate compact device—which now has been applied to both the Delaware and the Susquehanna—for dealing with the critical problems of water quality management.

Some of the best recent work has been done under the auspices of Ralph Nader's Center for Study of Responsive Law. Despite shortcomings of analysis and oversimplification in their recommendations for change, these investigators have taken the lead in revealing the truly monumental failures of our water pollution control program. *Water Wasteland* by David Zwick and Marcy Benstock (New York, Grossman Publishers, 1971) is a broad attack on the entire water pollution control program while *The Water Lords* by James M. Fallows (New York, Grossman Publishers, 1971) provides the detailed case study of the Savannah River and the unwillingness of regulatory agencies to grab hold of this problem.

Political scientists have paid far less attention to air pollution. The most perceptive analytical study is by a planner, George H. Hagevik, entitled *Decision-Making in Air Pollution Control* (New York, Washington, London: Praeger Publishers, 1970). Hagevik stresses alternative strategies for achieving improved air quality, including bargaining, and raises important questions about the decision-framework involving regional entities, states, the federal agencies and a multiplicity of local units of government. Utilizing a community power framework of analysis, Matthew A. Crenson has examined *The Un-Politics of Air Pollution: A Study of Non-Decision-Making in the Cities* (Baltimore and London: Johns Hopkins Press, 1971). He concludes that the power structure has prevented solutions to air quality problems by preventing these problems from becoming problems on the political agenda. The Ralph Nader Center also examined air pollution in its devastatingly critical way in *Vanishing Air* by John C. Esposito (New York. Grossman Publishers, 1970).

The Cooley and Wandesforde-Smith volume contains case studies dealing with outdoor recreation, but political scientists have not done much more empirical work in this area. One notable exception is the lengthy analysis by Daniel M. Ogden in "Outdoor Recreation: Policy and Politics" in *The Political Economy of Environmental Control* (Joe S. Bain and Warren F. Ilchman, eds., Berkeley: Institute of Business and Economic Research, University of California, 1972). He examines outdoor recreation policy in the context of "power cluster" politics, which is very reminiscent of Douglass Cater's "subgovernments."

The concept of the "spaceship earth" and the perceived world-wide dangers of ecological destruction have made the adoption of an ecological framework a natural thing for students of international politics. Notable in this regard are three recently published works: *In Defense of Earth: International Protection of the Biosphere* by Lynton K. Caldwell (Bloomington, Indiana, Indiana University Press, 1972). *Toward a Politics of the Planet Earth* by Harold and Margaret Sprout (New York: Van Nostrand Reinhold Company, 1971) and *This Endangered Planet: Prospects and Proposals for Human Survival* by Richard A. Falk (New York: Random House, 1971). The Sprouts' volume tends toward the traditional text in international politics with an environmental gloss whereas the Falk book makes a more thorough-going effort to suggest the distinctive character of ecological imperatives for the international political system. The solutions recommended do not suggest anything remarkably new in international politics as means of achieving a balanced political and ecological order. The Caldwell study reflects his experience with the IUCN and the NAS Committee for Environmental Programs. It is a careful and scholarly examination of the institutional problems of international environmental management.

Another area of potentially great concern to political scientists are the perceptions and attitudes of both elites and masses concerning environmental conditions and policy. Geographers have perhaps done the most extensive work in this area—Gilbert White, W. R. Derrick Sewell, David Lowenthal, Frank Quinn, Tom Saarinen—are names that stand out. Various articles and polls are available on public perceptions and attitudes, some done by political scientists, but the most comprehensive collection is probably *Perceptions and Attitudes in Resources Management,* W. R. Derrick Sewell and Ian Burton, eds., (Resource Paper No. 2, Policy Research and Coordination Branch, Department of Energy, Mines and Resources, Ottawa, Canada, 1971). This collection draws on both Canadian and U.S. experience with respect to public atttitudes and participation of publics and elites in the decision-making process.

The concepts of the environmental movement have been little investigated by political scientists in terms of relating them to broader political thought. The historians of political ideas have been helpful, however. Two notable examples are Samuel P. Hayes, *Conservation and the Gospel of Efficiency* (Cambridge, Massachusetts: Harvard University Press, 1959) and Roderick Nash, *Wilderness and the American Mind* (New Haven and London: Yale University Press, 1967). Among political scientists, perhaps Grant McConnell has been most insightful with his analysis of the relationship between the ideology of decentralization and disaggregation of power and the consequences for the conservation movement. This is to be found most fully in his *Private Power and American Democracy* (New York: Alfred A. Knopf, 1966).

Obviously, there is much to be done by political scientists in the area of environmental policy. Whole areas of environmental concerns such as pesticides, nuclear power plant effluents and radiation dangers, power plant siting, and aesthetics are almost virgin territory. Moreover, political scientists ought to be endeavoring to meet the challenge of designing political institutions that will achieve the public purposes embodied in law but so often disemboweled in administration. This probably means considerable boning up on the economics of environmental control, but it also means careful examination of the incentives created by public law and organization and the consequences of the adoption of alternative strategies to the various publics involved. These implications may be examined in both political and economic terms and neither should be ignored in undertaking such policy analysis.

Much has been left out of this brief essay. Many original works that have appeared in article form or in readers have been ignored. Two areas of direct relevance to political scientists in which considerable work has been done are studies of environmental law and international ecological/institutional problems.

II. Basic Facilities and Institutions[a]

A. *University and Other Programs*

There is, unfortunately, no readily available and up-to-date inventory of college and university programs that deal in large part with environmental policy analysis. It seems likely on the basis of available information that such an inventory would be brief.

In December, 1969, the House Committee on Science and Astronautics published the results of an analysis by the Environmental Policy Division of the Legislative Reference Service (now the Congressional Research Service) which showed that the social sciences generally were poorly represented in environmental studies programs then under way in 106 colleges and universities (U.S. Congress, House, Committee on Science and Astronautics, *Environmental Science Centers at Institutions of Higher Education*, 91st Congress, 1st Session, Committee Print, 1969). The same committee is now surveying programs in science policy, including environmental policy, and the results of this study may reveal some progress.

Another 1969 report, based upon a detailed analysis of multidisciplinary programs at six institutions (USC, Cornell, Harvard, Michigan, MIT, Johns Hopkins), also found, in general, poor representation and integration of the social sciences (U.S. Executive Office of the President, Office of Science and Technology, *The Universities and Environmental Quality: Commitment to Problem Focused Education*, September, 1969). The report called for policy analysis of specific problems to be given much greater attention.

Some institutions have a reputation for natural resources policy analysis that has presumably taken an environmental focus in recent years. Programs in these schools should provide opportunities to pursue environmental policy analysis at both the graduate and undergraduate levels. The School of Natural Resources, not the Institute for Environmental Quality, at the University of Michigan comes to mind, as does the Department of Political Science at Colorado State University.

---

[a]For some information on obtaining grants for environmental research, see Harriet Berlin "Federal Support for Environmental Research," and *Environment Reporter* (Bureau of National Affairs, December 10, 1971).

For some information on environmental interest groups, see *Groups That Can Help: A Directory of Environmental Organizations* (Washington, D.C.: U.S. Environmental Protection Agency, 1972).

Other institutions have launched new programs in environmental studies that either have very flexible undergraduate degree programs allowing students to acquire training in political science or have associated faculty with environmental policy interests. The University of Massachusetts at Amherst, Williams College, Dartmouth College, Purdue University, the University of Wisconsin at Green Bay, the State University of New York, Albany, and the University of California campuses at Davis, Santa Barbara, and Santa Cruz are examples in this category. At the graduate level environmental policy analysis is being pursued within established programs, such as that of the Graduate School of Public Affairs at the University of Washington, and through new programs, such as that of the new School of Public and Environmental Affairs at Indiana University. Others have environmental research and teaching associated with pre-existing research centers such as the water resources centers at Purdue, at the Universities of Oregon and Manitoba, and the School of Forestry at Yale.

At many institutions courses are offered that deal with one or another aspect of environmental policy as part of the political science curriculum, although they may not form part of a program in environmental policy analysis. Analysis of the questionnaires distributed at the PSO Environmental Policy breakfast meeting, during the 1972 APSA convention, can be expected to provide a useful listing of such courses as well as more complete information about new and developing programs.

Finally, mention should be made of the role of law schools. A brief analysis of developments in environmental law at law schools in the United States will be found in a paper by Frances Irwin in the April, 1972, issue of the *Natural Resources Journal*. Other interesting developments are reported from time to time in the *Journal of Environmental Education* and *Man-Environment Systems*.

B. Journals and Other Publications

With the burgeoning interest in environmental policy there has been an explosion in the number of publications dedicated to a concern for the environment. Moreover, other journals that had somewhat narrower orientations have altered their perspective to include the broader considerations of environmental quality. The following discussion is not intended to be exhaustive but it may provide some awareness of the literature now available to the student of environmental policy.

Given the central concerns of political scientists generally it is hardly to be expected that their major journals would prove to be significant outlets for articles on environmental politics. During the years 1969-1972 one article—Charles O. Jones' "Gold to Garbage: A Bibliographic Essay on Politics and the Environment," appeared in the *American Political Science Review* (Vol LXVI, No. 2, June 1972, pp. 588-595. The period 1969-1972 was chosen simply because one might have expected that environmental concerns which became prominent in the late 1960's might have found scholarly expression by that time period). A quick survey of the other leading journals—*Journal of Politics, Midwest Journal of Political Science, Western Political Quarterly, Political Science Quarterly* and *Polity* revealed not a single article that remotely concerned environmental or natural resource policy during that period. *Public Administration Review* did publish several articles during the period and appeared to be the only political science journal of more or less general circulation that was attractive to or responsive to those interested in research and writing on the environment.

As we move away from journals of interest principally to professional political scientists and toward journals having more of a policy focus, we find more interest and concern for the environment. *Public Interest* and *Public Policy* are two journals which publish the results of research related to a broad range of public policy issues. Both have recently published important articles dealing with ecology as a public issue, water pollution control, and population policy. (See the Winter 1972 issue of the former and the Winter 1971 issue of the latter.)

More clearly in the environmental field but having a strong scholarly and interdisciplinary character are five excellent journals. For more than a decade political scientists and other social scientists have found *The Natural Resources Journal,* published by the School of Law at the University of New Mexico, to be important reading in the resource field. Of considerable interest to but seldom the outlet for articles by political scientists is *Land Economics* which has a broad concern for land use and land use planning. Three new additions are *Environment and Behavior*, a Sage publication, which describes itself as "an interdisciplinary journal concerned with the study, design, and control of the physical environment and its interaction with human behavioral system." Even more recent is *Environmental Affairs,* published by the Environmental Law Center of Boston College. Its articles cover a broad range of environmental topics. Their authors include lawyers, scientists, publicists, economists and other academic types although no political scientists appear in its columns. Beginning also in 1971 was the *Journal of Environmental Systems*, edited at Brooklyn Polytechnic Institute, which devotes itself to "the analysis and solution of problems which relate to the system-complexes which make up our total societal environment." The Journal clearly emphasizes conceptual approaches and models and appears to focus on the urban environment.

The most impressive of the journals providing more popular, but nevertheless authoritative discussions of the entire range of environmental issues is *Environment*, published by the Committee for Environmental Information at St. Louis. It dedicates itself to the publication of "information about the effects of technology on the environment and about the peaceful and military uses of nuclear energy." Other journals are more concerned with providing current information or with inciting their readers to do battle with the enemy. *The Environmental Monthly* tends toward the former, providing highlights of current issues and events. *Not Man Apart*, published by Friends of the Earth, the John Muir Institute for Environmental Studies and the League of Conservation Voters, provides more in-depth treatment but is fully committed to action on the specific issues it highlights such as Mineral King or nuclear power plant safety. Far more propagandistic and less scholarly are such publications as *Ecology Action* which calls itself a "Journal of Cultural Transformation" and *Environmental Action*.

In a legalistic society, lawyers are quick to mobilize informational resources and they have done so with respect to the environment. The most authoritative law journal is the *Ecology Law Quarterly,* published by the School of Law, University of California, Berkeley. Beginning in Winter 1971, this journal has published lengthy treatises and comments on a wide range of issues of importance to environmental policy. Northwestern Law School at Lewis and Clark College, Portland publishes *Environmental Law*. While emphasizing legal matters, this journal tends to be more eclectic in its approach and less exhaustive in its treatment.

In a somewhat different category are the environmental law reporting publications. Two are noteworthy: the *Environment Reporter* published by the Bureau of National Affairs, providing a weekly report on such topics as federal and state laws, federal regulations, air, water, solid waste, and land use laws, and judicial decisions. Providing more exhaustive and analytical treatment of these issues while reporting current happenings is the *Environmental Law Reporter* published by the Environmental Law Institute. Its authoritative treatment has been cited by the courts in rendering decisions on such matters as the interpretation of the National Environmental Policy Act.

For those interested in particular environmental issues, there are journals that deal with selected elements in the environment. The *Journal of the Air Pollution Control Association* and the *Journal of the Water Pollution Control Federation* contain mainly technical articles but there are a considerable number of thoughtful articles on such topics as environmental planning, strategies of control, research, training, etc. *Air and Water News* supplies current information on what is happening with respect to "the law, markets, technology." *Water Resources Research* is heavily weighted toward technical discussions but has an occasional article on water policy and institutions of interest to the political scientist. Other journals that have been around a long time such as the *Journal of Forestry* and *Soil and Water Conservation* contain articles that make relevant their principal concerns to environmental issues. Last but not least, there is even a publication entitled *Shore and Beach* which has been around a long time and seems concerned with preserving shoreline values by means of technology.

Clearly, there are others: the publications of various interest groups and trade associations such as the Sierra Club, the National Wildlife Federation, the Audubon Society, the petroleum industry. The concerned student of environmental policy will presumably become acquainted with these and many other publications having something important to say on environmental matters.

III. Comparative Research on Environmental Policy

A. A New and Promising Field for Comparative Research

A most conspicuous political development in the last decade is the speed with which "environmental quality" has emerged as a top priority issue on the political agenda in many countries around the world. While perhaps somewhat extreme, Japan presents us with a vivid illustration to this rapid development. In 1955, there was no mentioning of *kogai,* i.e., environmental deterioration, in Japanese dictionaries. However, ten years later, *kogai* inflicted unprecedented sufferings upon large segments of the Japanese population. In most industrialized countries, the period between 1965 and 1972 brought an ever increasing number and variety of policies, programs, laws, and institutional changes in response to the environmental problem.

The industrialized countries adopting comprehensive environmental policies are rather similar with regard to economic development. On the other hand, they show wide ranges of variation with respect to cultural, ideological, and institutional characteristics. Thus the emergence of environmental policies in the same short span of time in so many and so different national contexts opens up promising avenues for comparative research. This policy field is also characterized by a wide variation of theoretical approaches and analytical concerns. Some scholars study the societal response to environmental issues in order to yield an analytical understanding of important aspects of political and social systems. Others share more "applied" concerns; they are interested in the peculiarities of national policies, approaches, and institutional designs, and their transferability among different national contexts. This variation, along with the "newness" of the issue, makes it difficult to give more than a partial picture of the present, very dynamic research developments.

B. Finished Research Efforts

With regard to theoretical and conceptual developments in comparative environmental policy research, some interesting contributions are found in *Environmental Policy: Concepts and International Implications*.[1] In their search for theories and concepts, comparative scholars should also consult the rich literature on environmental economics.[2]

Economists had an early start also in empirical comparative research, with the reports of the 1970 Tokyo symposium as a familiar example.[3] Comparative legal studies have been published, such as Peter H. Sand's report on environmental legislation in Japan, Sweden, and the United States, which provides some interesting notes on the developments in environmental law.[4]

The recently published *Environmental Policies in Canada, Sweden, and the United States: A Comparative Overview* is a study of societal response to environmental problems. A comparison is made of national processes of the "agendization" of the environmental issue, the making and implementation of policies, and the impact of environmental policy on institutional structures, administrative performance levels, and existing power relations.[5] A similar study on Japan, the Soviet Union, and the United States finds some interesting relationships between differences in institutions and patterns of public participation, and the processes and content of environmental policy-making and implementation.[6] Several papers delivered at the 1973 IPSA Congress in Montreal are of interest to comparative scholars. They have been collected in a special issue of the *American Behavioral Scientist*.[7] One should also mention a recent UN publication on environmental policy and administration, which besides comparisons of urban environmental planning and nature conservancy legislation in a number of countries also contains a very elaborated bibliography.[8]

C. Ongoing and Planned Research Efforts

A most comprehensive research effort is represented by the joint American-European proposals which were developed in 1973 under the auspices of the inter-university *Council for European Studies*. The proposed "Program of Comparative Studies of Environment and Society" is meant to function as an umbrella for several comparative projects, and to provide ways and means of cooperation for participants in America and Europe. In combining two related levels of analysis, (a) system behavior and response to new social problems, and (b) specific programs, approaches, institutions, and methods used by countries to deal with environmental problems, the proposed program identifies ten specific research areas, many of which are already "occupied" by American research projects.[9]

One specific research area being given attention on the European side concerns the comparative study of international cooperation in water basin areas. Coordinated by the Department of Political Science at Uppsala University, an inter-Nordic project comprising four disciplines in six universities is planned to start in 1976. The project will deal with the processes and arrangements for international cooperation to solve environmental and natural resources problems in the Baltic Sea basin. The obvious differences among the political systems around the Baltic Sea point toward a rich potential for the comparative study of different national policies, such as pollution control, coastal zone management, and nature conservancy, and their relationship to international environmental cooperation.[10]

Comprehensive comparative studies of the determinants of national policies and approaches and of the transferability of different management options are carried out in a program conducted by the OECD *Environment Directorate*. Originally geared towards a comparison of the member countries' implementation of OECD "Guiding Principles Concerning International Economic Aspects of Environmental Policies"—such as the "polluter-pay"-principle—the program first concentrated on a specific case study of Sweden's environmental policy. This case study covered Sweden's approaches to such environmental problems as pollution control, environmentally hazardous chemicals, and land-use planning.[11]

Since November 1973, much of the comparative efforts of the Environment Directorate have concentrated on selecting a set of "management options," suitable for the continued comparative review. By the spring of 1974, several member countries had delivered reports on national approaches to pollution control of stationary sources, land-use planning, and the use of "best available technology" and economic charges to reach environmental policy goals. Proposals for the further development of the OECD comparative program were discussed at the OECD Meeting of Environmental Ministers in November 1974, under the main theme of "Environmental Policies Looking Ahead to the 1980's: The Responsibilities of Industrialized Societies and the Role of the OECD." Specific comparative reviews of governmental involvement in "environmental economics" were started in November 1974 by the Economic Unit of the OECD Environment Directorate.[12]

The *UNESCO Man and the Biosphere Program* (MAB) contains several elements of interest to students of comparative environmental policy. *MAB Project 13*, "Perception of Environmental Quality" aims at developing comprehensive policy-planning models from the results obtained in cross-cultural comparisons of environmental quality perceptions and findings concerning their impact on national policies.[13] Closely related to Project 13 is the *ICSU/SCOPE Core Project 7*, "Communication of Environmental Information and Societal Assessment and Response" (CEISAAR), administered by the Holcombe Research Institute at Butler University, Indianapolis. The objectives of CEISAAR are (a) to assess the methods and channels of disseminating scientific information on environmental hazards and the individual and societal response to such information, and (b) to analyze related political and legal issues to provide a basis for policy recommendations concerning the relationship between scientific knowledge and policy-making.[14] A related study covering the case of mercury pollution in Sweden was published in August 1974.[15]

SCOPE is also carrying out *Core Project 9*, "Environmental Policy and National Institutional Infrastructures." This project involves comparisons of environmental policy-making systems in a number of nations, with specific emphasis on the implementation of scientific judgment through administrative actions. Coordinated by the *IUCN Commission on Environmental Policy, Law and Administration*, the project is scheduled to finish in 1976.[16]

Numerous comparative studies are underway outside the comprehensive research programs just mentioned. One such study, lead by the School of Law of the University of Washington, Seattle, compares water quality management policies through intensive studies of two selected river basins in France, Great Britain, Hungary, Sweden, and West Germany respectively. Among other things, the study is concerned with what factors determine the content and use of "best available" or "best practicable" technology in different national contexts.[17] A study under way at the University of Uppsala compares the effects of socioeconomic, cultural, and institutional differences on the selection of air pollution control policies in Canada, Sweden, and the United States. It also analyzes the socioeconomic, institutional, and cultural impact of selected and implemented policy alternatives.[18] With respect to land-use planning and environmental control a two-year comparative study undertaken by the Conservation Foundation analyzes the protection of environmentally sensitive areas, the location of industrial and urban activities, and the techniques of environmental impact assessment in eight countries.[19]

D. Research Resources: Institutions and Information Channels

The already mentioned *IUCN Commission on Environmental Policy, Law and Administration* is an obvious resource for exchange of information on comparative research. Its chairman, Professor L.K. Caldwell at Indiana University, has lead the work on a *Guide to Advanced Study of Environmental Policy, Law and Administration*. This Guide contains detailed bibliographies covering the whole range of environmental policy-related issues.[20]

The International Social Science Council (ISSC), has established a Standing Committee on Environment with representatives from all international social sciences associations. The Committee issues an *Information Circular* with communication concerning past, present, and future policy research, planned meetings, conferences, etc. Special issues on different aspects of the environmental problem are contemplated.[21] Among those represented on the ISSC Committee is the International Political Science Association (IPSA), which in turn has its own Group of Specialists on Environmental Policy. The Group is composed of researchers working on common problems, and provides a genuinely cross-national setting with prospects of continuous cooperation in a future research committee.[22]

Information on issues pertinent to comparative environmental policy research is found in a number of periodicals and publications already mentioned elsewhere in this chapter.[23] Scholars in the field should consult the *Environment Abstracts,* formerly *Environment Information Access* (New York: Environmental Information Center). A similar publication, also containing abstracts of articles on legal, administrative, and socioeconomic aspects of environmental issues is the *Environmental Health and Pollution Control* (Amsterdam: Excerpta Medica). A valuable bibliographical tool is the recently published *Guide to Information Sources on Environmental Science and Technology*.[24] Finally, one should mention *The Directory of Published Proceedings,* which publishes a special series on environmental issues beginning March 1974.[25]

Notes

1. A.E. Utton and D.H. Henning (eds.), *Environmental Policy: Concepts and International Implications,* (New York: Praeger, 1973).

2. See, e.g., A.V. Kneese and B.T. Bower (eds.), *Environmental*

Quality Analysis: Theory & Method in the Social Sciences (Baltimore: Johns Hopkins Press, for Resources for the Future, 1972).

3. S. Tsuru (ed.), *Proceedings of International Symposium on Environmental Disruption* (Tokyo: Asahi Evening News, 1970).

4. Peter H. Sand, *Legal Systems for Environmental Protection: Japan, Sweden and the United States* (Rome: FAO Legislative Studies No. 4, May 1972).

5. L.J. Lundqvist, *Environmental Policies in Canada, Sweden and the United States: A Comparative Overview*, (Beverly Hills: Sage Professional Paper in Administrative and Policy Studies, No. 03-014, 1974).

6. D.R. Kelley, K.R. Stunkel, and R.R. Wescott, *The Economic Superpowers and the Environment* (San Francisco: W.H. Freeman & Co. forthcoming).

7. *American Behavioral Scientist* 17 (May-June 1974).

8. UN Department of Economic and Social Affairs, *Organization and Administration of Environmental Programmes* (New York: UN,ST/ESA/16, October 1974).

9. For information on the CES "Program of Comparative Studies of Environment and Society," write to Council for European Studies, University of Pittsburgh, Penn. 15215.

10. "Prospects and Problems of International Cooperation for Resource Utilization and Environmental Management: The Case of the Baltic Sea Basin," Uppsala, Department of Political Science, May 1974, mimeo.

11. The following OECD documents are related to the Swedish case study: ENV/SWE/73.1-7; see esp. ENV/SWE/73.5 and 73.7, which contain summaries and comparative discussions of the Swedish approaches.

12. See OECD documents ENV (73) 38, ENV (73) 39, and ENV (74) 11 for details of the development of the comparative review.

13. See UNESCO, MAB: *Expert Panel on Project 13: Perception of Environmental Quality, Final Report* (Paris: UNESCO SC.72/Conf.616/3, July 1973), p. 28 f.

14. *The Programme of SCOPE,* (mimeo, not dated), pp. 20 ff.; cf ICSU/SCOPE, "International Research on Human Response to Environmental Hazards, Working Paper 1" (Document ENV HAZ 1, March 1973), and several working papers from the Holcombe Research Institute, Butler University, Indianapolis.

15. L.J. Lundqvist, *The Case of Mercury Pollution in Sweden –Scientific Information and Public Response,* (Stockholm: NFR, FEK Report No. 4, 1974).

16. L.K. Caldwell, "Preliminary Draft Statement for Core Project 9: Environmental Policy Issues. The Administrative Implementation of Scientific Judgments, with particular reference to Core Projects 1-7" (Bloomington: Indiana University, Department of Political Science, July 1974).

17. Information from Professor Ralph W. Johnson, School of Law, University of Washington, Seattle, Wash. 98195.

18. A preliminary analysis of the impact of institutional differences on selected policy alternatives is found in L.J. Lundqvist, "Do Political Structures Matter in Environmental Politics? The Case of Air Pollution Control in Canada, Sweden, and the United States," *American Behavioral Scientist* 7 (May-June 1974): 731-750.

19. Information from John S. Banta, Project Coordinator, The Conservation Foundation, 1717 Massachusetts Ave. N.W., Washington, D.C. 20036.

20. L.K. Caldwell (ed.), *Guide to Advanced Study of Environmental Policy, Law and Administration* (Bloomington, Ind.: Indiana University, November 1974).

21. For further information, write to S. Friedman, Secretary-General, ISSC, UNESCO, 1 rue Miollis, 75015 Paris.

22. For further information, write to André Phillipart, Secretary-General, IPSA, 43 rue des Champs Elysées, B-1050 Brussels.

23. See contributions of Mann and Wandesforde-Smith.

24. J.O. Mekeirle (comp.), *Guide to Information Sources on Environmental Science and Technology* (Amsterdam: Flemish Economic Association, 1974).

25. *The Directory of Published Proceedings, Series PCE, Pollution Control and Ecology* (Harrison; N.Y.: Interdok Corporation, March 1974).

7

Free Speech and Civil Liberties Policy

Samuel Krislov

I. Basic Issues and References

Since in one sense every legal decision is a question of policy, a summary of policy implications in the domain of civil liberties could be isomorphic with leading issues of constitutional law in the area. But the area is sharply delimited if one deals with those issues which suggest immediate potential for behavioral research. Some of these areas, hopefully the major ones, are discussed below.

A. *The Community of Tolerance*

The First Amendment presupposes a tolerant and civilized community. The paradox of American society is that studies indicate a lack of operational understanding of the principles of liberal democracy on the part of the community, [McClosky; Mack; Selven; Prothro-Grigg] yet the system works.

The explanation of the 50's and 60's was unequivocal, the key lay in the tolerance of elite groups. [Stauffer; Lipset; McClosky.] The argument of the "participatory democrats" is that only inexperience and lack of understanding produces the discrepancy between follower and leader respect for liberty. By expanding experience we will expand tolerance.

Recent research on these basic questions is meager. Even the more immediate relations of public opinion and the court has been explored only by Murphy and Tanenhaus and a handful of others. What is needed is a broad study of the climate of liberty, the minimum of order needed for tolerance, a study of the scope and sweep of Bay's *The Structure of Freedom*. Oddly the most relevant material in current times is the literature on violence and social change [Gurr; Flanigan and Fogelman; Fierabend, Nesvold and Fierabend].

B. *Media Consequence and Civil Liberties*

The push toward expanding expression has eroded many old differences in law on regulation of media. This has proceeded in the absence of any definite findings of harm in the area of pornography, where a body of experimental literature now suggests it is unlikely a danger exists. Existing regulations distinguishing between adults and children seems based more upon individual observation and episodic evidence rather than any experimental or quasi-experimental evidence. However, some evidence of deleterious effects of pictured violence in visual media has been tenuously advanced.

Interestingly enough the best evidence on the lack of effect of pornography, the consequences of visual representation of violence, and the causes of social violence, were all prepared under governmental auspices. Perhaps, effective work on racial prejudice and media consequences could be developed as well. Whether deleterious effects of media are sufficient to justify censorship could, of course, remain as a normative problem.

There are also real dilemmas as to the consequence of governmental regulation or its absence. Community pressures may be less reliable, more chilling and arbitrary than governmental action.

C. Security Publicity and Discretion in Government

The Pentagon Papers have effectively dramatized the problem of classification of materials and withholding information on policy groups. In general, this is an area where scholarship and past experience provide impressive guidance for the policy-maker. While empirical evidence of a scientific nature is scarce, historical and episodic experience is probably adequate and would serve as a valuable corrective to the administrator's preoccupation with restricting coverage to favorable information.

This issue dramatizes an even broader and more seminal issue of American government: the dilemma of discretion. This is one of the great antimonies of any political order. Have we erred in over-extension of discretion, especially executive freedom? This is a recent theme where the new left and old right merge with occasional agreement from the Old New Dealish Center.

D. Equality of Educational Opportunity

In no area has the behavioral sciences been more evident than this—from Myrdal's *An American Dilemma*, to the evidence in *Brown* v. *Board of Education*, the Coleman Report, and countless effectiveness studies. Neither the inconclusiveness nor the controversy should be excessively discouraging. The quality of debate would be lowered even further without such testimony.

Evidence as to the impact of various types of programs may well be doomed to relative inconclusiveness. The variables manipulated are so linked to others (often in subtle fashion) that these studies have often been true proving grounds of our standard research designs and statistical methods. Considering the importance of the issue, our propensity to overgeneralize has also not been adequately held in check.

In one sense the debate in this area represents a collision of civil liberty and equalitarianism. In the name of the latter, efforts to suppress types of research have occurred. Those efforts, designed to unscramble the eggs of heredity and environment, are probably misguided. In terms of policy, the established fact of intra-group variation so dominates the possible intergroup difference, as to make the enterprise almost trivial. Nonetheless the essence of scientific freedom involves the right to even clear error, subject to criticism, not suppression.

It is not only with respect to pedagogical patterns that behavioral research in this area has addressed itself. One of the major thrusts of research has involved fiscal structures and their consequence. The work of Jack Coons and his associates together with their attack on localism and the property tax has resulted in a Texas state decision now to be reviewed by the U.S. Supreme Court.

E. The Equality Revolution

A recent and significant decision has exempted Amish children from compulsory education at the high school level where this conflicts with their religious ethic on family involvement in agriculture and the avoidance of extensive worldly wisdom. In balancing the very high value of education against this religious claim, the Supreme Court noted the state has not proven compelling need, and the absence of alternative ways of achieving its objective. In emphasizing the empirical record of the Amish community in providing for the welfare of its members, the Court may well have inaugurated a less rigidly conceptual approach to such problems.

Similarly decisions on rights of illegitimate children, pupils in schools, teachers, wives, children in relation to parents, etc., betoken the immense benefits accrued to other groups in the wake of the civil rights movement. (So far, only in the field of welfare payments has the Burger Court reacted against extension of claims—a reaction which began in the Warren days and is rooted in traditional court reluctance to dictate fiscal policy.) These developments generally are assented with strong evidence on impact of restriction on the life styles and chances of the non-privileged group.

The cutting point on these developments has bended to involve the rights of institutionalized members of society. Reform of prisons and the correctional system and sanction system is being debated vigorously in virtually every state. The rights of mental patients has been vigorously pressed by such writers as Thomas Szass, who reject involuntary commitment outright. Paul Meehl has taken a more behavioral approach, stressing the great lack of danger and inertness, the vast bulk of inmates, such as in institutional populations have abnormally low crime rates. He therefore argues for a drastic change in the risk-rating patterns of committing agencies. Recent court decisions have begun to receive more favorably Judge D. Bazelon's audacious suggestion that if a mental institution did not in fact provide therapy—and many if not most don't—that courts begin to reassess the confinement of those called patients, but who are actually merely prisoners.

II. Basic Facilities and Institutions

Civil Liberties-Civil Rights policy issues have been at the heart of American policy conflict in recent years. As a result the sources of information and research are almost coextensive with the media.

Ideas, issues and evidence are part and parcel of such intellectual and semi-intellectual publications as the *New York Review of Books, The Public Interest, Atlantic Monthly*, etc. The use of such aids as the *Reader's Guide*, the *Public Affairs Information Service, Social Sciences and Humanities Index* is a sensible short-cut. *Journalism Quarterly, Columbia University Forum, Editor and Publisher, Publishers Weekly, Nieman Fellows Report* are other sources from a media viewpoint. Law journals are also useful; the most likely sources are Harvard, Yale, Columbia, and Stanford. The *Index to Legal Periodicals* is indispensible, though peculiarly classified. For legal trends on the Supreme Court *Harvard Law Review's* annual summary, The American Jewish Committee's Annual Summary of Civil Liberties cases, and the *Supreme Court Annual* are unrivaled. *Public Opinion Quarterly* prints regular poll summaries of relevance. The major law schools now have second rung law reviews much oriented to the concern of this section: The *Harvard Civil Rights-Civil Liberties Review*, the *Columbia Survey of Human Rights Law*, and the *Yale Review of Law and Social Action* come to mind. Symposia issues are run on elated problems by such journals as *The Annals, Law and Contemporary Problems,* the *Journal of Social Issues*, and *Daedelus*. Law and social science journals include *Law and Society* and the more economics-oriented *Journal of Legal Studies*. Help on the rich range of journals can be gained from Ulrich's *International Periodical Directory* (particularly under the rubrics of *Law and Political Science-Civil Rights*).

A large number of action groups are involved. These range from the

American Civil Liberties Union, the Center for Constitutional Rights, the National Emergency Civil Liberties Committee, and the Anti-Defamation League to specialized groups like the Citizens Advocacy Center and the Lawyers Committee for Civil Rights under Law. Many of these have their own publications. The Alexander Meiklejohn Institute at Berkeley publishes a unique *Civil Rights Handbook* which updates cases and suggests techniques for attorneys. The National Civil Liberties Clearing House in Washington co-ordinates some forty organizations, and has a house organ. The Clearinghouse for Civil Rights Research at Catholic University also does related research and publishes a monthly periodical.

Among research agencies the American Bar Foundation, Institute for Judicial Administration of NYU, the Vera Institute of Justice, the Western Center on Law and Poverty at Southern California, Freedom House in New York City, the A. Phillip Randolph Institute in New York City, and the Center for the Study of Democratic Institutions at Santa Barbara develop largely in-house research and ideas. Some individual programs can be worked out with these and other centers like Brookings and Twentieth Century fund.

Virtually all the major sources of funding are (in line with the current emphasis on research on social problem-solving) available for projects in this area, especially NSF (Several divisions including R.A.N.N., Law, and Political Science), NIMH, and Ford. The Russell Sage Foundation has interests especially focusing on professional roles. (In this respect its one year residencies for social scientists interested in law and lawyers with social science interests is relevant, as is Harvard Law School's program for Liberal Arts teachers.) The OEO, NIMH, the Office of Education, have action oriented grant programs. The Council on Law Related Studies has a program embracing very specific topics one of which is the rights of prisoners. The Charles Warren Center at Harvard and National Endowment for the Humanities fund less "scientific" projects than most of the above. Both have strong civil liberties orientations. In addition, many governmental agencies, e.g., LEAA, The Civil Rights Commission, the Civil Service Commission, have scholar-in-residence programs. Finally many small foundations—e.g., the Louis Rabinowitz and Field Foundation—have special interests in race relations, social change, and similar topics.

References

The Community of Tolerance

Hanan C. Selvin and Warren Hagstrom, "Determinants of Support for Civil Liberties," *British Journal of Sociology* (March 1960): 51-73.

Raymond Mack, "Do We Really Believe in the Bill of Rights," *Social Problems* (1956): 264ff.

Herbert Hyman and Paul Sheatsley, "Trend in Public Opinion on Civil Liberties," *Journal of Social Issues* No. 6, (1953).

Herbert McClosky, "Concensus and Ideology in American Politics," *APSR* (1964): 361.

Herbert Hyman, "England and America: Climates of Tolerance and Intolerance," in Bell (ed.), *The Radical Right* (New York: Anchor, 1964).

Samuel Krislov, *The Supreme Court and Political Freedom* (New York: Free Press, 1967).

Murphy and Tanenhaus, "Public Opinion and the Supreme Court," *Law and Society Review* (May 1968): 357-384.

Krislov et al., *Compliance and the Law* (Beverly Hills: Sage 1972), includes (inter alia) Fierabend, and Nesvold and Fierabend.

Gurr, *Why Men Rebel* (Princeton: Princeton University Press, 1970).

Prothro and Grigg, "Fundamental Principles of Democracy," *Journal of Politics* (1960): 276-294.

Media Consequence and Civil Liberties

Report of the Commission on Obscenity and Pornography (1970).

Technical Reports of the Commission on Obscenity and Pornography (1970).

Kronhausen and Kronhausen, *Pornography and the Law*, (New York: Ballantine Books, 1959).

Cairns, Paul and Wishner, "The Assumptions of Anti-Obscenity Laws and the Empirical Evidence," *Minnesota Law Review* (1962): 1009-1041.

R. S. Randall, *Censorship of the Movies* (Madison: Wisconsin University Press, 1968).

J.P. Levine, "The Supreme Court and Sex Censorship," in Fizman, *The American Political Arena* (Boston: Little Brown and Company, 1970).

Security Publicity and Discretion in Government

Davis, *Discretionary Justice* (Baton Rouge: Louisiana State University Press, 1969).

Lowi, *The End of Liberalism* (New York: Norton, 1969).

Rourke, *Secrecy and Publicity* (Baltimore: Johns Hopkins University Press, 1961).

Shils, *The Torment of Secrecy* (Glencoe: Free Press, 1956).

Equality of Educational Opportunity

Coons et al., *Private Wealth and Public Education* (Cambridge: Harvard University Press, 1970).

Katz and Gurin, *Race and the Social Sciences* (New York: Basic Books, 1969).

Coleman et al., *Equality of Educational Opportunity* (Washington, D.C.: Government Printing Office, 1966).

Deutsch, Katz and Jensen, *Social Class, Race and Psychological Development* (New York: Holt Press, 1968).

Gurin, "A Expectancy Approach to Intervention Programs," in V. Allen (ed.), *Psychological Factors in Poverty* (Chicago: Markham Books, 1970).

The Equality Revolution

Miller and Robgy, *The Future of Inequality* (New York: Basic Books, 1970).

Mayer, *The Lawyers* (New York: Harper Books, 1967).

Szass, *Life, Liberty and Psychiatry* (New York: Collier Books, 1969).

Meehl, "On the Justification for Civil Commitment," 117 *University of Pennsylvania Law Review* 75, 117 (1968).

8

Economic Regulation Policy

James E. Anderson

Political scientists have not devoted much time or resources to the study of economic regulation in recent years. The paucity of books and professional journal articles dealing with regulatory topics attests to this fact. Hopefully, though, the growing interest within the political science discipline in policy matters will alter this condition. There is no sound reason for leaving this field to journalists, law writers, and economists. Clearly, by focusing on policy problems with a policy approach much can be learned concerning political and administrative processes and behavior as well as the content and impact of policy.

In this chapter attention will be given first to some recent issues and developments in national economic regulation. Secondly, some sources for the study and research of economic regulatory policy will be discussed.

I. Recent Issues and Developments

A. Regulatory Commissions

Existent in the literature is a life-cycle theory of independent regulatory commissions, which depicts them as moving through the stages of gestation, youth, and maturity into old age, where they become essentially "captives" of the regulated.[1] This life-cycle theory has been accepted rather uncritically by political scientists although, to the best of my knowledge, it has never been fully documented by anyone. The activities of the Securities and Exchange Commission, recent expressions of vigor by the Federal Trade Commission, and the overall history of the National Labor Relations Board raise questions concerning the validity of this theory. A critical look at it is thoroughly in order.

Reform of the regulatory commissions has been a frequent issue in the past, with major efforts at reform occuring every decade or so. (E.g., the *Report of the President's Commission on Administrative Management*, 1937; the first *Hoover Commission Report*, 1949; James M. Landis, *Report on Regulatory Commissions to the President Elect,* 1960.) Most recently, the Ash Council in *A New Regulatory Framework* (1971) has proposed converting a number of the commissions into single-headed agencies subject to presidential control. The "new conceptual framework" on which the Council's recommendations are premised essentially embodies the precepts of the strong executive model of organization.[2] However, no action has been taken on the recommendations and, once again, the commissions appear able to resist drastic reform.

Dissatisfaction with the operation of some commissions, the impact of regulatory programs, or both, have produced some calls for de-regulation of some activities. A Kennedy Administration proposal for abandonment of some railroad rate regulation failed to win acceptance in the early 1960s because it would also have ended the antitrust exemption for railroad rate conferences by which rates are fixed. Many railroads apparently preferred continued regulation to the loss of their antitrust exemption, which in turn could have exposed them to the rigors of competition. Recently, various officials, including the chairman of the Federal Trade Commission and the head of the Antitrust Division, have levied criticism at some regulatory agencies and programs for doing more to protect producers against competitive pressures than consumers against corporate abuses. Especially singled out for criticism by "de-regulators" have been the Interstate Commerce Commission and the Civil Aeronautics Board.

Will "de-regulation" succeed? In most cases the prospects do not seem especially good. Although the persistence of controls is most commonly attributed to the political support of the regulated, such as what the ICC gets from its rail, motor carrier, and barge line clientele, this does not seem to be the most significant factor. More important is congressional support. Regulatory commissions are viewed as "arms of Congress" and hence more subject to congressional control than other agencies. To abandon commissions, on this perspective, would be to enhance executive power. Moreover, many members of Congress, especially Democrats, believe in regulation as a matter of faith. When an industry, such as the railroads, develops economic problems, subsidies rather than de-regulation is the preferred congressional response.

Interestingly, three new regulatory commissions have been recently created by Congress, namely the Consumer Products Safety Commission (1973), the Nuclear Regulatory Commission (1974), and the Commodity Futures Trading Commission (1974). Congress clearly has not lost interest in the commission form of agency. The relationship between Congress and the regulatory commissions needs further examination by policy analysts, as does comparison of the merits of commissions and regular agencies for the administration of regulatory programs.

B. Consumer Protection

For decades, the sad plight of the consumer, disorganized and inarticulate, in the politics process has been remarked and lamented. Consumer politics, however, has greatly increased in vigor and saliency since the early 1960s and a substantial volume of consumer legislation has flowed from Congress. Subjects include meat and poultry inspection, automobile safety, drug testing, truth-in-lending, truth-in-packaging, and natural gas pipeline safety.[3] One matter worthy of more examination here is the development of public interest lawyers and public interest research groups, such as Nader's Raiders, and their effect on public policy formation. What are their implications for traditional group theory?

Controversy still continues in Congress over the creation of a Consumer Protection Agency, which would serve as the advocate of consumer interests before regulatory agencies. Senate action on the proposed agency was blocked by a filibuster in 1974 after favorable House action. While some might view the establishment of a consumer agency with no substantive programs of its own as essentially symbolic, conservative and business interests have strongly resisted its creation. Interests that are articulated are more difficult to ignore than those that are not. In a somewhat different context, note the effect of the requirement of environmental impact statements by the National Environmental Protection Act on various agencies. It is a procedural requirement but it has had significant substantive consequences.

C. Industrial Safety

Greater concern with the quality of life, and itself, is undoubtedly one factor contributing to national legislative activity concerning industrial satety. Another is the failure of the states to act, or to act adequately, in this area to satisfy important claimants. Two major statutes should be noted. The Federal Mine Health and Safety Act of 1969 attempted to significantly strengthen mine safety requirements following a major coal mine disaster. The Occupational Health and Safety Act of 1970 represents a major movement by the national government into the area of general industrial safety, which previously had been left largely to the states. The ongoing struggles over the implementation and enforcement of these two statutes reveals the importance of the administrative process in shaping the real content and impact of public policy.

D. Antitrust

Antitrust action has been bipartisan in recent decades, with Republican and Democratic administration displaying equal vigor, or non-vigor, in enforcement.[4] No major substantive changes have been made in the statute law since the adoption of the Celler Antimerger Act of 1950. Most cases are settled by consent decrees informally negotiated by the Antitrust Division and the alleged offenders. The recent brouhaha over the ITT cases, apart from its partisan political aspects, has provided some insight concerning how major antitrust cases are handled by the government and some of the influencing considerations. Dispassionate economic and policy considerations may become quite secondary to the struggle for advantage, political skulduggery, and superficial policy biases. (E.g., consider the statement of former President Nixon that trust-busting was "all right fifty years ago but it's not a good thing for the country today," which was made in the course of his telling an antitrust official not to appeal one of the cases against ITT.)

The Nixon administration proved more willing to act on conglomerate mergers, a major policy issue, than the Johnson administration, whose officials contended they lacked authority to do so under the antitrust laws. Five major cases were started but all, however, were settled informally by consent decrees. As a consequence the legal issue of whether conglomerate mergers were covered by the amended Clayton Act was left unresolved.[5] Recently, price-fixing or non-price competition by professional groups such as realtors, accountants, and civil engineers, even when confined to a single locality, has come under antitrust scrutiny. In late 1974 legislation was passed increasing the penalties for antitrust violations. The maximum jail sentence was increased to three years and maximum fines to $100,000 for individuals and $1,000,000 for corporations. The legislation also provided for greater publicity for consent decree proceedings. Given the reluctance of judges to impose harsh penalties in the past, especially jail sentences, the increase in penalties may be largely symbolic, coming as it did at the time when many people were concerned about high prices and the possibility of price manipulations.

E. Economic Stability

The maintenance of economic stability has been a major focus of public policy since the adoption of the Employment Act of 1946, with fiscal and monetary techniques being the primary policy instruments. In August 1971, to deal with continuing inflation, which had been touched off by the Johnson administration's desire to have both "guns and butter" in the late 1960s, the Nixon administration instituted direct price and wage controls on the authority of the Economic Stabilization Act of 1970. This legislation, which had been passed at the behest of liberal Democrats in Congress, and which delegated almost unlimited authority to the executive, had been unwanted and opposed by the Nixon administration. Initially, the administration's action was well-accepted by the public, notwithstanding its rather drastic nature. Subsequent administration of price and wage controls, as they moved through Phases I to IV, and were finally terminated, indicated the political and administrative difficulties in implementing a program of direct controls on a peacetime (let's assume this anyway) economy. E.g., the tripartite wage board representing business, labor and the "public," which had been set up to win labor support for controls, soon broke down because of labor's dissatisfaction. How effective the controls really were remains a matter of some contention.

Inflation continued and in 1973 and 1974 reached the "double-digit" stage of 10 percent or more annually. Economists, who in the early 1960s sometimes spoke of their ability to "fine tune" the economy lost some of their glamor. The standard fiscal and monetary means for combating inflation no longer seem as workable or acceptable as they once did. How, indeed does one deal with "stagflation," that is, increasing price levels in an economy characterized by growing unemployment? This is not the way the economy is supposed to operate. What changes in the economy, and public policy, have contributed to this? Would a good dose of antitrust to restore competition, as some suggest, be helpful?

F. Energy

Traditionally, energy policy in the United States has been rather fragmented. Some controls, as on electricity and natural gas rates, were imposed for the purpose of protecting consumers. Others, as in the regulation of domestic petroleum production and oil imports, were designed primarily to protect prices for domestic production. Some thought was given but little was done to develop some kind of overall, coordinated policy, or set of policies, on energy development and useage. Some spoke of a possible energy shortage, but few listened. This situation changed in late 1973 with the Arab oil boycott. Since then much has been said, many proposals have been made, but little has thus far been accomplished toward providing a "solution" for the "energy crisis." Those who believe that the science and technology can provide a solution are really doomed to disappointment, as the problem is not really scientific in nature. In the long run, science and technology may increase the supply of energy but, among other things, what happens to demand at the same time? Some would say the solution should be economic, but there does not seem to be widespread faith in economic solutions. Moreover, is such a proposal as one to heavily increase federal gasoline taxes, and then leave allocation of supply to market forces, really an economic solution? Does it not blend politics and economics? Ultimately it would seem that whatever particular form "the solution" takes, it must involve a weighing and balancing interests, and this is a political task in the classic sense. This task maybe performed in more or less rational manner, depending upon the participants and processes involved.[6]

G. Agriculture

During the 1950s and early 1960s, the "farm problem" was a persistent item on both the societal and congressional policy agendas. Then, as such issue-areas as civil rights, welfare, the Vietnam War, the urban crisis, and environmental pollution, not necessarily in that order, drew the attention of policymakers and the public, the farm problem drew less attention. Also contributory was the enactment of legislation in 1965 and 1970 having a longer legislative life, which reduced the frequency with which Congress had to confront the problem. Customarily the farm problem had been defined in terms of surplus production, low farm prices, and inadequate farm incomes. Central features of farm policy were the regulation of production and the subsidy schemes to increase farm prices and incomes.

The Agriculture and Consumer Protection Act of 1973 marks a basic shift in the nature of agricultural policy. Guaranteed price support payments divorced from prevailing market prices were eliminated for several major commodities and replaced by target prices. In 1974 market prices were substantially above the target prices, notwithstanding less control of production, and consequently governmental costs for the price support were quite low.

Moreover, world conditions have changed and now our attention is focused on a shortage rather than a surplus of agricultural production, or to put it in a more human term, food. How to increase food supplies has become an issue with which policymakers are called upon to deal. The international food conference held in Rome in the fall of 1974, while producing no meaningful solutions, reflects the growing concern with this "new" policy problem.

II. Sources for the Study of Economic Regulatory Policies

The focus here will be on printed information and data sources for research and analysis of economic regulatory policies. Much can be gleaned, inferred, and learned from careful and imaginative use of such materials concerning the formation, substance, and impact of regulatory policies. Although interviews and other field research techniques are often necessary and yield much valuable data, we should not fall into the trap of assuming that primary recourse must always be had to such methods. Many readers have undoubtedly interviewed officials who gave rather self-serving or dissembling responses to questions on matters of controversy. The printed records serve as both safeguard and supplement in such cases. Instructive on the use of formal records to gain behavioral insights is an early article by Ralph Huitt based on Senate hearings on World War II price controls. ("The Congressional Committee: A Case Study," *American Political Science Review* 48 (1954): 340-365.)

What is presented here can be viewed either as a guide for the beginner or a checklist for the more experienced hand in policy analysis.

Political science journals in recent years have contained very little dealing with economic regulation policy, its formation or impact, which probably accurately reflects the interest of the discipline as a whole. The standard economic journals have done better, although their contents now reflect economists' fascination with public choice theories, model building, and econometrics. Much of this yields little insight into the actual processes of policy formation. Economists have made a variety of efforts to assess the impact of various regulatory policies. Note, for example, several of the articles by economists in Paul MacAvoy (ed.), *The Crisis of the Regulatory Commissions* (New York: W.W. Norton, 1970). Also, many of the economic studies published by the Brookings Institution involve policy assessment. *Public Policy* and the *Public Administration Review* should be consulted as they frequently carry articles of interest to students of economic regulation.

A number of the general law reviews carry articles with some regularity which relate to both the procedural and substantive aspects of regulatory policies. Some that I have found especially useful are the California, Columbia, George Washington, Harvard, Michigan, Stanford, University of Pennsylvania, and Virginia *Law Reviews, Yale Law Journal, Journal of Public Law,* and *Journal of Law and Economics*. Law writers, it should be noted, sometimes appear too uncritical in their use of formal records and printed sources. Arguments or claims may be accepted as facts. However, as we well know, agency statements of intention, for example, do not always describe agency action. As with economists, law writers tend to have little to say about the politics and informal aspects of policy formation.

There are also a variety of more specialized legal publications which can also yield useful information. A sampling includes such items as the *Administrative Law Review, Antitrust Bulletin, Banking Law Journal, Journal of Air Law and Commerce, ICC Practitioners Journal, Labor Law Journal, Natural Resources Journal,* and *Law and Contemporary Problems*. In all, the student of economic regulatory policies can benefit substantially from the efforts of law writers, notwithstanding the caveats expressed above. The *Index to Legal Publications* is a convenient guide to their voluminous output. Chester Newland's "The Supreme Court and Legal Writing: Learned Journals as Vehicles of an Anti-Antitrust Lobby?" indicates how it may be utilized in an attempt to influence judicial decisions.[7]

Some of the privately published legal reporting services should be consulted for current information and commentary on agency policy actions. Some meriting note are the *Antitrust and Trade Regulation Reporter* (BNA), *Labor Law Reporter* (CCH), *Federal Securities Law Reporter* (CCH), and *Pike and Fischer's Radio Regulation*. More general in coverage is the *U.S. Code, Congressional and Administrative News* (West Publishing Company).

Government documents are, of course, a major research resource in this area as in most other areas of public policy. Careful and imaginative use of them can yield much useful and valuable information and many insights into the regulatory process and impact of regulation on societal conditions. The *Congressional Record*, committee reports and hearings, and committee staff and sponsored studies can all be drawn upon. Appropriations committee hearings afford an annual insight into at least some of the affairs of most regulatory programs and agency-committee relationship. What agencies do in part reflects pressures from the appropriations committees. For example, Congressman John Rooney, long chairman of the House Appropriations subcommittee dealing with the Antitrust Division, has been much concerned with quantitative results (e.g., numbers of cases won and lost, amount of fines levied) and little interested in the economic impact of antitrust. This has undoubtedly contributed to the Division's inclination to deal mainly in lesser antitrust violations and to settle cases informally. A good won-lost record is built by such means.

Annual reports and other publications by agencies provide numerical data, as on policy enforcement patterns, and official policy viewpoints, among other matters. Periodic news releases such as those of the Federal Trade Commission and the Department of Justice may also be of some utility. Formal policy outputs are recorded in such sources as the *U.S. Statutes at Large*, the *Federal Register,* the *Code of Federal Regulations*, and the volumes of decisions of such agencies as the Federal Trade Commission, National Labor Relations Board, and Interstate Commerce Commission. Such sources can be used in seeking the substantive content of policy. They also provide much of the data needed for research on such topics as the voting behavior of independent regulatory commissioners. (See Bradley C. Canon, "Voting Behavior on the FCC." *Midwest Journal of Political Science* 13 (1969): 587-612, for an illustration of what can be done.)

A comparatively new agency, the Administrative Conference of the

United States is concerned with developing improvements in the legal procedure involved in regulatory and other programs. As a part of its operations it sponsors and publishes studies on various facets of regulatory procedure. (See *Recommendations and Reports of the Administrative Conference of the U.S., 1968-1970.*) These should not be neglected by those concerned with the procedural side of economic regulation. Neither should the four volume *Administrative Law Treatise* by Kenneth C. Davis.

A few other sources can be briefly noted. Trade journals and publications can yield information on the attitudes and perspectives of the regulated. Newspapers such as the *Washington Post, New York Times,* and *Wall Street Journal* contain both analytical and reportorial articles. The *Wall Street Journal* is the most thorough, extensive, and valuable in its coverage of economic regulation. Two especially useful periodicals are the *Congressional Quarterly Weekly Report* and the *National Journal Reports*. The *CQ* emphasizes congressional action while the *National Journal* includes many analytical and case study type articles on regulatory policies and programs. The publications of public interest advocates, such as Ralph Nader's Center for Study of Responsive Law, deserve attention. The Nader reports on the FTC, ICC, Food and Drug Administration, and Antitrust enforcement, for instances, contain much solid material, notwithstanding their normative biases and sometimes easy generalizations, on these agencies and their policy concerns.

In conclusion, the data sources mentioned here deal mainly with national economic regulatory policies. Collectively, they constitute a substantial body of data and information. The person who wants to do research on state regulatory policy will normally confront a more challenging task because of the usually limited and fugitive nature of pertinent published or printed materials. Field research becomes much more essential under such conditions. To date, relatively little has been done to investigate the states as economic regulators or to compare their actions and impact in this area. (Some of the input-output studies using quantitative measures of state policies have sometimes touched on this topic, but they have not been very enlightening.) In the era of "energy crisis," such matters as state regulation of strip mining and oil production are pertinent and challenging topics for research and should get more attention from policy analysts. Soundly-executed studies could yield important data both for political scientific and policy formation purposes.

Notes

1. Marver Bernstein, *Regulating Business by Independent Commission* (Princeton, N.J.: Princeton University Press, 1955).

2. Cf. Norman C. Thomas, "Politics, Structure, and Personnel in Administrative Regulation," *Virginia Law Review* 58 (1971): 1033-1068.

3. See Mark Nadel, *The Politics of Consumer Protection* (Indianapolis: Bobbs-Merrill, 1972), for an excellent analysis.

4. Richard Posner, "A Statistical Study of Antitrust Enforcement," *Journal of Law and Economics* 13 (1970): 365-388.

5. A good standard survey of antitrust policy is A.D. Neale, *Antitrust Laws of the U.S.A.* 2nd ed. (London: Cambridge University Press, 1970). Also see Mark J. Green, *The Closed Enterprise System* (New York: Grossman Publishers, 1972). This is the report of the Nader Study group on antitrust enforcement. It contains much useful information.

6. Three recent studies of value are David Howard Davis, *Energy Politics* (New York: St. Martin's Press, 1974); Richard B. Mancke, *The Failure of U.S. Energy Policy* (New York: Columbia University Press, 1974); and Robert H. Connery and Robert S. Gilmour (eds.), *The National Energy Problem* (Lexington, Mass.: Lexington Books, D.C. Heath and Company, 1974).

7. *Georgetown Law Journal* 48 (Fall 1959): 105-143.

9

Electoral Policy

William Crotty

I. Basic Issues and References

A. Voter Registration

The "pure" research in this area is scanty, yet the effect of arbitrary registration practices is limiting (by millions of people) those who can effectively speak, through the vote, to policy issues is beginning to be appreciated.

The only broad study of registration practices and their evolution, and it is both limited in the problems it chose to treat and dated, is Joseph Harris' *Registration of Voters in the United States,* published by the Brookings Institution in 1929. Since then there have been a smattering of studies executed out of curiosity. Those include Andrews' challenging exploration of the extent of the "actual" electorate, that is those legally eligible to participate as against the bloated estimates of political and official agencies, such as the U.S. Bureau of the Census, and the investigation by Stanley Kelley and associates of the relationship between the severity of registration demands and voter turnout in the nation's 104 largest cities during the 1960 presidential elections. Kelley and his co-researchers concluded that the greatest barrier to the vote was registration. Beyond doubt, it is the greatest institutional obstacle to the vote and one that can be effectively minimized.

In 1963, President Kennedy demonstrated an official concern by establishing a commission on registration and voting, with Richard Scammon as chairman and Donald Hersberg as staff director. The Report of the Commission constitutes a fine overview of the problems implicit in a limited electoral participation. Regrettably, the Report and its recommendations were scheduled to be presented to the president on November 26, 1963, as it turned out, four days after his murder. While the Report was presented to President Johnson approximately a month later, many of its proposed changes were lost in the rush of events.

To explore means for creating a more representative electorate, a Task Force (the Freedom to Vote Task Force) was established under the direction of former Attorney-General Ramsey Clark. The Task Force concentrated in particular on the problems posed by registration practices, seeking to advance proposals to insure more equitable practices. The dearth of information resulted in the need to do original research and to call on available data whenever it could be found. Based primarily on my work and data supplied by Walter Dean Burnham on registration effects on voter participation, the group was able to produce two reports that spoke to a major, and neglected, aspect of democratic politics, the role of the state in arbitrarily limiting political involvement. The reports were persuasive enough to initate attempts at legislative remedies. One sweeping proposal for a federal enrollment of voters is now before the Congress. Several more modest proposals are also pending before the Congress to modify substantially present registration actions. These drew on the expertise and data developed by the Task Force. Some organizations, including Common Cause and the National Municipal League, have begun to undertake support of change. The social consequences in expanding the electorate to the poor, the young, the blacks, those in the military and the more mobile could lead to more representative and equitable social policies.

The League of Women Voters has become interested in the problem —at the same time that Common Cause, through the abolition of its Voter Education Project under the able leadership of Anne Wexler, appears to be withdrawing. The League has published the results of its year-long study on barriers to the vote in *Obstacles to Voting,* a publication of the League of Women Voters Education Fund (1972) and available from their Washington office (1730 M St., N.W.). The National Municipal League has scheduled a forthcoming report on legislative remedies as a companion piece to the League of Women Voters.

Policy Objectives. The courts recently have begun a quiet revolution in questionning the acceptability of franchise limitations. The Supreme Court's decision is upholding the Voting Rights Act of 1970; a lower court's voiding of a Texas statute closing registration in January of election years (registration formerly was open for four months, October of the year before election to the end of January of the election year), an extremely effective method for maintaining a restricted electorate; and the Supreme Court's March, 1972 decision in *Dunn* v. *Blumstein* endorsing a 30 day residency period as sufficient for voting in federal elections. The Court has switched from assuming that state requirements are valid to where they now require a state to prove "a compelling state interest" before accepting restrictions on the vote. Additionally, the Court has increasingly related the criteria applied to the real needs of protecting the integrity of elections and to the administrative duties directly related to the conduct of decisions. Any actions intended to prod the states into action would be helpful. Law suits along the lines of the above should be well received by the courts at all levels.

The second agency that has demonstrated some intention to modify current restrictions is the Congress (the Nixon administration is actively hostile both to fundamental change and to enforcing the statutes now on the books). Three bills currently before the Congress deserve attention: the Inoyue-Udall Universal Voter Enrollment Act; Senator Gale McGee's postcard registration proposal; and Senator Edward Kennedy's bill to grant funds for modifying registration practices to the states, as well as introducing postcard registration on a voluntary basis and establishing a Census Bureau agency to deal with registration and voting problems. All three bills are related, but at this point the McGee and Kennedy bills are active candidates for Senate passage.

B. *The Voting Research*

There is an abundance of valuable research (I am thinking here primarily of the Survey Research Center research and the works resulting from it) on voter motivations. The research speaks to a major concern of the practicing politician, yet the latter seems dimly aware of its existence. An appreciation of the well-springs of the vote could lead to more informed, policy-conscious attempts to communicate substantive concerns to the public. Eventually such efforts could lead to a higher level of policy awareness and more impressive attempts to deal with outstanding social concerns.

Policy Objectives. There has been an effort to have the National Committees join the Inter-University Consortium for Political Research and conduct their own analyses with the ICPR data. The hope was to provide the best information possible on the nature of the electorate to both of the major (or any other) political parties, thus upgrading their conduct of campaigns, improving their curiously limited appreciation of voter motivations, and, if all went well, culminating in more issue-oriented campaigns directed to real (as distinguished from Washington, congressional or presidential) national concerns. When the parties showed a willingness to move, one political scientist (who shall remain nameless) retained as a consultant by one of the parties felt that ICPR would result in an unusual advantage for one party and thus delayed endorsing the idea. As financial concerns and the 1972 election came front stage, the plan was held in abeyance. It remains, however, a live possibility.

C. *Money in Politics*

One of the most blatantly odious, discriminatory and hypocritical areas of political concern relates to the role of money in politics. The most extensive information in this area has resulted from the work of such political scientists as Alexander Heard, Jasper Shannon and Herbert Alexander, among others. The continuing research of the Citizens' Research Foundation under the able leadership of Herbert Alexander may eventually result in the passage of further congressional legislation, provide realistic safeguards to financial abuse and equalize the political opportunity to serve in elective office. The recently enacted congressional legislation and the informal agreements among the Democratic presidential contenders to limit the spending in their primary campaigns are steps in the right direction. The new spending law is far more comprehensive and specific than anyone could have expected. Yet much remains to be done. Research stimulated by a researcher's academic curiousity and supported by a variety of sources can have wide social ramifications.

Policy Objectives. A refinement of the present legislation and the introduction of similar bills at the state level. Particular vigilance will be needed to insure that candidates meet the requirements of the law. Vigilance will be needed to make sure that the Congress does not repeal, emasculate or simply render the law ineffective through administration of the law's provisions (attempts along these lines are now underway). Consequently, of greatest immediate importance, is the need for a serious monitoring of the enforcement of the present legislation.

D. Political Parties

The 1968 Democratic National Convention was a disaster for anyone concerned with American political processes. The problems encountered and their significance went well beyond any one political party, presidential nomination, police actions, policy representation or city, and in fact well beyond the limited aspect of the problems encountered that will be dealt with in the following. For all its problems, the Democratic Convention of that year did see fit to call for the establishment of reform commissions to recommend procedures for more open political participation, particularly as it relates to the entire selection process for the party's nominee for the president, the most powerful single office in the entire political spectrum. The Democratic party established two "reform" commissions early in 1969. In their work, both drew on the research and training of political scientists. The Republican party also established a "reform" commission to deal with a wide range of political problems. Their operations are less clear as is the extent to which any political research affected their deliberations. One outcome will be a modernized—and more open and democratic—party system. Also, the present proposals call for instituting a more representative set of party institutions with party support drawn more from stands on relevant policy than issue than was true previously.

E. Nominating Conventions

Paul David, Malcolm Moos and Ralph M. Goldman wrote *Presidential Nominating Politics in 1952*, a major and distinguished work. The study, along with works directly developed from it, such as the several editions of the David, Goldman and Richard Bain co-authored *The Politics of National Party Conventions* (the original edition of which was published by Brookings), serve as the most comprehensive knowledge available on our national party conventions. The study was undertaken by the American Political Science Association in association with Brookings. It was intended to increase our knowledge of the workings of a key instrument of democratic leadership selection. There are other works of this nature, such as those financed by the now defunct National Center for Education in Politics (see the reports included in Paul Tillett, ed., *Inside Politics: The National Conventions*, 1960).

This information, personified in Paul David, the consultant to the Committion on Rules (the O'Hara Commission) of the Democratic National Committee, served as one basis of knowledge for reform of the convention system. In listening to the deliberation of the committee on convention reform, one became aware of how restricted the "pure" research into the many facts of the convention remains, and thus could be of no "applied" significance, regardless of how crucial the individual questions being debated. One also became aware of how much more knowledge the political scientists had to contribute on the implications of proposed convention changes, even conceding their limits, than did the practicing politicians charged with making the actual choices.

F. Delegate Selection Procedures at the State Level

There is virtually no literature of specific relevance to this problem. There have been studies of various aspects of primary elections in general by political scientists such as those by the late V. O. Key, Jr., and Austin Ranney (e.g., Key's *Southern Politics* and *American State Politics* and Ranney's March, 1972 article, "Turnout and Representation in Presidential Primary Elections" in the *American Political Science Review*).

Fortunately, to the extent the knowledge existed, it was available to the commission, the McGovern-Fraser Commission (or the Commission on

Party Structure and Delegate Selection of the Democratic National Committee), charged with recommending and, to a large extent, implementing change in these areas, through the appointment to the body of two noted political scientists, Austin Ranney and Samuel Beer.

The Commission was also fortunate in another respect. A well-trained political scientist, Kenneth Bode, was appointed as research director, insuring qualitatively thorough examinations of present procedures as well as the ramifications of change. The research conducted was extensive, and funded, it should be added, by public contribution and one political party. The goal, to provide an "open" and responsible party which gave those interested a "meaningful" opportunity to participate, should be of broad social value, and should represent the objective of every public institution.

Policy Objectives. The enforcement of the McGovern-Fraser guidelines needs the support of everyone at the state and local levels interested in seeing these changes realized.

G. Political Assassination

The assassination of Martin Luther King followed within months by the assassination of Robert Kennedy led a worried president to establish a national commission to inquire into the causes and prevention of such acts, as well as other forms of violent behavior. Little was known then and to a large extent little is known now concerning the implications of political assassination. Little funding was put into research related to the topic prior to 1968, despite the 1963 assassination of President John Kennedy and the continuing assassinations during the 1960's of political and civil rights figures. To my knowledge, outside of the millions of dollars invested in the short-run National Commission on the Causes and Prevention of Violence, little to no research funding has been invested in research into the political consequences of such acts since 1968.

When the Task Force on Assassination and Political Violence was formed, the only studies of direct concern to this work were the on-going "pure" research studies that developed indices of violent behavior (including political assassinations) and compared these cross-nationally. The work of the research teams (headed by Professor Ivo Feierabend and associates at San Diego State College and Professor Carl Leiden and associates of the University of Texas at Austin) were of direct relevance and helped place the American experience in comparative perspective. The research also was used to isolate the social and political factors that related to a high incidence of assassination, and to infer the potentially enormous political consequences for a nation of a leader's death by an assassin's hand. The research into the political and social ramifications of assassination should be continuing, particularly after the major investments of the Violence Commission, the seriousness of the act, and the demonstrated ability of assassinations to persist within the nation. There is little evidence that this is the case.

H. *Miscellaneous*

A number of other areas deserve attention. The multitude of studies on the legislative process could have immediate relevance in giving direction to intelligent congressional reform, but in my opinion have not been adapted to these ends. Our present knowledge of campaigning and voting perceptions could be employed to argue for more "rational" campaigning, a subject that takes on increasing urgency given the tragic death of Robert Kennedy in 1968 and the increasingly more frantic, exhausting and expensive nature of these efforts. A specific technique developed by Kenneth Janda to harness effectively large quantities of printed data on political parties, the MIRACODE system, can serve as an example of how the methodological technique intended to serve the substantive needs of one research project can have wide technical utility. The Janda system has been adopted by the Republican National Committee to organize their materials, and could be used to advantage by larger bodies such as the Congress to organize its records. Versions of it are in commercial production.

The applicability of "pure" political and social research to pressing social problems is virtually unlimited. It has been restricted to date only by the lack of attention given such research adaptations and the minimal expenses for pure, or applied, research outlay, in the relevant areas.

Conclusion

In each of these topical areas, the research has developed as outgrowths of academic interest. It has not been well funded and it has had to be adapted to applied uses in specific areas (voter registration, nominating conventions, etc.). The research has in all cases had a general effect on the thinking in given areas. The one exception to these broad comments would be the research in voter decision-making which has been well funded but which has had a less obvious impact on social concerns.

II. Basic Facilities and Institutions

Electoral politics suffers from a curious dilemma. There are a superabundance of first-rate academic studies but their impact on practical politics appears negligible. Conversely, an unknown but extraordinarily large, by any account, number of candidate-sponsored polls are undertaken every election year that make a meager contribution to any long-run understanding of electoral dynamics. Politicians who invest millions in polls assessing the concerns of voters are largely ignorant of the work done by academicians. Quite obviously, the solid core of academic works over the last two decades have influenced the efforts made on behalf of political candidates, mostly in refining the methodology of the better of the paid pollsters. The political candidate knows little of the changes in technique, and far worse, the substantive conclusions of the academicians. They have no access to the academic storehouses of knowledge—a condition that could be easily changed—and they depend for their data-gathering on hirelings of varying degrees of quality, competence and itegrity. Literally, millions of dollars are wasted.

Many of the polls are of dubious value even when conscientiously executed. They are superficial tappings of a given electorate and could profit from improvements on a series of fronts. Some candidates do manage to have fairly decent professional soundings taken. After they make whatever use they intend of them, the data are lost. They could supply basic demographic data and, the better ones, conceivably some useful attitudinal source materials (influences on cross-over voting, drop-off in different levels of election, attitudinal variations among constituencies, etc.). Poll data of this nature, at a minimum, could be integrated into some worthy analyses of campaign decision-making and the distortions, for example, that cloud resource distribution in an election contest.

Some of the millions invested by political contenders in these once-used polls could go further, serving to explore valuable conceptual and political problems. Richard Nixon in 1968 reportedly ran a back-up poll in a number of areas to check the accuracy of his principal opinion analysts. Whatever the sources of error or distortion are lost to future opinion researchers. Hubert Humphrey ran an original, academically-significant poll developed by a number of knowledgeable political scientists. Private efforts to retrieve the information for state-level political analyses had limited success. In this particular case, there was no funding available to establish an adequate staff to compile the data and clean it for serious and sustained examination.

The picture is then not bright at the present time. The campaigners often create the conditions and provide the stimulus for later analyses by political scientists. They then assess the groundwork through a series of polls commissioned also by them of potential benefit to academicians. With few exceptions, these are not retrievable. Louis Harris and Associates do have an agreement to deposit duplicates of most of their work in the data depository named after Harris at the University of North Carolina. Gallup and most of the major commercial outfits store the data that they do make available in the Roper Center located at Williams College. Beyond such efforts as these, the bulk of data is inaccessible.

The academic studies are available to researchers although the picture in this regard is not as encouraging as it was a few years ago. The Survey Research Center at the University of Michigan makes all of its past studies accessible to the members of the Inter-University Consortium for Political Research. These data have been liberally used. They are also available to such agencies as the Republican and Democratic National Committees under special provisions and upon payment of specified fees. Given the level most campaigns are conducted on and the faulty, and at times demeaning, conceptions of the electorate held by even the most intelligent politicians, the previous SRC tapes would appear to be a welcome addition to the basic knowledge either party could call on. At one time or another, the two parties have indicated a willingness to explore developing a working arrangement with academic enterprises, such as the Survey Research Center, in a special category of affiliation that would not give them power to influence decisions but would make completed work accessible to them for examination. The most recent effort (1970) along these lines was killed by a social scientist, prominent in the 1968 campaign, who when asked by one of the parties to recommend a course of action decided one party, not honored for the quality of its research efforts, might benefit more than the party to which he gave his allegiance. By the time that the Consortium was willing to admit one party independent of the other, financial problems and the anticipation of the upcoming presidential campaign became over-riding concerns. Much is to be done in this area; in fact, an intelligent beginning has yet to be made.

Of more directly academic concern, the promising Council of Social Sciences Data Archives, off to a struggling beginning a short while ago, is no more. The concept is a good one and the plan should be reviewed when adequate foundation or National Science Foundation funding becomes available. In addition to the ICPR, Roper and Harris data centers, the main repositories of information in the form of usable secondary survey materials are the International Data and Library Reference Service at the University of California, Berkeley, specializing mainly although not exclusively in cross-national surveys, and the Laboratory for Political Research at the University of Iowa.

To conclude on an upbeat note, a project initiated by the American Political Science Association and directed by Carl Beck of the University of Pittsburgh represents a promising beginning in standardizing the vocabulary and terminology relevant to the organizing of basic data resources, among other things. The project is funded by the National Science Foundation and is being assisted by an Advisory Committee chaired by

David Easton of the University of Chicago and including Richard Hofstetter of the Ohio State University, Kenneth Janda of Northwestern University and Samuel C. Patterson of the University of Iowa. The objective of the project is to decide upon a thesaurus of technical terms relevant to the discipline. Such a thesaurus would be the first step in abstracting the research completed in electoral politics, as in all of the discipline, for the use of political scientists or any other interested person. Such a work would stimulate dissemination of the knowledge on elections and voter decision-making to a broad public. It would provide a consensus meaning for terms in developing data repositories of both academic surveys and candidate-initiated polls, again open to both practitioner and researcher.

III. Comparative Electoral Policy

Exciting things have begun to happen in the study of comparative electoral behavior. This section will deal with three areas of endeavor—attitudinal and survey-oriented social psychological work as exemplified by the research instituted by or coordinated under the Center for Political Studies of the University of Michigan and its director, Warren Miller; the demographic and sociological comparative analyses pioneered in particular, although not exclusively, by European scholars and linked to such prominent names as Mattei Dogan, Juan Linz, Robert Alford, Erik Allardt, Stein Rokkan and S. M. Lipset; and the attempt to analyze a linkage institution, the political party, in aggegrating electors' opinions into meaningful policy alternatives, the International Comparative Political Parties Project directed by Kenneth Janda at Northwestern University.

A. *Comparative Electoral Surveys*

The survey-based electoral studies conducted in the United States by the Center for Political Studies of the University of Michigan over the last two and one-half decades have provided a good grasp of the dynamics of American voter motivation. The same principal components in the research model—the reliance on the in-depth personal interview as the data source, the implicit emphasis on the attitudinal and psychological dimensions of the voting decision, the increasingly sophisticated development of the empirical contours of the work, and the more recent efforts to attain higher levels of explanatory models—are now being applied to the study of voting behavior in other democratic nations. Two different time periods of study, if you will roughly analogize to the solid state and liquid fuel development programs in space exploration, are occurring coterminously. In varying degrees, all are connected with the Center for Political Studies. The first set of studies includes an analysis of the connections between voting decisions and policy alternatives as revealed through survey returns from elite and mass interviews. The study is modeled generally on the Miller-Stokes *American Political Science Review* article of 1963 "Constituency Influence in Congress," retaining the emphasis on both the policy objectives of voting and on matching the policy preferences of two populations, voters and decision-makers. While employing a common focus, the research varies in design as befits the interests of the chief investigators, usually an American and a scholar resident in the country being examined. Each of the studies is well along, with most of the field work having been completed and the impressive David Butler-Donald Stokes volume, *Political Change in Britain* (1969), coincidentally employing only part of the enormous store of British data, serving as a model for the others to emulate. The countries involved in the project and the principal investigators include: West Germany, Barbra Farah; Scandinavia, Bo Sarlvik; Italy, Samuel Barnes; France, Philip Converse and Roy Pierce; The Netherlands, Warren Miller, Hans Daadler and Jerrold Rush; England, Stokes and Butler; Japan, O. Kim; and Israel, Alan Arian.

A second generation of comparative electoral research, also under the tutelage of the Center for Political Studies, is occurring simultaneously with the first. These studies are being directed by a team of researchers, including Warren Miller, Samuel Barnes, Kent Jennings, Ronald Inglehard and academicians from each of the countries being surveyed (England, France, The Netherlands, West Germany, Italy, Austria, Switzerland, Japan, Belgium, and the United States). The research design results from a truly collaborative effort that brought the principals from the various nations together to construct an instrument intended to produce rigorous comparative findings. The studies are not as far along as the first series (for example, while most are just beginning to take to the field, the pre-tests have been concluded in two, West Germany and England, while at the other extreme funding uncertainties have delayed work on the American contribution to the project).

The potential pay-off from both sets of research enterprises is enormous. The data from both, happily, will be available through the Inter-University Consortium for Political Research.

B. *Comparative Demographic Analyses*

European scholars have long concentrated on the social components of voting behavior, although major American contributions in the area continue to be made. During the late 60's, a number of studies appeared in a series of publications that gathered together the best of the collective efforts. The research is related through the use of a common pool of empirical data, the nature of the questions examined and, more recently, the evolution of conceptual models designed to integrate the variety of explorations, provide a common and utilitarian focus and indicate the deficiencies as well as the attractions of the approach. The chief theoretical contributions in this vein have been the clevage-consensus, functional and developmental models, applied in particular to advanced democracies by Lipset, Rokkan, Allardt, Himmelstrand and Sartori.

Much of the work results directly from initiatives taken by the Committee of Political Sociology of the International Sociological Association and the foci of the analyses reflect this parentage. Among the most interesting developments in the series of comparative works, undertaken by individual scholars concentrating on a given country, have been (in addition to increasing the information available on more familiar concepts such as social class contributions to political cleavages) the introduction of constructs of geographic space into the explanation of elections and the effort to project developments over historical eras. The first provides a new and promising point of departure; the second contributes perspective to an area that characteristically over-concentrates on more recent events. Among the major publications reflecting these concerns have been the studies contained in Erik Allardt and Stein Rokkan's *Mass Politics,* Lipset and Rokkan's *Party Systems and Voter Alignments* and Rokkan's synthesizing volume, *Citizens, Elections, Parties.*

C. *Comparative Parties Research*

The third category of comparative electoral research makes an innovative attempt to explore the role planned by a mediating agency, the political party, in fifty nations in translating electoral preferences into policy outcomes. The study is markedly different from those discussed above and results from the creative efforts of Kenneth Janda to identify all extant documentary materials on one hundred and fifty parties in every type of political culture, organize the materials and, for the first time, analyze on a comparative basis the contributions and permutations of party types in differing political systems. The project is comprehensive. The conceptual design is an extended restructuring of basic ideas advanced originally by Maurice Duverger. The work will result in a contemplated five volume series comparatively assessing the major aspects of political parties throughout the world. To date, a number of extended monographs have been published, with potentially the most helpful introduction to the research being contained in the two hundred plus page 4th edition of the *ICPP (International Comparative Political Parties Project) Variables and Coding Manual.*

References

Voter Registration

Freedom to Vote Task Force, *That All May Vote* and *Registration and Voting in the States.* (Washington, D.C.: Democratic National Committee, 1970).

Joseph Harris, *Registration of Voters in the United States* (Washington, D.C.: The Brookings Institution, 1929).

President's Commission on Registration and Voting Participation, *Report on Registration and Voter Activities* (Washington, D.C.: Government Printing Office, 1963).

William Andrews, "American Voting Participation," *Western Political Quarterly* 19 (1966).

Stanley Kelley, Jr., Richard E. Ayres, and William G. Bowen, "Registration and Voting: Putting First Things First," *American Political Science Review* 61 (June 1967): 359-379.

The Voting Research

Angus Campbell, Philip Converse, Warren Miller, and Donald Stokes, *The American Voter* (New York: Wiley, 1960).

Angus Campbell, P. Converse, W. Miller and D. Stokes, *Elections and the Political Order,* (New York: Wiley, 1966).

Money in Politics

Alexander Heard, *The Costs of Democracy* (Chapel Hill: The University of North Carolina Press, 1960).

Herbert E. Alexander, *Financing the 1968 Election,* (Lexington, Mass.: D. C. Heath, 1971) and *Financing the 1964 Election,* (Princeton, N.J.: Citizen's Research Foundation, 1966). (Also see the other reports by Alexander or prepared under his direction and published by the Citizens' Research Foundation.)

Jasper Shannon, *Money and Politics* (New York: Random House, 1959).

Nominating Conventions

Paul T. David, Malcolm Moos, and Ralph M. Goldman, eds., *Presidential Nominating Politics in 1952*, 5 vols. (Baltimore: The Johns Hopkins Press, 1954).

Paul T. David, Ralph M. Goldman, and Richard C. Bain, *The Politics of National Party Conventions* (Washington, D.C.: The Brookings Institution, 1960).

Paul Tillett, ed., *Inside Politics: The National Conventions, 1960* (Dobbs Ferry, N.Y.: Oceana Publications, 1962).

Delegate Selection Procedures at the State Level

Mandate for Reform, (Washington, D.C.: Commission on Party Structure and Delegate Selection, 1970).

Political Assassination

W. Crotty, ed., *Assassinations and the Political Order* (New York: Harper and Row, 1972).

J. Kirkham, S. Levy, and W. J. Crotty, *Assassination and Political Violence* (Washington, D.C.: U.S. Government Printing Office, 1969 and New York: Bantam Books, 1970).

Carl Leiden et al., *The Politics of Violence*, (Englewood Cliffs, N.J.: Prentice-Hall, 1969).

I. K. Feierabend, "Aggressive Behaviors Within Politics, 1948-1962: A Cross-National Study," *Journal of Conflict Resolution*, Sept. 1966, pp. 249-271.

I. K. Feierabend and R. L. Feierabend, "Level of Development and Inter-Nation Behavior," in Richard Butwell, ed., *Foreign Policy and the Developing Nations* (Lexington: University of Kentucky Press, 1969), pp. 135-188.

Miscellaneous

Kenneth Janda, *Information Retrieval* (Indianapolis: Bobbs-Merrill, 1969); "Retrieving Information for a Comparative Study of Political Parties," in W. Crotty, ed., *Approaches to the Study of Party Organization* (Boston: Allyn and Bacon, 1968), pp. 159-216; and *ICPR Variables and Coding Manual* (Evanston: ICPR Monograph Series, No. 3.4, 4th ed., March, 1972).

10 Foreign Policy

Richard L. Merritt

The field of "foreign policy" is obviously a broad one. It has witnessed during the past decades an immense amount of debate and research —material that does not lend itself easily to succinct summarization or the specification of a few key sources. This chapter certainly does not seek to do so. For an excellent annotated listing of major sources, handbooks, and bibliographies, however, the student of foreign policy would do well to turn immediately to the five-volume work by Frederick Holler, *Information Sources of Political Science* (Santa Barbara, Calif.: American Bibliographic Center-Clio Press, 1974), especially volume 4, "International Relations & Organizations, Comparative & Area Studies of Politics & Government."

This chapter rather focuses upon two important aspects of the foreign policy process—the role and nature of public opinion, and approaches to the study of foreign policy leadership. It seeks to draw together both sources of relevant data and analytic studies. Moreover, it seeks to do this within a comparative framework, although it will quickly be noted that the bulk of germane items, particularly in a "behavioral" mode, stem from writers and publishers in the United States.

A concentration on public opinion and leadership studies should not be taken to imply that these are the sole types of information useful for foreign policy analysis, but only that these are often among the types most difficult to find. For a valuable set of abstracts of works using quantitative data, see Susan D. Jones and J. David Singer, editors, *Beyond Conjecture in International Politics: Abstracts of Data-Based Research* (Itasca, Ill.: F. E. Peacock Publishers, Inc., 1972). A comprehensive survey of studies currently under way using "events" data is: Philip M. Burgess and Raymond W. Lawton, "Indicators of International Behavior: An Assessment of Events Data Research," *SAGE Professional Papers in International Studies Series* (Series No. 02-010, vol. 1, 1972). A useful basis for research using quantitative indicators is: Leslie D. Wilcox, Ralph M. Brooks, George M. Beal, and Gerald E. Klonglan, *Social Indicators and Societal Monitoring: An Annotated Bibliography* (Amsterdam: Elsevier Scientific Publishing Company, 1972) On the problems of and publications in peace research, see my "Peace Research: The Search for Focus" in the appendix to this chapter. More generally, see also the propositional analyses that have appeared in various volumes of the *Political Science Annual: An International Review* (Indianapolis, Ind.: Bobbs-Merrill Company, Inc.).

I. Public Opinion and Foreign Policy

Rulers and scholars alike, regardless of political persuasion or the type of regime under which they live, have long recognized the relevance of public opinion to policy-making processes, including foreign policy. When it comes to more specific assertions about the nature of this relationship, however, disagreement sets in. A thorough analysis of public opinion and foreign policy must touch on several critical questions:

1. What do we mean by public opinion, and how do we determine what it is at any time on some set of issues?
2. How do officials charged with the responsibility of formulating and implementing foreign policy view and deal with various expressions of "public opinion"?
3. What role do foreign policy issues play in the lives of individuals, and can we determine what it is that guides their perspectives on such issues?
4. What is the relationship on the macroanalytic level between shifts in public opinion on the one hand and, on the other, public policy and international events?

In short, can we develop a model that *explains* the interaction between public opinion and public policy or, more specifically, foreign policy? Another concern, which goes to the very heart of democratic theory, is normative: What role *should* public opinion, however defined, play in the foreign policy formulation process? This section focuses less upon such philosophic questions than upon recent empirical research dealing with public attitudes toward foreign policy, their causes, and their consequences.

A. *The Nature of Public Opinion*

The debate on the nature of public opinion goes back to the earliest Greek philosophers and playwrights, and remains unresolved today. Some of the thinking of "classic" modern writers is contained in Bernard Berelson and Morris Janowitz, editors, *Reader in Public Opinion and Communication* 2d ed. (New York: The Free Press, 1966). And, of course, no library on public opinion is complete without Walter Lippmann, *Public Opinion* (New York: Harcourt, Brace and Company, 1922); and Vladimir O. Key, Jr., *Public Opinion and American Democracy* (New York: Alfred A. Knopf, 1964).

Other recent analyses that deserve serious treatment are Robert E. Lane and David O. Sears, *Public Opinion* (Englewood Cliffs, N.J.: Prentice-Hall, Inc., 1964), which neatly summarizes important empirical findings; Harwood L. Childs, *Public Opinion: Nature, Formation, and Role* (Princeton, N.J.: D. Van Nostrand Company, Inc., 1965); Bernard C. Hennessy, *Public Opinion* 2d ed. (Belmont, Calif.: Wadsworth Publishing Company, Inc., 1970); and James J. Best, *Public Opinion: Micro and Macro* (Homewood, Ill.: Dorsey Press, 1973).

Across the Atlantic the older debate continues, focusing more upon the idea of "publicness" than upon means to measure its dimensions. Excellent examples include Jürgen Habermas, *Strukturwandel der Öffentlichkeit: Untersuchungen zu einer Kategorie der bürgerlichen Gesellschaft* 5th ed. (Neuwied am Rhein and Berlin: Hermann Luchterhand Verlag, 1971); and Niklas Luhman, "Öffentliche Meinung," *Politische Vierteljahresschrift* 11, 1 (March 1970); 2-28.

B. The Role of Public Opinion in Foreign Policy-Making

Most of the above writers touch upon but do not deal extensively with the more specific question of the role of public opinion in the formulation of foreign policy. More directly germane are an early collection of essays by Lester Markel and others, *Public Opinion and Foreign Policy* (New York: Harper & Brothers, 1949); the pathbreaking volume by Gabriel A. Almond, originally published in 1950, *The American People and Foreign Policy* 2d ed. (New York: Frederick A. Praeger, Publisher, 1960); James N. Rosenau, *Public Opinion and Foreign Policy: An Operational Formulation* (New York: Random House, Inc., 1961); and Rosenau's essay, *The Attentive Public and Foreign Policy: A Theory of Growth and Some New Evidence* (Princeton, N.J.: Princeton University, Center of International Studies, Research Monograph No. 31, 1968).

How government officials actually perceive and use information about public opinion has proved to be a thorny question, primarily because of the elusiveness of the concept. Studies published to date suggest that poll data and other indicators of public opinion comprise only one desideratum—and not the most important at that!—for decisionmakers concerned with foreign policy. The most important of these studies is Bernard C. Cohen, *The Public's Impact on Foreign Policy* (Boston, Mass.: Little, Brown and Company, 1973).

The definitive analysis of this relationship nonetheless remains to be written. Other contributions include Bernard C. Cohen, *The Press and Foreign Policy* (Princeton, N.J.: Princeton University Press, 1963); Hadley Cantril, *The Human Dimension: Experiences in Policy Research* (New Brunswick, N.J.: Rutgers University Press, 1967), which contains a wealth of reports on Cantril's efforts to inject polling data into governmental decision-making processes; Richard L. Merritt, "The USIA Surveys:

Tools for Policy and Analysis," in *Western European Perspectives on International Affairs: Public Opinion Studies and Evaluations,* ed. Richard L. Merritt and Donald J. Puchala (New York: Frederick A. Praeger, Publishers, 1968), pp. 3-30, on the use by American government officials of worldwide data gathered by the United States Information Agency; Manfred Landecker, *The President and Public Opinion: Leadership in Foreign Affairs* (Washington, D.C.: Public Affairs Press, 1968); William O. Chittick, *State Department, Press, and Pressure Groups: A Role Analysis* (New York: John Wiley & Sons, Inc., 1970). A study on an earlier era is Doris A. Graber's *Public Opinion, the President, and Foreign Policy: Four Case Studies from the Formative Years* (New York: Holt, Rinehart and Winston, 1968). Other relevant studies are in Norman R. Luttbeg, editor, *Public Opinion and Public Policy: Models of Political Linkage* (Homewood, Ill.: The Dorsey Press, 1968).

It must be noted that the above studies focus almost exclusively upon the relationship of public opinion and foreign policy in the United States. Writers are aware that differences in political culture from one country to the next make this relationship highly variable cross-nationally. The same is true regarding political structures (the nature of the chief executive, electoral processes, the role of parliamentary bodies, bureaucracies), mass media, interest groups, and the like. The implication is clear: If we want to move beyond the parochial concern with policy formation in the United States in an effort to develop a valid model of such processes in even the rest of the industrialized world, then it will be imperative to focus more upon behavior in other countries.

C. Sources of Foreign Policy Attitudes

The development of sample surveys and other testing procedures opened a new world for scholars interested in the social and psychological sources of perspectives on world affairs. A pioneering thinkpiece was Harold D. Lasswell, *World Politics and Personal Insecurity* (New York: McGraw-Hill Book Company, Inc., 1935). An equally pioneering empirical effort, especially with respect to ethnocentrism and its correlates, was Theodor W. Adorno, Else Frenkel-Brunswik, Daniel J. Levinson, and R. Nevitt Sanford, *The Authoritarian Personality* (New York: Harper & Brothers, 1950).

Other major studies are M. Brewster Smith, Jerome S. Bruner, and Robert W. White, *Opinions and Personality* (New York: John Wiley & Sons, Inc., 1956); Bjørn Christiansen, *Attitudes toward Foreign Affairs as a Function of Personality* (Oslo: Oslo University Press, 1959); Robert E.

Lane, *Political Ideology: Why the American Common Man Believes What He Does* (New York: The Free Press of Glencoe, 1962), based upon lengthy interviews with fifteen men; the collection of important articles in Herbert C. Kelman, editor, *International Behavior: A Social-Psychological Analysis* (New York; Holt, Rinehart and Winston, 1965); William Eckhardt and Theo. F. Lentz, "Factors of War/Peace Attitudes," *Peace Research Reviews* 1, 5 (October 1967); 1-117, and William Eckhardt, "Ideology & Personality in Social Attitudes," ibid., 3, 2 (April 1969): 1-108; Johan Galtung, "Social Position, Party Identification and Foreign Policy Orientation: A Norwegian Case Study," in *Domestic Sources of Foreign Policy*, ed. James N. Rosenau (New York: The Free Press, 1967), pp. 161-193, and other articles in the same volume; and Joseph de Rivera, *The Psychological Dimension of Foreign Policy* (Columbus, Ohio: Charles E. Merrill Publishing Company, 1968).

A very useful compendium of attitudinal scales is John P. Robinson, Jerrold G. Rusk, and Kendra B. Head, *Measures of Political Attitudes* (Ann Arbor: University of Michigan, Institute for Social Research, Survey Research Center, 1968), especially pp. 279-409, dealing with world affairs, hostility, nationalism, and cosmopolitanism. Appendix B to this volume is John P. Robinson and Phillip R. Shaver, *Measures of Social Psychological Attitudes* rev. ed. (Ann Arbor: University of Michigan, Institute for Social Research, Survey Research Center, 1973).

D. Public Opinion Data on Foreign Policy

The postwar years have seen the generation of a plethora of empirical studies on attitudes toward foreign policy issues. The problem of collecting, storing, and distributing these data to other scholars has proved to be both time-consuming and expensive. Many universities and research institutes have created their own archives, which are more or less accessible to others. The two such archives with the most general concerns are:

> Inter-University Consortium for Political Research, P. O. Box 1248, The University of Michigan, Ann Arbor, Michigan, 48106. It concentrates particularly upon survey and other data produced by academic institutions.

> The Roper Public Opinion Center, Williams College, Williamstown, Massachusetts, 01267. The largest existing file, containing data from academic and commercial surveying institutes in a large number of countries.

Researchers at a university which belongs to these archival organizations can get surveys on cards or tape at nominal cost; those at non-member universities will find the costs somewhat higher. An important West European archive is:

> The European Consortium for Political Research (ECPR), The Chr. Michelsen Institute, Gamle Kalvedalsveien 12, N-5000 Bergen, Norway. Its newsletter, *European Political Data*, is published three times per year.

The ECPR also organizes seminars and workshops on substantive issues and methodological approaches.

Several periodicals, most of them now defunct, have carried survey data, sometimes from several countries. *The Public Opinion Quarterly*, which has appeared since 1937, continues to report findings, in additional to important articles and research notes. Earlier publications included *Opinion News*, published from September 1943 to October 1948 by the National Opinion Research Center; *Surveys of World Opinion*, issued from November 1945 to October 1948 on a quarterly basis by the American Institute of Public Opinion and later the International Association of Public Opinion Institutes, both associated with George Gallup; *International Journal of Opinion and Attitude Research*, five volumes of which, issued quarterly from March 1947 to Winter 1951-52, contained both scholarly articles and poll findings; and, more recently, the quarterly *Polls*, issued from Spring 1965 to Summer 1968 under the auspices of the Steinmetz Stichting in Amsterdam. In February 1973 the Roper Public Opinion Center began publication of its monthly *Current Opinion*, which presents news as well as data from its international survey holdings. In addition, as will be reported below, survey institutes in several countries issue periodic releases.

It goes virtually without saying that a wide variety of scholarly journals occasionally publishes relevant articles which, due to spatial limitations, are not included in this bibliographic essay. Among these journals are the *American Political Science Review, American Journal of Political Science, Journal of Conflict Resolution, International Studies Quarterly, Comparative Political Studies, Comparative Politics, Journal of Peace Research, Journal of Social Issues, American Journal of Sociology, American Sociological Review, British Journal of Sociology, Sociology, Journal of Social Psychology, International Journal of Comparative Sociology, Revue Française de Sociologie, Kölner Zeitschrift für Soziologie und Sozialpsychologie, Acta Sociologica, Archives Européennes de Sociologie*, and *SAGE Professional Papers* in such fields as comparative politics and international politics.

The wealth of periodical literature suggests that the time may be ripe for another extensive cross-national bibliography on public opinion and foreign policy. Excellent earlier examples are Bruce Lannes Smith, Harold D. Lasswell, and Ralph D. Casey, *Propaganda, Communication, and Public Opinion: A Comprehensive Reference Guide* (Princeton, N.J.: Princeton University Press, 1946), and Bruce Lannes Smith and Chitra M. Smith, *Communication and Political Opinion: A Guide to the Literature* (Princeton, N.J.: Princeton University Press, 1956).

E. Data and Analyses of Individual Countries

Cross-National Studies. Several scholars and commercial institutes have initiated extensive cross-national studies or reported cross-national data relevant to foreign policy issues. A monumental collection of data, mostly American but also some from other countries, was prepared by Mildred Strunk under the editorial direction of Hadley Cantril, *Public Opinion, 1935-1946* (Princeton, N.J.: Princeton University Press, 1951). An early, explicitly cross-national study, conducted in nine countries under the auspices of UNESCO, was William Buchanan and Hadley Cantril, *How Nations See Each Other: A Study in Public Opinion* (Urbana: University of Illinois Press, 1953). Cantril subsequently initiated an ingenious cross-national survey of 18,663 respondents in fourteen countries, aimed at uncovering people's hopes and fears, aspirations and sense of accomplishment for both themselves and their countries; this is reported in Hadley Cantril, *The Patterns of Human Concerns* (New Brunswick, N.J.: Rutgers University Press, 1965). Another effort deserving greater attention than scholars have given it consists of the worldwide surveys conducted by the United States Information Agency's Office of Research and Reference (now called Office of Research and Assessment). Periodic samplings going back more than two decades are reported in occasional memoranda, released two years after their date of issue and deposited in major American libraries.

United States. Relevant studies of public opinion and foreign policy processes in the United States are legion, particularly in the form of journal articles. This section can only supplement the items already listed under other headings (such as Almond's *The American People and Foreign Policy*) with some additional landmarks. An important collection, noted earlier, is *Public Opinion, 1935-1946*, prepared by Strunk and Cantril. Gallup International, Inc. (53 Bank Street, Princeton, New Jersey 08540) has also published periodic press releases and, since 1965, a monthly report, *The Gallup Opinion Index*. In 1972 appeared an immensely useful compilation: George H. Gallup, *The Gallup Poll: Public Opinion, 1935-1971* 3 volumes (New York: Random House, Inc., 1972). Commercial firms in several states, such as California and Texas, send out their own news releases, but only infrequently do these deal with problems of foreign affairs.

Some general volumes analyzing public opinion data in the United States include: Lloyd A. Free and Hadley Cantril, *The Political Beliefs of Americans: A Study of Public Opinion* (New Brunswick, N.J.: Rutgers University Press, 1967); Donald J. Devine, *The Attentive Public: Polyarchical Democracy* (Chicago, Ill.: Rand McNally & Company, 1970); Louis Harris and Associates, *The Harris Survey Yearbook of Public Opinion, 1970* (New York: Louis Harris and Associates, 1971); Leo Bogart, *Silent Politics: Polls and the Awareness of Public Opinion* (New York: Wiley-Interscience, 1972); Robert S. Erikson and Norman R. Luttbeg, *American Public Opinion: Its Origins, Content, and Impact* (New York: John Wiley & Sons, Inc., 1973); William Watts and Lloyd A. Free, editors, *State of the Nation* (New York: Universe Books, 1973); and Rita James Simon, *Public Opinion in America: 1936-1970* (Chicago, Ill.: Rand McNally College Publishing Co., 1974), particularly Chapter 6 on foreign policy.

Major substantive studies geared more to foreign policy include Leonard S. Cottrell, Jr., and Sylvia Eberhart, *American Opinion on World Affairs in the Atomic Age* (Princeton, N.J.: Princeton University Press, 1948); William A. Scott and Stephen B. Withey, *The United States and the United Nations: The Public View, 1945-1955* (New York: Manhattan Publishing Company, 1958); Raymond A. Bauer, Ithiel de Sola Pool, and Lewis Anthony Dexter, *American Business and Public Policy: The Politics of Foreign Trade* (New York: Atherton Press, 1963); Alfred O. Hero, Jr., *The Southerner and World Affairs* (Baton Rouge: Louisiana State University Press, 1965); Davis B. Bobrow and Allen R. Wilcox, "Dimensions of Defense Opinion: The American Public," in *Peace Research Society (International), Papers, VI, The Vienna Conference, 1966*, ed. Walter Isard and Julian Wolpert (Philadelphia, Pa.: The Peace Research Society [International], 1965), pp. 206-231; Tom Atkinson, *A Propositional Inventory of the Empirical Work Involving Foreign Affairs and National Security Attitudes, 1960-1966: A Non-evaluative Review* (Oak Ridge, Tenn.: Oak Ridge National Laboratory, Civil Defense Research Project, 1967); John P. Robinson, *Public Information about World Affairs* (Ann Arbor: University of Michigan, Institute for Social Research, Survey Research Center, March 1967); Urban Whitaker and Bruce E. Davis, *The World and Ridgeway, South Carolina,* Studies in International Affairs No. 5 (Columbia: University of South Carolina, Institute of International Studies, 1967); Charles C. Moskos, Jr., ed., *Public Opinion and the Military Establishment* (Beverly Hills, Calif.: SAGE Publications, Inc., 1971); Alfred O. Hero, Jr., *American Religious Groups View Foreign Policy: Trends in Rank-and-File Opinion, 1937-1969* (Durham, N.C.: Duke University Press, 1973); and John E. Mueller, *War, Presidents, and Public Opinion* (New York: John Wiley & Sons, Inc., 1973).

Canada. A continuing source of information is *The Gallup Report,* released periodically by The Canadian Institute of Public Opinion (364 Bessborough Drive, Toronto 17, Canada). Important substantive studies are John Paul and Jerome Laulicht, *In Your Opinion: Leaders' and Voters' Attitudes on Defence and Disarmament* (Clarkson, Ont.: Canadian Peace Research Institute, 1963); Claude Lemelin and Jean-Claude Marion, *Le Canada français et le Tiers-Monde: L'opinion publique au Canada français et l'aide aux pays sous-développés* (Ottawa: Éditions de l'Université d'Ottawa, 1963); and Mildred A. Schwartz, *Public Opinion and Canadian Identity* (Berkeley and Los Angeles: University of California Press, 1967).

West Europe. In early 1953 the Organization for Comparative Social Research interviewed 2,758 school teachers at the primary and secondary levels in seven countries. Unfortunately, the full set of findings was never published, but some of relevance to international affairs are reported in Stein Rokkan, "Party Preferences and Opinion Patterns in Western Europe: A Comparative Analysis," *International Social Science Bulletin* 7, 4 (1955): 575-596. Data from surveys conducted by the United States Information Agency in France, Great Britain, Italy, and West Germany are reported in Richard L. Merritt and Donald J. Puchala, editors, *Western European Perspectives on International Affairs: Public Opinion Studies and Evaluations* (New York: Frederick A. Praeger, Publishers, 1968). In early 1962 Gallup International polled citizens of the Common Market countries, reporting the results in brief form in "Public Opinion and the European Community," *Journal of Common Market Studies* 2, 2 (November 1963): 101-126, and in greater detail in *L'Opinion publique et l'Europe des six* (Paris: L'Institut Français d'Opinion Publique, 1962); the implications for Spain were spelled out in *La Opinion Publica en la Communidad Europea: España y el Mercado Común* (Madrid: Nuevo Horizonte, 1965).

Federal Republic of Germany. West Germany is doubtless the best surveyed of the Western European countries, and certainly the one for which the richest data are available. It is also the country in which have taken place some of the most serious disputes about the intellectual nature and practical political consequences of public opinion and surveying operations. Besides the two pieces mentioned earlier—Habermas, *Strukturwandel der Öffentlichkeit*, and Luhman, "Öffentliche Meinung" —see Kurt Rückmann, *Demoskopie oder Demogogie? Zur Meinungs-*

forschung in der BRD (Frankfurt-am-Main: Verlag Marxistische Blätter GmbH, 1972), which presents a Marxist critique; and Richard L. Merritt, "Public Opinion and Foreign Policy in West Germany," in *SAGE International Yearbook of Foreign Policy Studies,* Volume One, ed. Patrick J. McGowan (Beverly Hills, Calif.: SAGE Publications, Inc., 1973), pp. 255-274.

From 1945 until the late 1950s, the United States Army and subsequently the State Department conducted surveys in West Germany. Reports from the earlier period are summarized in Anna J. Merritt and Richard L. Merritt, editors, *Public Opinion in Occupied Germany: The OMGUS Surveys, 1945-1949* (Urbana: University of Illinois Press, 1970); those for the later period in Anna J. Merritt, editor, *Public Opinion in Semisovereign Germany: The HICOG Surveys, 1949-1955* (Urbana: University of Illinois Press, forthcoming).

For a quarter century two of the leading commercial organizations have published regular reports: *Allensbacher Berichte,* issued thrice monthly by the Institut für Demoskopie (7753 Allensbach-am-Bodensee, West Germany); and the monthly *Informationen,* distributed by EMNID-Institut GmbH & Co, (48 Bielefeld, Bodelschwinghstr. 23-25a, Postfach 2540, West Germany). The directors of the Institut für Demoskopie have also published occasional papers, entitled *Allensbacher Schriften,* and five "yearbooks" to date. The latter, edited by Elisabeth Noelle and Erich Peter Neumann and entitled *Jahrbuch der öffentlichen Meinung* (Allensbach-am-Bodensee and Bonn: Verlag für Demoskopie, 1956-1974), cover almost three decades, from 1947 to 1973; a shortened version appears in English under the title *The Germans: Public Opinion Polls, 1947-1966* (Allensbach-am-Bodensee and Bonn: Verlag für Demoskopie, 1967). Working primarily with data from the Institut für Demoskopie, Gerhard Schmidtchen wrote an interesting volume on public opinion and politics, *Die Befragte Nation: Über den Einfluss der Meinungsforchung auf die Politik* (Freiburg im Breisgau: Verlag Rombach, 1959).

Until the early 1960s the Deutsches Institut für Volksumfragen (DIVO-Institut) also published regular reports and produced four yearbooks, *Umfragen: Ereignisse und Probleme der Zeit im Urteil der Bevölkerung* (Frankfurt-am-Main: Europäische Verlagsanstalt, 1958-1962). Since 1966 the Institut für angewandte Sozialwissenschaft GmbH (INFAS, 53 Bonn-Bad Godesberg 1, Margaretenstr. 1) has published occasional reports, *Politogramm,* on both domestic and international topics. By now, too, three volumes of the *Sozialwissenschaftliches Jahrbuch für Politik* (Munich and Vienna: Günter Olzog Verlag, 1969-1972) have appeared, containing important analyses in German and English. A brief summary of some central trends is contained in the publication of the Press and Information Office of the Federal Republic, *Public Opinion* (Bonn: Press and

Information Office, 1971). See also, for an excellent analysis of a highly important topic, Gebhard Schweigler, *National Consciousness in Divided Germany* (Beverly Hills, Calif.: SAGE Publications, Inc., 1975).

France. Data and analyses of French public opinion appear in the quarterly *Sondages: Revue française de l'opinion publique*, published by the Institut Français d'Opinion Publique (20, rue d'Aumale, Paris 9e, France). In addition, several scholars at the Foundation nationale des sciences politiques have completed relevant studies, such as Guy Michelat and Jean-Pierre Hubert Thomas, *Dimensions du nationalisme: Enquête par questionnaire (1962)*, Cahiers de la FNSP No. 143 (Paris: Librarie Armand Colin, 1966), and Hélène Delorme and Yves Tavernier, *Les Paysans français et l'Europe,* FNSP research series no. 6 (Paris: Librarie Armand Colin, 1969). See also Jean Charlot, *Les Français et de Gaulle* (Paris: Librairie PLON, 1971); and Achille Lebrun, *L'Opinion des Français sur le Tiers-Mond* (Paris: Les Éditions Ouvrières, 1971).

Great Britain. British data appear in the *Gallup Political Index*, published monthly by Social Surveys Ltd. (202 Finchley Road, London NW3 6BL). See also Richard Hodder-Williams, *Public Opinion Polls and British Politics* (London: Routledge & Kegan Paul, 1970), which deals primarily with domestic political concerns; and I. Rauta, *Aid and Overseas Development: A Survey of Public Attitudes, Opinions and Knowledge* (London: H. M. Stationery Office, 1971).

Italy. Italian data are in the semi-monthly *Bollottino DOXA*, issued by DOXA, Istituto per le ricerche statistiche e l'analisi dell'opinione pubblica (Galleria S. Carlo 6, Milano). Collections of DOXA data and analyses of Italian public opinion were made by Pierpaolo Luzzatto Fegiz, *Il Volto Sconosciuto dell'Italia* (Milano: Dott. A. Giuffrè, 2 vols., 1956 and 1966).

Other Western European Countries and Israel. Some Belgian data appear in the symposium held at the Free University of Brussels, *L'Opinion publique belge*, XXXIe Semaine Sociale Universitaire (Brussels: Éditions de l'Institut de Sociologie de l'Université Libre de Bruxelles, 1971), especially pp. 92-162, entitled "L'Opinion publique belge et l'Europe." For Norway, see Nils Ørvik, editor, *Fears and Expectations: Norwegian Attitudes toward European Integration* (Oslo: Universitetsforlaget, 1972). In an earlier context a study discussing Spain and the European Community was mentioned: *La Opinion Publica en la Comunidad Europea*. More generally, the Instituto de la Opinion Publica (Doctor Arce, 16, Madrid-2) has published since 1965 a quarterly *Revista española de la opinion publica*, and, since November 1972, a monthly *Boletin*. For Israel, see

Aaron Antonovsky and Alan Arian, *Hopes and Fears of Israelis: Consensus in a New Society* (Jerusalem: Jerusalem Academic Press, 1972).

Eastern Europe. By and large, data on political attitudes of citizens of socialist countries have not appeared in the West. Some analysts of East European countries have therefore relied upon interviews with former residents of the area or visitors to the west. Examples include Siegfried Kracauer and Paul L. Berkman, *Satellite Mentality: Political Attitudes and Propaganda Susceptibilities of Non-Communists in Hungary, Poland and Czechoslovakia* (New York: Frederick A. Praeger, Publishers, 1956); and the series of interviews with refugees from the German Democratic Republic conducted by Infratest in Munich, reported in Gerhard Schröter, *Jugendliche Flüchtlinge aus der Sowjetzone* (Munich: Infratest-Verlag-GMBH, 1958) and Viggo Graf Blücher, *Industriearbeiterschaft in der Sowjetzone* (Stuttgart: Ferdinand Enke Verlag, 1959). Another such study, carefully and imaginatively carried out, was by Alex Inkeles and Raymond A. Bauer, *The Soviet Citizen: Daily Life in a Totalitarian Society* (Cambridge, Mass.: Harvard University Press, 1959). Similarly, the Audience Research Section of Radio Free Europe issues at irregular intervals reports based upon such interviews. Topics covered include reasons given by refugees for their flight, views of East-West politics, attitudes toward cooperation with the government, and international issues such as the Vietnam conflict and the Arab-Israeli conflict.

Occasionally, however, some survey data do appear, particularly in scholarly journals such as the *Journal of Peace Research,* published under the auspices of the International Peace Research Association at the International Peace Research Institute, Oslo. A unique publication is Jaroslaw A. Piekalkiewicz's *Public Opinion Polling in Czechoslovakia, 1968-69: Results and Analysis of Surveys Conducted During the Dubcek Era* (New York: Praeger Publishers, 1972), which includes data on economic, political, and social issues gathered by professional institutes independent of government or party control.

Japan. Along with the United States and West Germany, Japan is a thoroughly surveyed country. Considerable data from the first postwar decade appear in Allan B. Cole and Naomichi Nakanishi, editors, *Japanese Opinion Polls with Socio-Political Significance, 1947-1957,* published under the auspices of The Fletcher School of Law and Diplomacy, Tufts University, and The Roper Public Opinion Poll Research Center, Williams College (Ann Arbor, Mich.: University Microfilms S-220, 1967). These and other data are discussed in Douglas H. Mendel, Jr., *The Japanese People and Foreign Policy: A Study of Public Opinion in Post-Treaty Japan* (Berkeley and Los Angeles: University of California Press, 1961). The

Public Information Section of the Prime Minister's Office publishes in Japanese a yearbook of public opinion polls. Excerpts from the 1965 edition appeared in *Public Opinion in Japan, 1965*, Occasional Papers of Research Publications and Translations, Translation Series No. 26 (Honolulu: University of Hawaii, East-West Center, Institute of Advanced Projects, 1967), mimeographed.

Other Countries. In East Africa, Kenya Research Services (P.O. Box 21095, Nairobi, Kenya) publishes an irregular *Marco Surveys*. The Indian Institute of Public Opinion (P) Ltd. (2-A, National Insurance Building, Parliament Street, New Delhi-1, India) has published since 1955 its *Monthly Public Opinion Surveys*. And in Australia the Roy Morgan Research Centre Pty. Ltd. (130 Flinders Street, Melbourne; and 77 Pacific Highway, North Sydney) published Australian Gallup Polls until 1973 and now *Morgan's Gallup Poll*. Since mid-1973 the former has been published by McNair Surveys Pty. Ltd. In addition, surveys are conducted by the Australian Nationwide Opinion Polls Pty. Ltd. and the Australian Sales Research Bureau in conjunction with the Political Science Department of Melbourne University; the latter has published AGE Poll since March 1971. An interesting publication from New Zealand is by A. A. Congalton and M. J. Kirton, *Public Opinion and the United Nations*, Victoria University College Publications in Psychology No. 6 (Wellington: Victoria University College, Department of Psychology, 1955).

II. Foreign Policy Leadership

Although political theorists and policy scientists have long talked about the qualities of leadership and characteristics of leaders, efforts at systematic analysis are rather recent. This section focuses on some of these recent efforts, particularly in the area of foreign policy leadership—foreign policy views of political and other leaders in a society, the attributes and behavior of leaders active in formulating and implementing foreign policy, and the motivations underlying these perspectives and behavioral patterns.

A. The Comparative Study of Elites

Several general bibliographies or analytic summaries merit mention at the outset. Of particular importance to researchers is Carl Beck and J. Thomas McKechnie, *Political Elites: A Select Computerized Bibliography* (Cambridge, Mass.: The M.I.T. Press, 1968). Using the KWOC (Key Word Out of Context) approach, it indexes approximately 4,000 items from the years

1945-1966, of which 66 appear under the key word "foreign," another 20 under "international'" and several hundred under the names of individual countries.

Among numerous interpretations of the general role of elites in society, several stand out as classics or because of their relevance to foreign policy: Vilfredo Pareto, *The Mind and Society* (New York: Harcourt, Brace and Co., [1916-23] 1935, 4 vols.); Gaetano Mosca, *The Ruling Class* (New York: McGraw-Hill Book Company, [4th ed., 1923], 1939); Harold D. Lasswell, Daniel Lerner, and C. Easton Rothwell, *The Comparative Study of Elites: An Introduction and Bibliography*, Hoover Institute Studies, Series B, No. 1 (Stanford, Calif.: Stanford University Press, 1952); C. Wright Mills, *The Power Elite* (New York: Oxford University Press, 1956); Renzo Sereno, *The Rulers: The Theory of the Ruling Class* (New York: Frederick A. Praeger, Inc., Publisher, 1962); T. B. Bottomore, *Elites and Society* (London: C. A. Watts, 1964; and Baltimore, Md.: Penguin Books, 1966); Urs Jaeggi, *Die gesellschaftliche Elite: Eine studie zum Problem der sozialen Macht* (Bern and Stuttgart: Verlag Paul Haupt, 2d ed., 1967); and Robert Presthus, *Elites in the Policy Process* (New York: Cambridge University Press, 1974). A volume of essays viewing elites (and other variables) as linkages between national and international systems is James N. Rosenau, editor, *Linkage Politics: Essays on the Convergence of National and International Systems* (New York: The Free Press, 1969). Two recent collections of papers focusing on British elites are Ivor Crewe, editor, *British Political Sociology Yearbook,* volume 1: *Elites in Western Democracy* (New York: Halstead Press, 1974), and Philip Stanworth and Anthony Giddens, *Elites and Power in British Society* (Cambridge: Cambridge University Press, 1974). Finally, there are numerous popularly written studies of leadership of interest to students of foreign policy. One of the more recent and fascinating is David Halberstam, *The Best and the Brightest* (New York: Random House, Inc., 1972), which deals with, among other things, the origins of American involvement in Vietnam.

Among several analytic summaries of elite studies, the most thorough in substantive terms is Suzanne Keller, *Beyond the Ruling Class: Strategic Elites in Modern Society* (New York: Random House, Inc., 1963), especially pp. 284-326. Others are John R. Raser, "Personal Characteristics of Political Decision-Makers: A Literature Review," *Peace Research Society (International), Papers, V, Philadelphia Conference, 1965* (Philadelphia, Pa.: Peace Research Society [International] 1966), pp. 161-181; and my chapter, "The Comparative Study of Elites," in *Systematic Approaches to Comparative Politics* (Chicago, Ill.: Rand McNally & Company, 1970), pp. 104-139. There is also a large body of literature on leadership in local communities, which is beyond the purview of this essay. Similarly, no attention is paid here to the organizational aspects of leadership; in this regard, however, see Victor H. Vroom and Philip Y. Yetton, *Leadership and Decision-Making* (Pittsburgh, Pa.: University of Pittsburgh Press, 1973), and Ralph M. Stogdill, *Handbook of Leadership: A Survey of Theory and Research* (New York: The Free Press, 1974).

B. Social Background and Foreign Policy

It seems intuitively obvious that biographical information about elite members of a society—traits acquired at birth (nationality, race, caste, age-group), socialization experiences (education, membership in social organizations, occupational training), and adult career patterns (profession, marriage and family, political activity, participation in specific events such as a war or depression)—*should* help us understand significant aspects of their perspectives and behavior. It was to test such assumptions that, in the late 1940s, Harold D. Lasswell and his colleagues at Stanford University's Hoover Institute undertook their analyses of "world revolutionary elites": the Politburo (George K. Schueller), Italian Fascists (Lasswell with Renzo Sereno), the Nazi elite (Daniel Lerner with Ithiel de Sola Pool and Schueller), and the Kuomintang and Chinese Communists (Robert C. North with Pool). These investigations, reprinted in Harold D. Lasswell and Daniel Lerner, editors, *World Revolutionary Elites: Studies in Coercive Ideological Movements* (Cambridge, Mass.: The M.I.T. Press, 1965), set the pattern for a plethora of subsequent empirical elite analyses and research frameworks. Of the latter, one of the more influential has been Donald R. Matthews, *The Social Background of Political Decision Makers* (Garden City, N.Y.: Doubleday & Company, Inc., 1954).

Social background data have proved to be helpful more for describing patterns and trends than for explaining them. Here is not the place to go into the wealth of frequently interesting and relevant analyses (e.g., Lewis J. Edinger, "Continuity and Change in the Background of German Decision-Makers," *Western Political Quarterly* 14, 1 [March 1961]: 17-36; and Frederick W. Frey, *The Turkish Political Elite* [Cambridge, Mass.: The M.I.T. Press, 1965]). It is worth noting, however, that the range of propositions they can test is limited unless the analyst uses other kinds of data as well. Even then results to date have not been as encouraging as we might wish. Uwe Schleth ("Once Again: Does It Pay to Study Social Background in Elite Analysis?" in *Sozialwissenschaftliches Jahrbuch für Politik*, volume 2, ed. Rudolf Wildenmann [Munich and Vienna: Günter Olzog Verlag, 1971], pp. 99-118), analyzing data on 800 members of the West German elite, concluded that "it does not seem to be very promising to study social background . . . if from this inferences are to be made about attitudes or even about behavior of elites."

At best, as Byung-kyu-Woo and Chong Lim Kim discovered in their examination of South Korean legislators ("Inter-Elite Cleavages in the Korean National Assembly," *Asian Survey* 11,6 [June 1971]: 544-561), later experiences such as recruitment to political activity rather than traits acquired at birth or early socialization account for some variance in outcomes. But even this differs from society to society, and according to the attitude or behavior tapped (cf. Lewis J. Edinger and Donald D. Searing, "Social Background in Elite Analysis: A Methodological Inquiry," *American Political Science Review* 61,2 [June 1967]: 428-445; and Searing, "The Comparative Study of Elite Socialization," *Comparative Political Studies* 1, 4 [January 1969]: 471-500).

These and similar findings suggest that, although social background data can tell us much about a society, we must pursue other modes of analysis if we are interested in the perspectives (on foreign policy and other issues) held by the society's elites. One way to find out what people value and how they view their surroundings is simply to ask them. Less obtrusive approaches rely upon various kinds of content analysis.

C. Perspectives of Foreign Policy Leaders: Questionnaire Surveys

Surveying techniques, well understood in principle but frequently quite difficult to carry out in the foreign policy realm, have underlain numerous research projects. (For a discussion of general methodological issues, see Lewis Anthony Dexter, *Elite and Specialized Interviewing* [Evanston, Ill.; Northwestern University Press, 1970].) It goes without saying that practically every elite survey project includes at least a few questions germane to the foreign policy realm. Examples include Wendell Bell, *Jamaican Leaders: Political Attitudes in a New Nation* (Berkeley and Los Angeles: University of California Press, 1964); Lester G. Seligman, *Leadership in a New Nation* (New York: Atherton Press, 1964); Marvin Zonis, *The Political Elite of Iran* (Princeton, N.J.: Princeton University Press, 1971); Allen H. Barton, Bogdan Denitch, and Charles Kadushin, *Opinion-making Elites in Yugoslavia* (New York: Frederick A. Praeger, Publisher, 1973); Rudolf Wildenmann's extensive study of 800 members of the West German elite, to be reported in greater detail in a forthcoming volume of the *Sozialwissenschaftliches Jahrbuch für Politik*; and still others are listed in the Beck-McKechnie bibliography mentioned earlier. Many but not all such studies have used national legislators as their sample.

Other projects have focused especially upon foreign policy issues, often in a comparative framework. These include Lloyd A. Free, *Six Allies and a Neutral: A Study of the International Outlooks of Political Leaders in the*

United States, Britain, France, West Germany, Italy, Japan and India (Glencoe, Ill.: The Free Press, 1959); John Paul and Jerome Laulicht, *In Your Opinion: Leaders' and Voters' Attitudes on Defense and Disarmament* (Clarkson, Ont.: Canadian Peace Research Institute, 1963), and Laulicht's subsequent "An Analysis of Canadian Foreign Policy Attitudes," *Peace Research Society (International), Papers, III, Chicago Conference, 1964* (Philadelphia, Pa.: Peace Research Society [International], 1965), pp. 121-136; Mark Abrams, "British Elite Attitudes and the European Common Market," *Public Opinion Quarterly* 29, 2 (Summer 1965): 236-246; Karl W. Deutsch, Lewis J. Edinger, Roy C. Macridis, and Richard L. Merritt, *France, Germany and the Western Alliance: A Study of Elite Attitudes on European Integration and World Politics* (New York: Charles Scribner's Sons, 1967); Daniel Lerner and Morton Gorden, *Euratlantica: Changing Perspectives of the European Elites* (Cambridge, Mass.: The M.I.T. Press, 1969); and Robert L. Peterson, "European Bureaucrats in European Regional Organizations: Attitudes and Administrative Structures," *International Review of Administrative Sciences* 36,4 (1970): 3-16.

In a unique project, George Modelski gathered social background and behavioral data on 175 foreign ministers throughout the world, and compared these data with information from questionnaires he had mailed to the ministers, 16.7 percent of whom filled them out; see "The Foreign Ministers as a World Elite," *Peace Research Society (International), Papers, XIV, Ann Arbor Conference, 1969* (Philadelphia, Pa.: Peace Research Society [International], 1970), pp. 31-46; and "The World's Foreign Ministers: A Political Elite," *Journal of Conflict Resolution* 14, 2 (June 1970): 135-175.

Studies focusing upon national subelites have been able to shed considerable light upon the foreign policy process, particularly the relationship between foreign policymakers and interest groups in the United States. Among the more notable are Raymond A. Bauer, Ithiel de Sola Pool, and Lewis Anthony Dexter, *American Business and Public Policy: The Politics of Foreign Trade* (New York: Atherton Press, 1963); James N. Rosenau, *National Leadership and Foreign Policy: A Case Study in the Mobilization of Public Support* (Princeton, N.J.: Princeton University Press, 1963); Lloyd Jensen, "American Foreign Policy Elites and the Prediction of International Events," *Peace Research Society (International), Papers, V, Philadelphia Conference, 1965* (Philadelphia, Pa.: Peace Research Society [International], 1966), pp. 199-209; Frank Bonilla and José A. Silva Michelena, editors, *A Strategy for Research on Social Policy,* volume 1 of *The Politics of Change in Venezuela* (Cambridge, Mass.: The M.I.T. Press, 1967); William O. Chittick, *State Department, Press, and Pressure Groups: A Role Analysis* (New York: John Wiley & Sons, Inc., 1970); and

Bernard C. Cohen, *The Public's Impact on Foreign Policy* (Boston, Mass.: Little, Brown and Company, 1973).

Less attention has been paid to the operations of what Karl W. Deutsch *(The Nerves of Government: Models of Political Communication and Control* [New York: The Free Press, 1963], p. 154) has termed "the decisive middle level of communication and decision" in such areas as foreign policymaking. In one such study, Chihiro Hosoya (cf. "Miscalculations in Deterrent Policy: Japanese-U.S. Relations, 1938-1941," *Journal of Peace Research* 5, 2 [1968]: 97-115) found that officers of the rank of commander and captain systematically distorted information flowing to flag officers of the Japanese Imperial Navy in 1941, with the effect that the latter finally saw no viable alternative to the decision preferred by the former, namely an attack on Pearl Harbor.

D. Perspectives of Foreign Policy Leaders: Content Analysis

A different set of approaches analyzes systematically the communications of foreign policy leaders, using the manifest content of these messages to infer consistent patterns (latent structure). Some of the more interesting of these have been "nonquantitative"—that is, not actually using numerical indicators, although clearly relying upon some (implicit) judgments about the frequency with which certain variables usually occur or covary. Thus Nathan Leites examined the behavior of Soviet elites to delineate *The Operational Code of the Politburo* (New York: McGraw-Hill Book Company, Inc., 1951), and in *A Study of Bolshevism* (Glencoe, Ill.: The Free Press, 1953). Alexander L. George compared wartime statements with information discovered subsequently, in his *Propaganda Analysis: A Study of Inferences Made from Nazi Propaganda in World War II* (Evanston, Ill.: Row, Peterson & Company, 1959). And Ole R. Holsti elaborated Secretary of State John Foster Dulles's image of the Soviet Union in "Cognitive Dynamics and Images of the Enemy: Dulles and Russia," in *Enemies in Politics,* by David J. Finlay, Ole R. Holsti, and Richard R. Fagen (Chicago, Ill.: Rand McNally & Company, 1967), pp. 25-96.

Especially in its earlier years, quantitative content analysis concentrated upon indicators of elite sentiments rather than their direct expression. The most influential study was begun in the late 1940s at Stanford University's Hoover Institute under the general guidance of Harold D. Lasswell. Its analyses of the elite press in several countries, which was presumed both to reflect and to shape elite attitudes, appeared in 1951-1952, and were republished in Ithiel de Sola Pool et al., *The Prestige Press: A Comparative Study of Political Symbols* (Cambridge, Mass.: The

M.I.T. Press, 1970). Later scholars have developed other techniques to derive "elite" attitudes from "prestige" or special-interest publications. These include Robert C. Angell, "Social Values of Soviet and American Elites: Content Analysis of Elite Media," *Journal of Conflict Resolution* 8, 4 (December 1964): 330-380; J. David Singer, "Soviet and American Foreign Policy Attitudes: Content Analysis of Elite Articulations," *Journal of Conflict Resolution* 8, 4 (December 1964): 424-485; J. Zvi Namenwirth and Thomas L. Brewer, "Elite Editorial Comment on the European and Atlantic Communities in Four Countries," in *The General Inquirer: A Computer Approach to Content Analysis,* by Philip J. Stone, Dexter C. Dunphy, Marshall S. Smith, and Daniel M. Ogilvie et al. (Cambridge, Mass.: The M.I.T. Press, 1966), pp. 401-427; Milton C. Lodge, *Soviet Elite Attitudes Since Stalin* (Columbus, Ohio: Charles E. Merrill Publishing Co., 1969); and J. Zvi Namenwirth and Harold D. Lasswell, "The Changing Language of American Values: A Computer Study of Selected Party Platforms," *SAGE Professional Papers in Comparative Politics Series* (Series No. 01-001, vol. 1, 1970).

A more direct attempt to treat quantitatively the communications of top-level foreign policy decisionmakers stems from the work of Robert C. North and his colleagues, most notably Ole R. Holsti, Richard A. Brody, and Dina A. Zinnes. Their analyses of diplomatic dispatches, private letters, public statements, and other documents pertinent to such crises as the outbreak of war in 1914 and the Cuban missile confrontation of 1962 have produced a large number of articles in the scholarly literature and, so far, three books: Robert C. North, Ole R. Holsti, M. George Zaninovich, and Dina A. Zinnes, *Content Analysis: A Handbook with Applications for the Study of International Crisis* (Evanston, Ill.: Northwestern University Press, 1963); Ole R. Holsti, *Crisis, Escalation, War* (Montreal, Que.: McGill-Queen's University Press, 1972); and Ole R. Holsti, P. Terrence Hopmann, and John D. Sullivan, *Unity and Disintegration in International Alliances: Comparative Studies* (New York: Wiley-Interscience, 1973). For a critique, see Gordon Hilton, "The 1914 Studies—A Re-assessment of the Evidence and Some Further Thoughts," *Peace Research Society (International), Papers, XIII, Copenhagen Conference, 1969* (Philadelphia, Pa.: Peace Research Society [International], 1970), pp. 117-141.

Data and propositions produced by this type of study may also be used for simulations of crises, relying either entirely upon computers as in Ithiel de Sola Pool and Allan Kessler, "The Kaiser, the Tsar, and the Computer: Information Processing in a Crisis," *American Behavioral Scientist* 8, 9 (May 1965): 31-38, or upon interaction between live participants and computers, as in Charles F. Hermann, *Crises in Foreign Policy: A Simulation Analysis* (Indianapolis, Ind.: Bobbs-Merrill Company, Inc., 1969). Valuable discussions of these various projects are contained in Charles F.

Hermann, editor, *International Crises: Insights from Behavioral Research* (New York: The Free Press, 1972).

E. Motivations of Foreign Policy Behavior

For some analytic purposes, knowledge of the perspectives of foreign policymakers is sufficient, but frequently we want to know what it is that leads them to say what they say and act as they do. As noted earlier, social background data may provide some interesting hypotheses but few opportunities for concrete tests. Depth interviewing, only infrequently possible given the busy schedules of policymakers, might permit the trained analyst to gain greater insights, as could such techniques as interaction analysis (see John Spiegel, *Transactions: The Interplay Between Individual, Family, and Society* [New York: Science House, Inc., 1971]) to the extent that they can be applied. Current analytic routines based upon social-psychological models of behavior (such as Stone's "General Inquirer," noted in the previous section) are useful for drawing inferences from a leader's communications.

A more comprehensive approach is what Lewis J. Edinger has called the "developmental biography." It matches the known behavior and communications of a person throughout the course of his life with more general personality models that have been developed through psychiatric interviews, experimental techniques, and in-depth discussions with volunteers; it uses the findings to "explain" or even predict key decisionmakers' behavior. The basic model stems from the writings of Sigmund Freud.

Most biographers working in this mode, however, deviate considerably from the original model. Perhaps the purest application came from Freud himself, in a collaborative study with William C. Bullitt, written after World War I but not published until thirty-five years after its completion, *Thomas Woodrow Wilson: Twenty-Eighth President of the United States; A Psychological Study* (Boston, Mass.: Houghton Mifflin Company, 1967). Harold D. Lasswell showed the political relevance of the model in his work of the 1930s, especially *Psychopathology and Politics* (Chicago, Ill.: University of Chicago Press, 1930), and *World Politics and Personal Insecurity* (New York: McGraw-Hill Book Company, Inc., 1935). More recently, scholars have sought to specify the elements of a leader's developmental biography most critical for explaining his political views and behavior; the most substantial of these is by Lewis J. Edinger, "Political Science and Political Biography: Reflections on the Study of Leadership," *Journal of Politics* 26, 2 (May 1964): 423-439, and 26, 3 (August 1964):648-676.

Within the course of the last two decades, a number of developmental biographies relevant to foreign policy have appeared in print. At least two were performed at the direct request of branches of the American government: Walter C. Langer's analysis of *The Mind of Adolf Hitler* (New York: Basic Books, Inc., 1972), performed originally during the course of World War II; and Bryant Wedge's examination of "Khrushchev at a Distance—A Study of Public Personality," *Trans-action* 5, 10 (October 1968): 24-28.

Others include Alexander L. George and Juliette L. George, *Woodrow Wilson and Colonel House: A Personality Study* (New York: John Day Company, 1956); Arnold A. Rogow, *James Forrestal: A Study of Personality, Politics, and Policy* (New York: Macmillan Company, 1963); Lewis J. Edinger, *Kurt Schumacher: A Study in Personality and Political Behavior* (Stanford, Calif.: Stanford University Press, 1965); Betty Glad, *Charles Evans Hughes and the Illusions of Innocence: A Study in American Diplomacy* (Urbana: University of Illinois Press, 1966); E. Victor Wolfenstein, *The Revolutionary Personality: Lenin, Trotsky, Gandhi* (Princeton, N.J.: Princeton University Press, 1967); James David Barber's examination of American presidents since Theodore Roosevelt, *The Presidential Character: Predicting Performance in the White House* (Englewood Cliffs, N.J.: Prentice-Hall, Inc., 1972); and Bruce Mazlish, *In Search of Nixon: A Psychohistorical Inquiry* (New York: Basic Books, Inc., 1972). A useful analytic summary of various approaches is in Betty Glad, "Contributions of Psychobiography," in *Handbook of Political Psychology,* ed. Jeanne N. Knutson (San Francisco, Calif.: Jossey-Bass, Inc., 1973), pp. 296-321.

F. Foreign Policy Leaders and Conflict Resolution

Most experimental work in interpersonal behavior has been conducted with college students which, as far as the conduct of foreign policy is concerned, cannot account for a wide variety of socialization, institutional, and environmental constraints. For this reason developers of simulations, such as Harold Guetzkow, have occasionally tried to enhance the degree of reality by having persons at moderately high levels in national decision-making structures participate in sessions. Similarly, other imaginative scholars have developed "action research" programs, which bring together representatives of conflicting countries as a means to develop and test ways to manage and resolve international conflicts. One such program, reported in John W. Burton, *Conflict & Communication: The Use of Controlled Communication in International Relations* (New York: The Free Press, 1969), brought Greek and Turkish Cypriotes to London; a second, reported in Leonard W. Doob, editor, *Resolving Conflict in Africa: The Fermeda Workshop* (New Haven, Conn.: Yale University Press, 1970), included Somalis, Ethiopians, and Kenyans who were invited to discuss a common border dispute. The potentialities of such programs for ameliorating conflict, their limitations, and clues about their usefulness for learning about leaders' behavior in conferences are discussed by Herbert C. Kelman, "The Problem-Solving Workshop in Conflict Resolution," in *Communication in International Politics,* ed. Richard L. Merritt (Urbana: University of Illinois Press, 1972), pp. 168-204.

Systematic studies of foreign policy leadership, like those on the nature of public opinion and its role in the foreign policy process, have made great strides in recent years. That much remains to be done is nonetheless clear. Of prime concern to scholars may be linkages among these phenomena. But policymakers have a focus that puts such issues of theory in second place, well behind questions about the types of data that can best be used and means of actually using them in the policymaking process. Closing such gaps, far from trivial, between theorists and practitioners will doubtless remain a central task for the field of policy studies in the years to come.

Appendix 10A: Peace Research—The Search for Focus

The heart of the study of international relations has traditionally been questions of war and peace, the worldwide distribution of valued resources, and the opportunities of individuals and groups to enjoy these values with at least a modicum of liberty, spontaneity, and security. The very diffuseness of such concerns has nonetheless made it extremely difficult to achieve widespread agreement upon scope, underlying premises, or research strategies. Withal, the student of foreign policy faces yet another problem: Is research activity to be aimed more at developing theory, however relevant or irrelevant this may be to the practical issues of making and implementing foreign policy, or should it rather be geared to the more immediate needs of policymakers for information, analytic tools, and forecasting?

The newest subfield of foreign policy studies to confront this issue directly focuses on peace research. The rubric "peace research" itself implies its ambiguity of orientation. On the one hand, it suggests research designed to aid national policymakers attain their oft-proclaimed goal of peace. But, as is well known, one nation's idea of peace is another nation's definition of enslavement. Research oriented specifically toward national foreign policy processes and goals is thus "peace research" only in the symbolic sense that it identifies these goals with peace—a symbolic identification that researchers and policymakers in other countries are quite likely to deny!

The rubric "peace research" suggests on the other hand *basic* rather than applied research. Policymakers may well reject current formulations and data generated by peace researchers as too "theoretic" for use in their day-to-day work. Such basic research may of course have long-run payoffs. If persistent patterns among variables are discovered, then policymakers may be able to use this knowledge in their future behavior. Still other frameworks and findings, constituting a radical critique of the methods and goals previously adopted by national policymakers, are likely to be rejected out of hand by the latter as equally irrelevant. It is largely for this reason that one proponent of the radical perspective, William Eckhardt ("A Brief Review of the Radical Critique of Peace Research," in *Proceedings of the International Peace Research Association Fourth General Conference* [Oslo: International Peace Research Association Secretariat, 1973], pp. 125-135), notes that the main audience for such analyses must remain the international academic community.

A glance at the major institutions and journals that have explicitly embraced peace research as a focus reveals far more interest in basic research than in that designed to be immediately policy-relevant. This certainly does *not* mean, however, that analysts associated with these institutions and journals agree basically on either substance or approach. Part of the reason for this lies in the historical background of modern peace research.

A. Some Developmental Trends

Peace research is a new "discipline" with deep emotional and intellectual roots. From the earliest times people have longed for peace—albeit often only on their own terms. And writers down to the present day, while crying for peace, have sometimes devoted as much attention to the art of (and reasons for) waging war more efficiently or stabilizing great-power hegemony as to the tasks of preventing wars or encouraging modes of cooperation that rest on international equality. It was peace, though, that continued to fire both imaginations and rhetoric. And it was the expressed desire for peace that remained a central organizing focus of international studies.

Why, then, did the emergence, less than two decades ago, of a distinguishable subfield of peace research seem to be such a revolutionary development? How can we account for the emotionalism it engendered? One answer lies in the disrepute into which the term "peace" fell as an intellectual issue. The 1920s and 1930s saw too many scholars sincerely concerned with peace who identified themselves all too closely with pacifism. Hitler's aggressions and ultimately the Japanese attack on Pearl Harbor in 1941 undercut their position, and left ardent advocates of peace exposed to buffeting from left and right. Then, too, the Soviet appropriation of the term in the late 1940s to justify its international behavior at every turn seemed to complete its debasement. It was no mere accident that the new breed of peace researchers began their work under such banners as "conflict resolution" or "arms control."

Another answer lies in the intellectual diversity of the subfield's roots. From the outset scholars and others interpreted variously the notion and implications of peace research. Moreover, not all these different intellectual strands were mutually compatible.

Perhaps the oldest stems from "utopian" peace plans that can be traced back to such classic writers as Dante and Kant. Toward the end of the nineteenth century writers began to approach the concept of universal peace from a more empirical perspective. Of particular interest were those who tried to examine what we would call today the cost/benefit ratio of wars—most prominent among them being Norman Angell, with his 1910 book *The Great Illusion* (New York: G. P. Putnam's Sons). These and similar concerns led to a focus on international organization as the major deterrent to war. By the 1920s writers were engaged in the analysis and critique of and plans for restructuring the League of Nations; and two decades later many were expounding some form of federal world government.

Although justly criticized as overly legalistic or institutional in their approach, these scholars nonetheless laid a foundation for the study of the prerequisites of a peaceful world order. More recent writers, such as Karl W. Deutsch and Ernst B. Haas, have focused less on the structural aspects of international organizations than upon processes of integration at all levels—a changing concern reflected in such journals as *International Organization*.

Another strand of contemporary peace research sprang from the analytic interests of Quincy Wright and Lewis Frye Richardson. Wright, in his monumental *A Study of War* (Chicago, Ill.: University of Chicago Press, 1942, 1965), sought to move from strategic analyses, anecdotal reports, and moral judgments to the scientific investigation of the characteristics of wars. Richardson, in his posthumously published *Statistics of Deadly Quarrels* and *Arms and Insecurity* (Chicago, Ill.: Quadrangle Books, 1960), focused upon the mathematics of arms races. More recent analysts—such as J. David Singer and Melvin Small, in their careful study, *The Wages of War, 1816-1965: A Statistical Handbook* (New York: John Wiley & Sons, Inc., 1972)—have initiated a vast wealth of quantitative studies of societal conditions attending the outbreak of wars, perceptual processes in warmaking, patterns of alliance, integrative processes, and means for terminating wars and mitigating tensions.

A third strand developed in reaction to the intensive concern of other American scholars of the 1950s and early 1960s with how best to carry on covert (and, if need be, overt) warfare against potential aggressors, particularly the Soviet Union. If complete disarmament is indeed impracticable, said some analysts, then let us concentrate our attention upon arms control or conflict management. This interest produced a wave of analytic schemes for producing international stability, ranging from disengagement in central Europe to nuclear-free zones to such imaginative plans as Charles E. Osgood's GRIT, or *Graduated* and *Reciprocal Initiatives* in *Tension-reduction*, proposed in his *Perspectives in Foreign Policy* (Urbana: University of Illinois Press, 1965). Still others launched tightly-reasoned but impassioned attacks against the prevailing reason of the nuclear strategists. The most impressive of these were Anatol Rapoport's *Strategy and Conscience* (New York: Harper & Row, Publishers, Inc., 1964) and Philip Green's *The Deadly Logic* (Columbus: Ohio State University Press, 1966).

Still a fourth strand came in reaction to the perceived status-quo bias of scholars interested merely in understanding wars or ending them. Peace is not merely the absence of organized warfare, its adherents argue. It requires the elimination of "structural" as well as open violence. National decision-making structures ("the military-industrial complex") or international business arrangements ("Madison Avenue imperialism") that enrich a privileged few at the expense of whole nations, or which ensure the continued hegemony of American commercialism over the communication processes of less developed as well as industrialized societies, the argument continues, do as much violence to people's liberty, spontaneity, and security as does military intervention or an escalation of the arms race. Exemplary of such arguments are the articles of Johan Galtung, published in the *Journal of Peace Research*, or Herbert I. Schiller's *Mass Communications and American Empire* (New York: Augustus M. Kelley, 1969).

A plurality of approaches characterizes the organization as well as intellectual content of the emerging subfield of peace research. Research institutes have sprung up in several countries, sometimes even competing with one another for national research funds. (Philip P. Everts reports that the number of institutes concerned with peace and conflict research grew from 81 in 1966 to 267 five years later; cf. his *International Repertory of Institutions for Peace and Conflict Research* [Paris: UNESCO, 1972].) National and international associations tend to have looser structures than is the case for most academic disciplines. And, under the cover of a common concern with peace, these associations sometimes seethe with ideological and methodological disputes.

B. Literature on Peace Research

The plethora of intellectual stances regarding peace research, together with the wide variety and growing number of research institutions, means that there is no easy way for the interested person to get thoroughly acquainted with the subfield. Indispensable for keeping abreast of developments, such as conferences, publications, and activities of national organizations and research institutions, is:

> *International Peace Research Newsletter,* 1963+. Published several times yearly by the International Peace Research Association (United States editorial office: Institute of Behavioral Science, Bldg 3, University of Colorado, Boulder, Colorado, 80302).

Given the importance of journals in this emerging discipline, doubtless the best way to get an overview of what research is being performed as well as the assumptions upon which it rests and the methods it uses is to examine carefully the major publications. As a starter, one journal is particularly important for summarizing writing and research relevant to peace:

> *Peace Research Abstracts Journal,* 1964+. Published monthly by the Canadian Peace Research Institute, 119 Thomas Street, Oakville, Ontario, Canada. An official publication of the International Peace Research Association. For a small fee CPRI provides a searching service (98,349 abstracts in the first eleven volumes).

More analytic surveys appear in yet another journal, each issue of which deals with a particular topic, such as theories of deterrence, initiatives and responses in foreign policy, and Inter-Nation Simulation:

> *Peace Research Reviews.* 1967+. Published bimonthly by the Canadian Peace Research Institute, 119 Thomas Street, Oakville, Ontario, Canada.

Lengthy abstracts of particular peace proposals, as well as scholarly articles, appear in:

> *Bulletin of Peace Proposals.* 1970+. Quarterly, edited at the International Peace Research Institute, Oslo, under the auspices of the International Peace Research Association. Subscriptions are available from Universitetsforlaget, P. O. Box 142, Boston, Massachusetts 02113.

The *Bulletin*'s aim "is to present various plans, proposals and ideas for development, justice and peace, in a systematic manner, and to compare and discuss them in the light of general peace research theory."

Several other journals report on thinking and research in the field of peace research. Some are more general publications, such as (in English) *International Interactions, International Studies Quarterly, SAGE Professional Papers in International Studies Series, World Politics,* and sometimes *Foreign Affairs* or *Foreign Policy.* Others geared specifically to aspects of peace research include:

> *International Organization,* 1947+. Published quarterly under the

sponsorship of the World Peace Foundation and The University of Wisconsin Press, Box 1379, Madison, Wisconsin 53701. Recent changes in editorial policy have introduced greater emphasis upon integrative processes and quantitative data.

Journal of Conflict Resolution, 1957+. Quarterly. Subscriptions are available from SAGE Publications, Inc., 275 South Beverly Drive, Beverly Hills, California 90212. Usually, each issue contains articles, reviews, and a gaming section.

War/Peace Report, 1961+. Published bimonthly by Gordon and Breach (One Park Avenue, New York, N.Y. 10016) in association with the Center for War/Peace Studies of the New York Friends Group, Inc. Contains articles, reviews, and documentation.

Journal of Peace Research, 1964+. Published quarterly by the International Peace Research Institute, Oslo, under the auspices of the International Peace Research Association. Subscriptions are available from Universitetsforlaget, P. O. Box 142, Boston, Massachusetts 02113. Contains articles, review articles, and book reviews.

Peace Science Society (International), Papers, 1964+. Appearing irregularly, but roughly twice per year, each volume comprises papers presented at a given PSS(I) conference. Available free to members of The Peace Science Society (International); apply at Department of Peace Science, The University of Pennsylvania, Philadelphia, Pennsylvania 19174. Note: The PSS(I) was formerly called The Peace Research Society (International).

IPRA Studies in Peace Research, 1966+. The five volumes published between 1966 and 1973 by the IPRA Secretariat in Oslo contain proceedings of the International Peace Research Association's general conferences.

Peace Research, 1969+. Published at first monthly but now quarterly by Canadian Peace Research Institute, 119 Thomas Street, Oakville, Ontario, Canada. Current issues are obtainable free of charge. Contains original research.

Instant Research on Peace and Violence, 1972+. Published quarterly by the Tampere Peace Research Institute, Tammelanpuistokatu 58 B V, 33100 Tampere 10, Finland. The journal "concentrates on actual problems and phenomena related to questions of peace and war, of open and structural violence," and stresses research results more than methodologies.

In addition, from 1907 until 1972 the Carnegie Endowment for International Peace published *International Conciliation* five times yearly. Each issue was devoted to a particular topic, such as that of March 1972 (No. 587): *The*

Arms Race: Steps toward Restraint, by Herbert Scoville, Jr., Betty G. Lall, and Robert E. Hunter.

Numerous national and international associations also publish their own newsletters to advise members of organizational and other matters. IPRA's *International Peace Research Newsletter* was mentioned earlier. The *Newsletter* of the Peace Science Society (International) gives information about forthcoming meetings of its several sections in various parts of the world. The Stockholm International Peace Research Institute publishes occasional papers as well as, since 1969, the *SIPRI Yearbook of World Armaments and Disarmament.* The Lancaster Peace and Conflict Research Programme at the University of Lancaster, Bailrigg, Lancaster, has published since 1971 its *Programme Newsletter,* the editorial page of which is open to "anyone who has a concern for Peace." The Hessische Stiftung Friedens- und Konfliktsforschung (6 Frankfurt/Main 1, Eschersheimer Landstrasse 14, Federal Republic of Germany) issues occasional *Mitteilungen.* And recently the Leonard David Institute for International Relations (The Hebrew University, Jerusalem, Israel) has begun a series, *Jerusalem Papers on Peace Problems.*

The extent and nature of the debate and publications reveal that, as yet, a unified discipline of peace research—with commonly accepted intellectual underpinnings, concerns, methodologies, and styles of discourse—has not emerged. For some it is doubtless little more than a fad or temporary specialty; for others, peace research institutes and publications may merely serve propaganda purposes. For still others, however, and these are the scholars on whom this note focuses, the business of developing a science of peace is a serious one that reflects a continuing commitment of time and intellectual resources. They are seeking to perform a variety of vital tasks: integrating the wealth of relevant findings and ideas into coherent peace theory; generating new research, and testing new tools of analysis; reconceptualizing the central issues; and, more generally, working toward a scientific discipline with functional equivalence across nations, ideological lines, university campuses, and individual research units.

11 Crime and Criminal Justice Policy

John A. Gardiner
and
John Conrad

I. Crime and Criminal Justice Policy Issues in the United States

A. Policy Issues of the 1970s

Recent public interest in crime as a national problem appears to date from the presidential campaign of 1964, with an ever-increasing number of presidential commissions, government agencies, private foundations, and other groups advocating that something be done about crime, law enforcement, and the nation's criminal justice system. Apart from the one-hundred-year-old inquiry into the nature and causes of delinquent and criminal careers, social science research related to crime and criminal justice seems to be of equally recent vintage. The newness of the crime issue as a matter of national debate, and as a topic for serious research, to some extent makes it difficult to list an agreed upon set of issues, but I will attempt to describe some of the major debates currently under way.

1. Is there an increase in crime? Since the mid- and late-1960s, there has been a substantial increase in the number of crimes reported to the police and summarized in the FBI's *Uniform Crime Reports*. Public surveys conducted for the National Crime Commission in the mid-1960s indicated that there was also a large amount of crime which was never reported to the police, and which therefore did not show up in the official reports. Finally, there is an issue of the appropriate denominator to be used in calculating the crime *rate*: the Uniform Crime Reports cite crime per 100,000 of the total population, rather than per "population at risk," e.g., the potential victims of particular crimes. Despite these conflicting definitions and data insufficiencies, it is generally accepted that there has in fact been an escalation in the crime rate (both per total population and per population at risk), but that it is not as great as the rise indicated by the *Uniform Crime Reports*. Further light will be shed on this issue as the Law Enforcement Assistance Administration begins publication of crime statistics based upon repeated interviews with a national panel of households and businesses to ascertain their victimization experience.

Section I of this chapter was authored by John A. Gardiner. Section II was authored by John Conrad.

2. Can crime be reduced? By how much? Studies of offenders over the past forty years show a high correlation between criminality and poverty, race, low education, lack of job skills, poor housing, birth defects, and other pathologies. While research into the causes or etiology of crime has been inconclusive—there is as yet no accepted deterministic model to predict criminality—it is generally accepted that there is some degree of criminality which is essentially opportunistic and which can be deterred by making the target less accessible or by increasing the perceived costs of crime through more effective police action, speedier trial, or more certain punishment. While the proportion of crime which is deterrable is unknown, extensive efforts are now underway to increase the crime reduction potential of target-hardening, police patrol, adjudication, and correctional programs. At the same time, there has been a great increase in the use of evaluation research to identify the crime-reduction consequences of new programs. The Law Enforcement Assistance Administration, NIMH, and other federal, state, and local agencies are now conducting and sponsoring extensive evaluations of public and private crime-reduction programs.

3. What are the nature and consequences of interactions between the public and agents of the criminal justice system? Surveys over the past ten years have documented the varying and often ambivalent nature of public attitudes toward police and the criminal justice system; inner city residents particularly feel both a lack of protection and unsympathetic treatment from police, prosecutors, and courts. Conversely, the police recognize public apathy or hostility toward their activities. On the other hand, Wilson, in *Varieties of Police Behavior,* notes a general congruence between the values of local communities and the styles or policies adopted by local police departments. While the general lines of these public-system interactions are becoming clear, their consequences (beyond the generation of mutual alienation and antagonism) are less well known; whether an improvement in police-community relations will lead to more effective crime reduction programs remains to be seen.

4. How do the organizational characteristics of criminal justice agencies affect their performance? It has become common to introduce undergraduate courses with the statement "The criminal justice system is a non-system—police, court, and correctional agencies are unable to cooperate on anything." Despite the fact that local crime problems are, or could be, influenced by all of these agencies, they usually tend to reject the idea of common responsibility for problem-solving, and only recently have been willing to cooperate in developing plans and proposals for federal funding. It is possible, however, that current forced cooperation to develop these proposals will lead to actual system integration.

A second organizational characteristic of criminal justice agencies has been extreme decentralization—policemen, judges, and correctional personnel generally make decisions on their own; unlike the geographically dispersed agents described by Kaufman in *The Forest Ranger* who internalized and acted upon detailed codes of operating procedures, criminal justice agents typically have a great deal of discretion and latitude in deciding how to deal with the victims and offenders before them. The result, unsurprisingly, is wide variation in the way that similar problems are handled. Over the coming years, it will be interesting to measure the degree of acceptance of guidelines being promulgated by the American Bar Association, the LEAA National Advisory Commission on Criminal Justice Standards and Goals, the National Crime Commission, and other groups.

B. Resources for Crime Policy Studies.

While many political scientists have addressed research problems associated with crime or the administration of criminal justice, their projects have generally been relatively small, using limited data sources and research staffs. Unlike such areas as voting behavior or foreign policy, no university department of political science has established a sustained interest in or national reputation for crime-oriented research; as will be indicated below, large-scale research enterprises have been limited to interdisciplinary teams, law schools, and sociology departments with major interests in criminology.

The identification of resources for crime policy studies is further complicated by the fact that since criminal justice administration has been a state and local responsibility, data resources, whether quantitative or qualitative, are usually scattered throughout the country, each subject to unique problems of accessibility, reliability, and interpretation. While there are signs of marked improvement in the availability of quantitative data on a national scale (see below), one must keep in mind the old observation that crime data ultimately are based upon watchmen "writing down whatever they damn please." As research problems are defined, therefore, the analyst must be continually cautioned to verify—in the field—the agency policies which affect when and how events are reported.

A third aspect of crime policy research which provides both an opportunity and a limitation is that much of the work done to date might be characterized as evaluation for operational purposes: a police chief wants to learn a better way to conduct his patrol operations, a judge wants to reduce court delay, or a correctional administrator wants to know how to deal with a particular type of offender, so they sponsor or invite analyses addressed to these problems. Evaluations of this type present a number of problems for the scientist interested in contributing to a generalized body of literature (see my comments in the November, 1971, issue of the *Law and*

Society Review), but they provide innumerable opportunities for acquiring access to agency operations, familiarity with data sources, and exposure to "real world" problems. Unfortunately, few of these evaluative studies ultimately appear in the general literature.

C. Major Journals in the Field

Much of the research which has been done to date on issues of crime and criminal justice is conducted by scholars with only a passing interest in the area. As a result, they tend to publish in journals focusing on their professional specialty rather than in crime-oriented journals. From time to time, therefore, many of the social science and law journals have presented individual research reports on crime and law enforcement problems.

The major journals which are specifically addressed to professionals and scholars dealing with crime, law enforcement, and the administration of criminal justice are:

American Journal of Correction (American Correctional Association, published bi-monthly)

Abstracts of Criminology and Penology (Criminologica Foundation, bi-monthly)

British Journal of Criminology (Institute for the Study and Treatment of Delinquency, London, quarterly)

Canadian Journal of Criminology and Corrections (Canadian Criminology and Corrections Association, quarterly)

Crime and Delinquency (National Council on Crime and Delinquency, quarterly)

Crime and Delinquency Literature (National Council on Crime and Delinquency, quarterly)

Federal Probation (Administrative Office of the United States Courts in cooperation with the United States Bureau of Prisons, quarterly)

Issues in Criminology (University of California School of Criminology, quarterly)

Journal of Criminal Law and Criminology (Northwestern University School of Law, quarterly)

Journal of Research in Crime and Delinquency (National Council on Crime and Delinquency, semi-annually)

Judicature (American Judicature Society, ten times per year)

The Police Chief (International Association of Chiefs of Police, monthly)

Journal of Police Science and Administration (International Association of Chiefs of Police, quarterly)

D. *Sources of Grants*

In addition to those agencies which provide broad support for social science research, political scientists should investigate the availability of funds from criminal justice agencies and regional and state criminal justice planning agencies. In addition to whatever funds these agencies allocate for research, they are increasingly providing funds for the evaluation of federally funded action programs.

Among the private foundations presently funding research on crime, law enforcement, and criminal justice are:

> Council on Law-Related Studies, Harvard Law School, Cambridge, Massachusetts 02138
>
> Law and Government Programs, Ford Foundation, 320 East 43rd Street, New York, New York 10017
>
> Russell Sage Foundation, 230 Park Avenue, New York, New York 10017

The major federal agencies funding research in the area are:

> Office of Research Programs, National Institute of Law Enforcement and Criminal Justice, Law Enforcement Assistance Administration, Washington, D.C. 20530
>
> Center for the Study of Crime and Delinquency, National Institute of Mental Health, 5600 Fishers Lane, Rockville, Maryland
>
> Research Addressed to National Needs Program, National Science Foundation, 1800 G Street Northwest, Washington, D.C.
>
> Social Sciences Division, National Science Foundation, 1800 G Street Northwest, Washington, D.C.
>
> National Center for Educational Research and Development. U.S. Office of Education, Washington, D.C. 20021
>
> Office of Research and Development, Manpower Administration, U.S. Department of Labor, 1111 20th Street Northwest, Washington, D.C.

Since the funding levels and priorities of each foundation and federal agency change from year to year, it is advisable to write for program descriptions and indications of interest in particular topics before preparing full proposals.

E. *University Programs*

As was mentioned earlier, there are no major groups of political scientists looking at crime policy issues. The major interdisciplinary research programs (in no particular order) are:

Center on Administration of Justice, University of California-Davis

Center for the Advancement of Justice, Harvard Law School

Center for Studies in Criminal Justice, University of Chicago Law School

Center for Studies in Criminology and Criminal Law, University of Pennsylvania

Criminal Law Education and Research Center, New York University

Institute for Court Management, University of Denver

Institute of Judicial Administration, New York University

John Jay College of Criminal Justice, City University of New York

School of Criminal Justice, Michigan State University

Public Systems Research Institute, University of Southern California

Southeastern Correctional and Criminological Research Center, Florida State University

School of Criminal Justice, State University of New York—Albany

Center for the Study of Law and Society, University of California—Berkeley

School of Criminology, University of California—Berkeley

School of Social Work, University of Michigan

Center for Criminal Justice Research, University of Illinois at Chicago Circle

F. Non-Academic Research Institutes

The major research groups with continuing interest in crime and criminal justice, frequently working with both endowments and grants and contracts from other sources, are the American Bar Foundation, Chicago; The American Justice Institute, Sacramento; the International Association of Chiefs of Police, Gaithersburg, Maryland; National Council on Crime and Delinquency Research Center, Davis, California; Rand Institute, New York City; and the Vera Institute of Justice, New York City.

G. Information Sources

Several major reference services or clearinghouses contain information (primarily abstracts of journal articles and research reports) pertaining to crime. Since their areas of specialization, subject classifications, and fee schedules vary, it is advisable to contact them for general information before requesting specific searches.

> National Criminal Justice Reference Service, Law Enforcement Assistance Administration, Washington, D.C. 20530
>
> Information Center, National Council on Crime and Delinquency, Continental Plaza, 411 Hackensack Avenue, Hackensack, New Jersey 07601
>
> National Clearinghouse for Mental Health Information, National Institute of Mental Health, 5600 Fishers Lane, Rockville, Maryland
>
> Science Information Exchange, 1730 M Street Northwest, Washington, D.C. 20036

For other information sources and periodically updated lists of publications dealing with crime and law enforcement, contact the Librarian, Law Enforcement Assistance Administration, Washington, D.C. 20530.

H. Statistical Data Sources

I indicated earlier that most statistical data on crime and law enforcement are collected and stored locally or at the state level. There is a growing movement to establish statewide crime data centers, with information on both crimes reported to the police and activities of police, court, and correctional agencies. Information on the appropriate point of contact in individual states can be obtained from the National Criminal Justice Information and Statistics Service, Law Enforcement Assistance Administration, Washington, D.C. 20530.

On some specific topics, data are available on a national basis. Crime figures, based on incidents reported to the police, are available from the Uniform Crime Reporting Section of the Federal Bureau of Investigation, and are published annually in *Crime in the United States*. Data on persons released from prison on parole are published in the *Uniform Parole Reports* by the National Council on Crime and Delinquency Research Center at Davis, California. LEAA also collects and publishes materials on prison populations, local jails, and criminal justice employment and expenditures. Beginning in 1974 LEAA has published the results of the National Crime Panel survey, an on-going program involving 60,000 households and about 15,000 businesses throughout the United States. Respondents in the Crime Panel are asked questions concerning their victimization experience, their responses to being victimized (e.g., did they report the offense to the police, did they take preventive measures, etc.), and their attitudes toward crime and criminal justice.

I. Interest Groups

It is impossible to identify on a national basis the various groups which seek to influence crime policy, since the vast majority of crime policy decisions are made at a local or state level. In each instance, decisionmakers must react to shifting influences from the personnel involved (policemen, judges, correctional officials), citizens' groups (both permanent and ad hoc), and, in some cases, ex-offender organizations. On a national level, criminal justice professionals are primarily represented by the American Bar Association, the American Correctional Association, and International Association of Chiefs of Police, the National District Attorneys Association, the National Legal Aid and Defender Association, the National Sheriffs Association, and the North American Judges Association. Interest groups representing cities, counties, and states seek to influence the level and allocation of federal funding for crime control programs. The major citizens group in the field is the National Council on Crime and Delinquency.

II. The European Perspective on Policy Issues in Crime Control

Any attempt to encapsulate European criminal policy research in the space assigned me would misrepresent a wide variety of scientific activity. The range extends from a fundamental examination of the instrumentalities of social control to a maintenance of continuity from the classical criminology of the nineteenth century. The sense of urgency which characterizes American work is naturally lacking in Europe, where metropolitan streets are noticeably safer and the volume of crime is exponentially lower. But despite data generated by these enviable conditions, many European criminologists have a wary concern about the future. They note the metropolitanization of their societies and the increasing geographical mobility of all classes. Upward trends in rates and volumes are so far insufficient to justify sweeping changes or bold new programs, but their significance for a less orderly future is not lost on social scientists. No one seriously expects that the American experience will be duplicated, but many of the same questions which confront students in this country are formulated in the accents of anxiety about the consequences of social change.

In what follows I shall draw on notes from a recent tour of criminological institutes in Oslo, London, and Rome. I hope that this account will not be construed to be either comprehensive or conclusive, but that it will be suggestive enough to instigate an interest in the ideas and methods of contemporary European scholarship. The value of cross-cultural comparisons in social science seems to me to rest primarily on their potentiality for the generation of new ideas. Surely American students of the crime problem stand in need of conceptual innovation from whatever source it can be derived.

A. *Norwegian Studies of Social Control*

In spite of a crime rate which is the second lowest in Europe, Norway has for many years enjoyed the benefits of one of the most distinguished criminological institutes in the world. The work of Andenaes on deterrence is classic; around him there have gathered younger social scientists such as Christie, Aubert, Bratholm and Mathiesen, all of whom have published in English. Their work demonstrates the influence of empirically supported theory on the evolution of public policy. As a result of their studies, alcoholism has been decriminalized and work camps for drunken vagrants have been abolished in favor of detoxification centers. They now hope that a somewhat similar impact on legislation will ensue from their current studies of correctional facilities for youth.

This strategy for research is based on the examination of the nature of social control. It is thought that the sources of crime are to be found in structural dysfunctions of society which are manifested in excessive reliance on control as the instrument for the resolution of social problems. Thus, the question which the criminal policy researcher should address is, To what extent is the control policy for the problem under consideration redundant or inappropriate? The corollary question should address the alternatives for existing controls.

An example is to be found in penology. As in most western countries, the correctional romance with various treatment ideologies is coming to a disenchanted end. Norwegian studies have been supported by Finnish and Danish research in the finding that correctional "treatment" produces no significantly positive results. The inference is strong that reliance on treatment has resulted in a needlessly oppressive sentencing policy. The specific question to be addressed has to do with the administration of justice in a context in which the use of control for the purposes of treatment is ruled out. This approach transfers attention from the prison, (where much outstanding research has been done by Norwegian social scientists), to the community. It now seems more important than ever to study the roles which can be played by the police and the extent to which the community can be involved in meaningful interaction with the police apparatus. To the Norwegian policy-maker it is not an outlandish notion to explore the potentiality of the police role for social work functions. Already some experimentation in this direction is under way in Oslo and more can be expected.

Norwegian social scientists take the reasonable point of view that although prisons ought to be as humane as possible, the nature of decent conditions of incarceration is not a subject for research. What is researchable, however, is the dialectic of reform. Currently, there is an active penal reform movement in Norway under the intentionally meaningless designation, KROM, not an acronym for anything. KROM is an amalgam of liberal intellectuals and inmates of Norwegian prisons. Its explicit objective is the abolition of incarceration and the reconstruction of the criminal justice system so that offenders can be dealt with in the community. The actual structure to supplant the present system is not described; the proponents believe it is enough to demonstrate the futility of our present methods. The use of research methods to study and further activism parallels the "reflexive" sociology of Alvan Gouldner and his followers in this country, but is of evidently indigenous origin.

B. The Conduct of Official Research in the United Kingdom

Under the leadership of Thomas Lodge, the Home Office Research Unit has for many years persevered at the difficult and unglamorous tasks of empirical research in criminology. The foundation is the annual publication of *Criminal Statistics for England and Wales*, surely the most comprehensive compilation of its kind published in any country, including our own. The Home Office research staff is also engaged in a wide range of evaluative research in which the search for a valid methodology has been a consistent concern. Perhaps the most famous work conducted in this setting was Wilkins' investigation of the base expectancy prediction method, which has been widely adapted for use in correctional research in the United States. This research theme has continued to the present time, with the recent publication of Frances Simon's impressive monograph, *Prediction Methods in Criminology* (Home Office Research Study No. 7, HMSO, 1971). The concern about methodology for evaluation has continued with the publication of *The Controlled Trial in Institutional Research*, by Clarke and Cornish (Home Office Research Study No. 15, HMSO, 1972). The re-examination of the experimental paradigm for evaluative research leads away from the massive studies of program variables so characteristic of evaluative research both in this country and England in the last fifteen years, toward the study of "constituent" variables on a much smaller scale.

The structure of the Home Office Research Units is an interesting solution of the problem of maintaining continuity and detachment in evaluative functions. The research unit supports a considerable amount of extramural research directed at specific needs of action departments of the

Home Office but at the same time maintains a large and versatile staff for the conduct of continuities in longitudinal research strategies and the study of methodology. The examination of penal institutions and the alternatives to incarceration has been under way for many years with results which fail to support the efficacy of treatment as an objective of penal action. The links between research and policy change are mostly to be found in a variety of commissions which review evidence and recommend legislation. It is not easy to discover connections between research and the conduct of ordinary correctional operations. This gap is recognized; during the coming year, conferences will be organized between Prison Department officials and the research community in which it is hoped that a systematic interaction can be created.

Criminological research at the universities is led by Cambridge and Oxford. At Cambridge, the Institute of Criminology under Sir Leon Radzinowicz has focused on the offender and his treatment by the criminal justice system. The Oxford Penal Research Unit, under Professor Nigel Walker, has been primarily concerned with the functioning of the system. Thus the exercise of police discretion, the functions of the jury, and the uses of the pre-sentance investigations made by probation officers have been the subjects of brief monographs. These are relatively recent papers and it is too soon to estimate their influence over a system which has yet to accustom itself to the uses of research.

For years British criminological research has been addressed to the practical problems of criminal justice administration as these problems have been defined by researchers themselves. As in this country, the administrative arms of criminal justice have yet to perfect a liason in which research becomes the foundation of managerial creativity. Nevertheless, the potential is considerable and the climate is good for rapid progress.

C. International Collaboration Under the United Nations

For the last twenty years the United Nations has maintained a Social Defence Unit which has been responsible for the collection and dissemination of information about crime and criminals. Every five years it has conducted a large and ponderous conference on the prevention of crime and the treatment of the offender in which eminent delegates from participating nations compare experience and policy. The value of conferences of this kind has never been confirmed, except that each conference has been better attended than its predecessor.

In 1968, the Social Defence Unit entered into a co-operative arrangement with the Italian government to establish a Research Institute in Rome principally directed at assistance to the developing countries in the utilization of western experience in the operation of correctional systems. For the most part the efforts of the Institute consisted of surveys and recommendations.

The Institute moved to a second stage in 1971 with the appointment of Dr. Peider Könz, a Swiss social scientist, as director, Könz enlarged the Institute staff and its program. Evidently concluding that in the field of crime control all nations must be regarded as "developing," he includes in the scope of the Institute's charge the development of research methods in criminology, collaboration with national research personnel in the conduct of specific research, and the provision of technical assistance in research design and methodology. Already this ambitious program has been implemented in an impressive array of projects, many of which will be completed for publication of findings during the present year. Subjects now under study range from a survey of contemporary prison architecture and its sources in public policy to a study of the impact of criminological research on decision-making by courts and parole boards. There is widespread interest in the engagement of public participation in criminal justice process and an investigation of various models for the achievement of this goal will be undertaken soon, to include collaboration with Eastern European scholars.

The Institute's program is intended to deal with issues in which policy change is possible and desired. For the most part, the actual conduct of research will be in the hands of investigators in the participating countries. The Institute's role for the foreseeable future will be essentially consultative. It will assist in the identification of problems and their formulation for trans-national study; its staff will be available for assistance with methodological difficulties; and it will assist in the dissemination of findings. In its present form, the Institute will be unlikely to undertake research independently.

An institute of this kind is a social experiment. Its success depends on the interest of the international research community in the exchange and comparison of findings. That interest must be supported by administrative recognition of the value of criminal justice research. An objective assessment of the present condition of criminology throughout the world must conclude that this recognition is precarious at best. But success feeds on success. The reception accorded to the array of publications to be expected from the Institute during this year and the next will determine whether the time is ripe for this kind of international collaboration.

D. A Note on International Problem-Solving

The culture of the international scholarly conference is well-established.

Its objectives, at least in criminology, are not. One of the functions of the Council of Europe is the maintenance of a forum in which the directors of criminological institutes can foregather for discussion of topics of common concern. In November 1972, they met for the eleventh time in the handsome city of Strasbourg. The topic was violence.

There could be no question as to the concern which all felt about the significance of violent crime. The persistence of primitive behavior in the advanced societies perplexes everyone; its apparent spread is serious cause for anxiety. For an international gathering of experts, the question is obviously pressing, but a format for its useful discussion is elusive.

Position papers were presented to the conference by an impressive array of well known scholars. The statistics of violence were compared so far as they were available, the outcome was that significant comparisons could not be made. The etiology of violence was discussed at great length, with primary, but not exclusive emphasis being placed in its psychological origins. The phenomenology of violence was discussed without an adequate definition of that term. In short, a good deal of the underbrush was cleared away for a meaningful discussion of action, but at that point the conference ended. It was as though criminologists could afford the interminable processes of analysis and interpretation but could not spare the time for a review of action to deal with the problem itself.

It is natural to attribute the inconclusive quality of a conference like this to the academic style. Certainly, the exchange of ideas, references and notions testified to the universality of the don. But it is inappropriate for the academic to conclude that nothing can be done about violence until it is thoroughly understood. Something is being done about violence without that understanding, and it requires description, understanding, and assessment by whatever means may be available to the scholar. The traditional means of deterrence and control may be all the protection that the state can offer its citizens. But there may be alternatives to our present management of the violent offender. Neither area of study is receiving systematic attention anywhere. It is not unreasonable to suppose that impaired access to administrative data is at least as much an obstacle to research as the interest of the criminologist in causation. The hesitance of the social scientist in the study of administrative alternatives in criminal justice is partly rooted in the administrator's reluctance to be studied.

The consequence is the creation of a cycle of ineffectuality. The criminologist's work is too often seen as irrelevant puttering with side issues, thereby showing the futility of reliance on that discipline for useful contributions to the solution of problems. But administrators and legislators persist in the same old ineffectual programs because they have no basis for their replacement or improvement. In the meantime, the tiger is at our gates, gaining constantly in size and vigor.

12 Educational Policy

Samuel K. Gove,
Frederick Wirt,
and
William Walker

I. Basic Issues and References

Prior to the early 1960s recognition of the political nature of educational policy-making was virtually absent from the political science literature. The landmark article on the political bases for educational policy-making was Thomas Eliot's "Toward an Understanding of Public School Politics."[1] This article, as the title would indicate, dealt with policy related to elementary and secondary schools but not with policy related to higher education.

There have been few applications of political science knowledge to policy-making situations simply because there has been little such knowledge to apply. The construction of theories on educational politics has been slow, and the work which has been done consists of the description and testing of relatively inexact hypotheses. More complete description and testing of somewhat more precise hypotheses have been accomplished on aspects of the politics of elementary and secondary education rather than on the politics of higher education.

A. Politics of Elementary and Secondary Education

Frederick Wirt has surveyed the literature on elementary and secondary education politics in "Theory and Research Needs in the Study of American Educational Politics."[2] He reviews the research that has been conducted in an Eastonian framework. Wirt expresses concern that his article may be taken to imply that more formulation and testing of hypotheses has occurred than is actually so. He stresses that most of the work cited consists of case studies, often conducted in restricted locales. More aggregate and less case research is needed. Specific suggestions for research directions to fill out more parts of the Eastonian framework are given.

Wirt identifies the Elementary and Secondary Education Act of 1965 as the focus of a significant amount of research. The political basis of both the passage and implementation of this act are examined.

Section I of this chapter was authored by Samuel K. Gove. Section II was authored by Samuel K. Gove and Frederick Wirt. Section III was authored by Samuel K. Gove and William Walker.

One aspect of political science research which already has had influence on actual educational policy is that of political socialization in the schools. Political scientists have identified currents of ethnocentrism in many high school civics curricula, have developed new materials to remove such currents, and have won acceptance for the new materials in many school systems.

At a conference on the politics of public schools held late in 1970, directions for research in the governance of public education were discussed. The papers prepared and a summary of the conference discussion are collected in *State, School, and Politics: Research Directions*, which was edited by Michael Kirst.[3] In an introductory presentation to the conference, Heinz Eulau expresses perhaps the central question political scientists face in approaching the politics of education. A model that postulates the primacy of politics in the relationship with education, he suggests, may well be more appropriate than the classical model which postulates the reverse primacy.[4] The directions for research discussed at the conference are summarized in Michael Kirst and David Grossman's "An Analysis of the Conference Discussion."[5] All participants agreed that more attention needs to be concentrated on who ultimately benefits from the outputs of the policy system. It was repeatedly stressed that identification of dependent variables was central to more fruitful policy analysis. No consensus could be reached, however, on what constituted the "important" dependent variables. There was general agreement that research on the governance of public education should be comparative and should work toward the development of generalized classificatory schemes. Two particular thrusts for research were suggested: (1) follow a policy from its birth and authorization through its administration at all levels of government from the federal downward; and (2) focus horizontally on one unit of decision-making to see what is happening to a wide variety of substantive policies. Areas which could not be fitted into the Eastonian framework but which were considered to demand urgent analysis are accountability and the political legitimacy of current educational institutions.

B. *Politics of Higher Education*

It is often difficult for a political scientist to be dispassionate in an analysis of the politics of higher education. He may be studying higher education in a particular state while he is employed by a public university in that state. Frequently he must examine roles in which he has at some time been a participant. The supply of political scientists writing about policy making in higher education is constantly changing. Political scientists who might have made a major contribution to the literature in this area have become actors in the politics of higher education and are now writing for different audiences.

Samuel K. Gove and Barbara Whiteside Solomon, in "The Politics of Public Higher Education: A Bibliographic Essay," reviewed literature written prior to 1968 which in any way related to the politics of higher education. They found "little material that has the relationship between higher education and the state political situation as its major focus."[6] The absence of much sustained analysis is further shown in Gladys Kammerer's call for the attention of political scientists to five aspects of the politics of public universities (relating to both internal and external relationships of the university) in a 1969 article, "The State University as a Political System."[7]

Political science literature related to the politics of higher education has focused on narrowly defined topics. Typically it has centered on the behavior of a particular institution or of individuals clustered around that institution.

A recent study for which data were systematically gathered is Heinz Eulau and Harold Quinley's *State Officials and Higher Education: A Survey of Opinions and Expectations of Policy-makers in Nine States*.[8] Data drawn from questionnaires and intensive interviews were used to elucidate the attitudes, opinions, and information about higher education held by legislators in the selected states. The report was prepared for the Carnegie Commission on Higher Education.

In the last three years interest in analysis of the politics of public higher education has increased. At the 1970 meeting of the American Political Science Association papers focusing on internal politics of the university were delivered by Leon Epstein and Victor Rosenblum at a panel on the university as a political system.

A panel on state education politics at the 1971 meeting of the Midwest Political Science Association included a paper by Joseph Tucker on the politics of public higher education in Ohio which focused on the external relationships of the university. At the 1972 MPSA a convention panel was devoted to "The Politics of Public Higher Education: A Comparative Analysis," and papers were prepared on the political configurations in the following states: Illinois (Gove and Carol E. Floyd), Nebraska (C. R. McKibbin), and Wisconsin (Alan Rosenbaum).[9] Each paper dealt with the political roles of state universities, of major figures in the state's political life, and of the coordinating agency for higher education, as well as the political resources of higher education. Each paper concluded with an analysis of the prospects for public higher education in the near future. During discussion of the papers, the question was raised, "So what? Where has all this analysis gotten us?" It was generally agreed that the papers offered little basis for generalization. Difficulties in comparing political configurations in highly urbanized and less highly urbanized states were noted.

The policy analysis done to date, both by political scientists and others, has not been based to any significant degree on sustained political analysis.

The policy studies which have received the most attention in policy-making circles are probably those carried out under the auspices of the Carnegie Commission. Eugene Lee and Frank M. Bowen in *The Multi-Campus University: A Study of Academic Governance*[10] examine a number of the characteristics of such systems and make suggestions as to how their functioning can be improved. Although limited political analysis on a few topics (the constituency of a state system, factors increasing and decreasing external political pressures on a state system) is present, the basis for the suggestions made is clearly administrative rather than political. A report of the Carnegie Commission, *The Capitol and the Campus: State Responsibility for Post-Secondary Education*,[11] makes no reference to explicit political analysis in reaching its major conclusion that only state assumption of responsibility for postsecondary education can preclude a greater degree of federal control over that level of education.

II. Resources for the Study of Education Policy[a]

A. Elementary and Secondary Education

The study of Elementary and Secondary Education (ESA) as part of the American policy field has traditionally not been a domain for political scientists. Sociologists, economists, psychologists, and educationalists have interacted for decades in this policy field. In the following resume of resources, we ignore much of the work of these specialists because it does not provide a direct linkage to public policy—thus, *American Educational Research Journal* or *Review of Educational Research*. Rather, we have provided those items which might prove most fruitful if one new to this field wished to apprise himself of resource allocation both within and outside the school. Much of this boils down to either the social context or the administration of education, which conforms to the titles of two major divisions of the national American Educational Research Association.

Journals. Aware of overlaps in what follows, we can distinguish between these contextual and internal administrative focuses in relevant journals, while some are even more general. Journals with an administrative focus would include: *Administrator's Notebook, Education Administration*

---
[a]In this section, Fred Wirt is mainly responsible for the material on elementary and secondary education policy, and Sam Gove for higher education policy.

Quarterly, American School Board Journal, Educational Leadership, and their foreign counterparts, such as the Australian *Journal of Educational Administration*. Articles here are mainly empirical analyses of administrative practices, both internal and in community linkages. The journal of the education administration honorary, *Phi Delta Kappan*, provides useful introduction to large research projects and findings of interest to such schoolmen.

Other journals focus more upon the social context in which education proceeds. Thus, *Sociology of Education, Teachers College Record, Harvard Educational Review, Education and Urban Society, School and Community, School Review*, and *Urban Education*. Some journals have a special focus, such as *Social Studies, Journal of Negro Education,* or *Integrated Education*, which still retains a contextual framework.

Few journals are oriented to a specific concern for the public policy consequences of the subject studied. But the *Harvard Educational Review* would be an exception, as would in many cases *Theory into Practice*. From time to time non-educational journals contain articles of importance in this field, such as *Public Administration Review, Public Administration Quarterly, National Tax Journal* (despite the wide availability of financial data and administrators' encompassing involvement with the subject, there is no journal specially focused on the subject), and the traditional sociology or political science journals.

Data Sources. ESA is awash with data on school's finances, personnel, and measurable academic outputs. Major sources of raw statistics are the National Education Association and the U.S. Office of Education, especially the National Center for Educational Statistics. Offices of public information in each will answer inquiries about all publications. The NEA is an umbrella organization for groups of specialized schoolmen with offices in Washington; they provide not merely statistics, such as yearbook of statistics by states, but specialized reports, such as the voluminous two-volume study of state education in this century, *Education in the States*, edited by Edgar Fuller and Jim B. Pearson (1969).

A promising development was the congressional authorization of the National Institute of Education by amendments to the Higher Education Act in 1972. However, at this writing no appropriations had been made, so the program is unsettled. Present indications are that much of the research function of the old USOE have been gathered into the NIE to provide more focused research programs in the future. Clearly it is an effort to duplicate the concept of the National Institute of Mental Health.

A highly useful bibliographic service is available in ERIC (Educational Resources Information Center) in NIE, which provides through regional centers print-outs of annotated items under a variety of subject headings.

The originals of such writings may be purchased in microfiche or full-size. The chief utility of ERIC is its coverage of the fugitive literature of the field.

More scattered data sources abound within the interstices of our federal system, of course. Private groups provide materials, such as the yearbook of the National Society for the Study of Education, which focuses upon a special topic. State departments of education in most cases have a statistics collecting and reporting service, and larger systems such as New York State generate their own research. Federal involvement in education, clearly increasing enormously in the last decade, brings with it even more numerous data sources. Congressional committees produce lengthy analyses, both specific and general. Thus, the House Committee on Education and Labor's *Federal Educational Polities, Programs and Proposals: A Survey and Handbook* (1968) is both an historical and topical analysis, while its *Books for Schools and the Treatment of Minorities* (1966) represents the more specialized treatment. The hearings by Senator Walter Mondale's subcommittee on Equal Educational Opportunities in the early 1970's represent a unique albeit disparate collection of viewpoints and detailed reports on that subject.

Political scientists should note, however, the curious lack of data on school elections. While the school district is the most numerous governing agency in America, and elections to the board and tax referenda provide the most frequent, direct data source on Americans' policy preferences, few scholars have written on the subject and few data sources exist.[12] Most states do not collect such data, and the only national collection is USOE's small annual report of local bond elections, by state and outcome (*Bond Elections for Public School Purposes,* National Center for Education Statistics).[13]

Grant Sources. It seems very likely that scholarship funds available for study in aspects of education will not merely increase in the near future, but will provide federal resources for this policy study far greater than for any other. Symptomatically, USOE officials met for a day at the 1971 convention of the APSA in Chicago to elicit suggestions for directing research funds into the politics of education. The uncertain status of the NIE at present precludes providing any guidelines about that particular research direction, however. But it does suggest potentially larger funds than has been the case.

Note that the USOE has in the past provided enormous amounts for study in many aspects of education, of which political scientists have had some use. But it seems likely that the NIE reorganization will bring both small and large grant functions within its boundaries, according to my interviews. Besides USOE, however, note the potential resources available in the wide array of other federal departments described in the report noted above *(Federal Educational Policies,* etc.).

Foundation support for innovation research has been a feature of much private funding in ESA. Thus, Ford's Division of Education and Research: Public Education has been the key element in recent years supporting research and litigation which resulted in the overturning of the present use of the local property tax for financing schools. Ford has recently been giving highest priority to research projects which have a high capacity for increasing community participation in schools. The Spencer Foundation of Chicago has been recently established for funding large-scale research into critical education problems, including desegregation impact. A quick glance at any directory of foundations will reveal unnumbered smaller groups willing to finance specialized aspects of ESA, but Ford and Spencer are of current importance.

University Programs. University interest in ESA as a public policy has most often focused in the educational administration section of the school of education. Typically, this work was designed to train principals and superintendents in the professional skills necessary for providing maximum school services.[14] Certain of these schools, however, have had another tradition, that of providing scholarly analysts of educational policy—thus Harvard, Chicago, Stanford. Newer ones are emerging, too, such as at Berkeley, Ohio State, Oregon, and Claremont. The traditional education school dominates the universities of this country, however, with its more narrow professional training emphasis. The policy analyst tradition, while smaller, has accounted for highly important research and analysts who have helped shape state and national school policy.

Interest Groups. Because of the notion of schoolmen that they are not in a political context, "interest groups" is a term alien to their perspective. But in reality, the organized legions of schoolmen—administrators, teachers, board members, staff—have developed an organizational base both for transmitting to one another ideas and skills but also for securing a more favorable allocation of resources and values from the political system. Nationally, the NEA has been a holding company interest group for schoolmen, while more recently the AFL teachers' union has introduced splits in that group and made much clearer the political nature of schoolmen's work.[15] At the state level exist congeries of school lobbies operating in different contexts and with different power.[16] Locally, one finds permanent groups, both professional (like teacher organizations) and private (like PTA's), as well as *ad hoc* growths for particular issues, such as communism in the schools, sex education, taxes, etc.

Of special interest to scholars is the Interest Group for Politics of Education of the American Educational Research Association. Now listing over a hundred members from political science and education, it reflects institutionally the recent development of scholarly interest in the interface between schools and the state.[17] They maintain a regular newsletter and arrange panels of interest at the AERA's annual convention.

Conclusion on Elementary and Secondary Education Policy. This too-brief report makes several important points about the study of ESA policy. Interest in the subject is growing rapidly, reflected both in funds, scholars, and reports. Too, there exists a surprising resource base for those interested in the field, with the usual nexus of universities, foundations, and government which one finds in other policies. Finally, as Gove made clear (*Policy Studies Journal*) 1, 1 (1972), only limited frameworks of analysis have been brought to bear by political scientists on ESA policy, dominated by the Eastonian conceptualization. In short, this policy fields displays signs of interesting possibilities for scholarly growth in the near future.

B. Higher Education Policy

Resources for policy studies in higher education are considerably fewer than those for secondary education. There is no one source of funding, and the journals are limited. Higher education is a very highly organized area; professional organizations range from accrediting associations to admissions officers associations to associations with broader concerns such as the American Council on Education and the Education Commission of the States. There are many many more, some of whose publications might be helpful to the policy analyst, most would not. The academic centers for the study of higher education are limited in number, and in most cases their areas of interest cannot be described as aimed primarily toward policy analysis. This is not to say that there is a shortage of data on higher education; this is not the case. In general, however, the data are widely scattered.

Journals and Other Publications. There are only a few journals devoted to general issues in higher education. Among them are two of note: the *Educational Record* (American Council on Education) and the *Journal of Higher Education* (American Association of Higher Education and Ohio State University). A new Elsevier journal, *Higher Education*, has potential for filling some of the present need for sources on higher education policy. In its third edition as of August 1972, it is "an international journal of higher education and educational planning." The *Bulletin of the American Association of University Professors* occasionally has some article of interest; its academic freedom and tenure cases frequently provide much insight into the internal and external politics of a particular university. Occasional articles appear in the political science journals, but these have been quite infrequent. The same is true for the *Public Administration Review* and *Daedalus*, the journal of the American Academy of Arts and Sciences.

In the past five years the literature on higher education has proliferated, and a number of new publications have been started. For example, the *Chronicle of Higher Education* now provides journalistic coverage on a wide variety of aspects of higher education. *Change: The Magazine of Higher Learning* is a new publication whose main concern is with recent innovations and developments in higher education. In 1967 the Jossey-Bass Publishers of San Francisco started a series of books on higher education which now includes a number of works touching on the political aspects of higher education. Lewis B. Meyhew has written three volumes which synopsize and comment on books of higher education, including the few written on the politics of higher education during the years 1969, 1970, and 1971. Particularly valuable is his essay, "Trends in the Literature 1965-1970," found in the 1971 survey. Probably the most influential of the new publications on higher education policy is the series of recently released Carnegie Commission on Higher Education reports and sponsored research reports.

Since 1968 *Current Issues in Higher Education,* the annual collection of papers presented at the conference of the American Association on Higher Education, has included more articles on political aspects than it had previously. That association now has in its newsletter *College and University Bulletin* a column "Research Currents" prepared by the ERIC Clearinghouse on Higher Education at the George Washington University, Washington. The ERIC Clearinghouse also prepares, on a semi-annual basis, *Current Documents in Higher Education: A Bibliography* published by the American Association for Higher Education. The AAHE compiles its own *Bibliography on Higher Education* for each of its national conferences. Another recent bibliography is The Council of Planning Librarians' *Administration and Planning in Higher Education: A Bibliography of Books and Reports* by Milo C. Pierce, September 1972 (Monticello, Ill.). The Education Commission of the States publishes ten issues a year of *Higher Education in the States*, which contains reports on developments in the states as well as bibliographies of state reports.

One other source of data on higher education, particularly finances, is M.M. Chambers personal newsletter *Grapevine* (Illinois State University, Normal). This monthly contains early data on appropriations as well as state-by-state information on administrative and other developments. Chambers has assembled much data from his monthly newsletter in books on finance, legal developments, and other topics in higher education published by the Interstate Printers and Publishers, Danville, Illinois.

University Programs and Other Organizations. The specialized centers of higher education on our campuses have generally been associated with schools of education, suggesting some possible limitations for the policy analyst. Some of the better known higher education centers or institutes are found at Berkeley, Michigan, and Columbia.

As mentioned above, the higher education system in this country is highly organized. For interested faculty, administrators, trustees, or students, the possibilities for memberships are great. One may choose from the academic discipline groups, the organization of business managers, the association for university trustees, plus the several student groups. At the national level many of the broadly based organizations are housed in One Dupont Circle, Washington. This proximity tends to encourage communication between the organizations.

Grant Sources. The possible sources for financial support of policy analysis studies in higher education are few. The National Institute of Education is an unknown quantity at this time. The Danforth Foundation has supported some higher education programs over the years, and the Carnegie Commission on Higher Education was supported from a grant from the Carnegie Foundation for the Advancement of Teaching. Other foundations, such as Ford, have supported higher education studies. No clear sources of funds have developed, however, and the best suggestion is to check the *Chronicle of Higher Education* for their listing of recent foundation grants. The just published *Securing Support for Higher Education: A Bibliographical Handbook* by Cletis Pride (Praeger) may also be helpful.

Conclusion on Higher Education Policy. Although higher education has become a more popular subject for policy studies, it seems clearly to be behind our brethren in elementary and secondary education. But the field seems to be growing: the body of literature is increasing, as are the sources of data. Interest in the topic is beginning to surface at political science meetings and in political science journals. Unfortunately, funding for such studies is far from abundant at this time.

III. Comparative Educational Policy[b]

A. Elementary and Secondary Education

The area policy studies in international education is indeed vast. As an

---

[b]In this section, William Walker is mainly responsible for the material on elementary and secondary education policy, and Sam Gove for higher education policy. Sam Gove wishes to acknowledge the valuable comments he received from Professor Robert E. Scott and the

example, a recent study concerned with the testing of only two theories in the context of the development of higher education in one state of Australia and in England lists no fewer than 850 references.[18] This section can provide only a resume of the literature by pinpointing current concerns for scholars and describing in a "comparative" context some developments in the study of educational policy making around the world. A detailed overview of the scholarly development of comparative education is found in Jones's excellent monograph.[19]

Suffice it to say here that for historical reasons policy studies in education have chiefly developed in the broad areas of "comparative" and "international" education. During the nineteenth century when systematic studies in these fields began, the emphasis was on what could be learned from other schools or school systems. In contrast, the emphasis today is more upon the planning process and upon the most economic and efficient use of resources. Further, while writers in the field around the turn of the century were chiefly educational administrators, today educators, political scientists, psychologists, demographers, sociologists, economists and organizational theorists all focus their expertise upon the field.

The author, in association with colleagues at the Universities of Alberta, Colorado, London and Victoria (New Zealand), has just completed a glossary of terms used in educational administration and policy making in five English-speaking countries.[20] The task was a salutary one for the student of policy studies since the simplest of terms can have half a dozen different meanings. The word 'college' in New Zealand, for example, may refer to a public (government) high school, a private (church) high school, a residential unit in a university, a teachers' college, an agricultural degree granting institution or a formal group of professional workers. In England a public school is, in effect, a private school; in Australia it can mean *either* a government or a private school; in the U.S.A. it can refer to an elementary or secondary school or to a university or college, and so on.

Furthermore, the present author proposed in 1964[21] and 1972[22] that, in discussions on centralization and decentralization, scholars should distinguish clearly between the governance dimension and the administrative dimension. But the literature on educational planning and policy making is remarkable for such lack of definition. It is possible, as Jones[23] shows, to distinguish among national, state, regional and local planning and among long-term, medium-term and short-term planning; it is also possible to distinguish among levels of policy making. Much of the literature, however, eschews any effort to do so. Even attempts at simplistic models, based on a macro-micro planning dimension on one coordinate and an ultimate-contributory policy dimension on the other, are rare.

Clearly, the problem of the relationships between planning and
─────────
assistance of Lawrence Mann. William Walker wishes to acknowledge the considerable assistance of Mr. P. E. Jones, Senior Lecturer in Education at the University of New England.

policy-making continue to challenge scholars. Diez-Hochleitner of UNESCO idealizes planning as

> . . . a cohesive force that co-ordinates and directs the many components of an educational system and ensures that widely accepted long-term goals, such as universal primary education, are approached more objectively.[24]

Eide, Director of Norway's Educational Planning Board, however, sees the planner more as a brake on the aspirations of policy-makers:

> . . . the planner may use the technique of formulating explictly the kind of objective function which in fact corresponds to an actual policy—thus provoking the policy-makers to state more explicitly their real value judgements.[25]

As planning—and especially manpower planning—has attracted the interest of economists, the long-standing emotive pleas by traditional educators for maximum education for all and education for its own sake have been put into a new perspective. *Economy* and *efficiency* are emphasized to a much greater degree than in the past. Ribiera typifies the economist's approach:

> The major problem of planning consists, in future, in manipulating the various possibilities in education so as to find the combination which offers optimum results for the lowest cost.[26]

Coombs[27] suggests that it is a categorical imperative to plan, to determine priorities. Yet it is clear that the practice of education like that of any other profession or semi-profession will always consist of part art and part science,[28] of value judgments and of fact.

In recent years, the earlier sweeping "manpower-unit" arguments of some economists have been tempered somewhat by planners. As Husen of Sweden puts it,

> Any educational planning is virtually impossible without certain basic information about some quantitative aspects both of education itself and of the society it is supposed to serve. But successful planning, particularly if it is carried out as a regular part of policy making, must also consider the qualitative aspects of education[29]

Manpower planning has come under attack in several quarters in recent years, for example by Anderson[30] and Campbell[31] of U.S.A. and Elvin[32] of Great Britain, and the development of the "human resources" movement has, if anything, grown apace. Schultz[33] of the University of Chicago points out that "people enhance their capabilities as producers and as consumers by investing in themselves and that schooling is the largest investment in human capital." Harbison[34] echoes this viewpoint with regard to developing countries, where the problem is usually not one of natural resources but of human capital. On the other hand, Foster points out that in Ghana the market demand for technical skills is small, unlike the usual conception that there is an insatiable need for technically trained people in underdeveloped areas.[35]

In another area there has been much discussion in recent decades of the policy making process. The sociologist Parsons,[36] who distinguishes among policy, allocative and coordinative decisions, has provided some useful guidelines for scholars. Truly, the question of policy making inside the organization as distinct from outside pressures, as highlighted by Lindblom[37] and Miller and Starr[38] is as fascinating as that raised by Cardozo[39] with regard to judge-made law a half-century ago. In the Netherlands[40] it has been shown that, because of this interior-exterior dichotomy, many institutional forces influence the system, so planning cannot be carried out exclusively by a ministerial unit. Planning is effected by negotiation with a variety of organizations concerned with education. Glasman's[41] description of policy making in Israel and Leila Berg's[42] English classic on *Risinghill* also raise issues regarding the crucial question: who makes policy?

A natural corollary of the interest of economists in policy making has been the development of predictive mathematical models. The work of Blaug[43] and Correa[44] has been very influential. Yet, as Tinbergen and Bos point out, "No models, however realistic or refined, will ever fully cover all the circumstances, be able to answer all the questions, or solve all the problems which might arise."[45] On the other hand, there seems to have been surprisingly little interest in the use of such predictive devices as the Delphi Technique; the recent University of Florida Report, "Changes in Organizational Structures of Large School Systems"[46] is an outstanding example of one study which *did* use the technique and which is, consequently, of major concern for U.S. educational policy-makers, at least. While the publication of "Designing Education for the Future"[47] and other projects are now readily available to students of policy making, it is problematical how many, even in the U.S.A., have taken this fine material seriously. One major recent U.S. educational study much influenced by Futurism and which *is* receiving wide acclaim is the publication of the National Conference of Professors of Educational Administration, "Educational Futurism, 1985."[48]

One finding which emerges from this brief review is that the study of policy making in education is growing rapidly in its appeal to scholars in many parts of the world. This will probably increase as the costs of schooling rise and as alternatives are sought for traditional educational structures. The question is reflected in the report of the OECD Directorate for Scientific Affairs on Swedish planning:

It is unrealistic to believe that new resources can be allotted on a substantially larger scale to any one sector than to others. The only possibility . . . of bringing about a more rapid development in education than in the economy as a whole is to introduce rationalisation measures having a comparatively rapid effect. By rationalisation we mean measures which yield the same output but which cost less per production unit than previously in respect of manpower or monetary investment.[49]

Similar problems are known to face Soviet[50] policy makers and, indeed, policy makers in most other parts of the world.

It is good that scholars have turned to the crucial social issue of educational policy making. One of the most distressing and depressing aspects of international educational developments since the end of World War II has been the large scale invasion of developing countries by "planners" and "advisers" whose knowledge of political or administrative theory was minimal.

Today there is an urgent need for literature to assist students of policy making in education around the world to comprehend another's problems. Periodicals like the *Journal of Educational Administration*[51] and books like Harman's recent *Politics of Education: A Bibliographical Guide,*[52] are too few and far between. There is, as Wirt pointed out in 1970,[53] a need for a much larger collection of aggregate data. There is a need, too, for a greater concern for theory, for the development of explanatory and predictive models of wider international relevance and, in general, for a more intense concentration of social scientists on the phenomena of comparative policy making *qua* policy making around the world.

B. Higher Education Policy

Relatively few studies had been conducted on the relationships between governments and higher education in the United States. A search of the English language literature shows that this situation exists to a greater degree internationally. Discussion of the politics of higher education[54] in other countries is virtually absent.

We will review the limited amount of English language literature that exists on the politics of higher education, that is, the interactions between governments and institutions of higher education. We will then consider the sources available to those who wish to read beyond this essay. Lastly we will raise some questions for research in other policy areas of higher education.

Reviewing the Literature. The question of university autonomy is the political issue that is most frequently analyzed. As will be noted from the following brief review of English language literature, virtually all the works discussed touch upon this question.

In Canada, a controversial 1970 report *The University, Society and Government–The Report of the Commission on the Relations Between Universities and Government* focuses upon existing and potential government education programs and the structuring of higher education.[55] The report, authored by Rene Hurtubise and Donald C. Rowat, recommends a move toward provincial and regional coordination and a lessening of the direct role of the federal government in the development of higher education. With this thrust, there would be less institutional autonomy. The report was strongly criticized by the Association of Universities and Colleges of Canada, the organization which had distributed federal funds to institutions of higher education and had helped sponsor the report. The association said, "The report's lack of appreciation of the inevitability of federal concern in matters related to higher education . . . ignores the complexity of Canadian political reality. . . . If there are problems of federalism in Canada, there equally are problems of undue provincialism in Canadian education." Although there have been other general analyses of higher education in various countries,[56] the Hurtubise-Rowat Report seems to be the most recent.

Another Canadian development that has received considerable attention is the 1971 University of Toronto Act, which restructured the governance of that institution. The new act eliminates the two-tier system consisting of an academic senate and a separate board of governors, and creates a new single governing council which will have representation of the public, faculty, students, alumni, and the administrative staff. Writing in *Minerva*, Murray Ross says, "It is quite clear that the government has substantially increased its control of the university. This is not immediately apparent, since previously the government appointed all members of the board, whereas now it appoints only a portion. But in the old arrangement the senate could be . . . a very stubborn antagonist. The board's power was limited by this fact. Now, without a senate, the government's representatives will meet with staff and students at the same table to decide both academic and administrative policy."[57]

The literature about British higher education is largely concerned with the University Grants Committee, the agency that distributes public funds to individual universities. An earlier study (1959) by a political scientist is Robert O. Berdahl's *British Universities and the State*.[58] In a recent debate in the British journal *Minerva*, Max Beloff[59] has argued that the grants committee poses serious threats to academic freedom and university autonomy. He also maintains that the grants committee has brought uniformity to the British university system by the homogenization of universities based upon egalitarian concepts. Beloff, an Oxford University professor of government and public administration, states that it is simply impossible to depend upon the public purse and expect autonomy at the same time. "If there is to be any real measure of university autonomy . . . the important thing is to increase the proportion of money obtained through private endowments and fees and lessen that which comes from the state. For this to come about, a change in the tax laws is essential . . . . In the second place, universities that can raise private funds should be given complete discretion over spending." The important thing is to "find some way of dismantling the controls that already exist, and of minimizing dependence upon the proceeds of general taxation."

The University Grants Committee and the British Department of Education and Science are defended in a *Minerva* article by Sir Eric Ashby, a scholar of higher education around the world and a member of the committee.[60] Ashby denies that these two agencies have placed the "dead hand of uniformity" on British universities. The grants committee, composed of 75 percent academics, prevents Parliament, civil servants, and the Department of Education and Science from interfering with the universities' autonomy. Parliament's role is limited to making "perfectly legitimate political decisions" regarding allocation of "massive grants of money with very few constraints attached to them." Parliament leaves the universities free to use the money as they see fit. Although the grants committee has issued guidelines of what is expected from British universities, fundamental educational issues (such as control of admissions, curricula, and appointment and tenure of faculty) are decided by the universities. In concluding, Ashby asserts that "hands of some sort will eventually be laid upon universities." Cognizant of such a reality, he urges that universities work *with* government so that government influences "overall social policy" and not the specifics of educational policy.

Lord Bowden in another *Minerva* article looks at the roles the comptroller and the auditor general should have in reviewing the fiscal matters of universities.[61] He says that some form of state intervention can be valuable and that government auditing need not violate academic freedom. In fact, he favors increased governmental auditing, for he believes British universities have been less productive in aiding society than have universities in the United States. He concludes that the university system in Britain is less efficient than its American counterpart: it could be doing much more for government and society with its government money.

In other countries, the issue of autonomy frequently arises. In West Germany the federal government's power over the universities has been increased, writes G. Kloss in *Minerva*.[62] When in the late 1960s state efforts failed to produce fundamental university reform, the federal government intervened with the Financial Reform Act of 1969. The federal government now has powers to regulate student grants, to make rules regarding basic principles governing the universities, to collaborate with the states on "common tasks," and to cooperate with the states in general educational planning and in support of research institutions. It now seems plausible, according to Mr. Kloss, that if the states do not take the initiative in enacting reforms, the federal government may soon acquire complete control over higher education.

Autonomy is also an issue in India. S. R. Dobgerkery is the author of a book *University Autonomy in India*.[63] It is his thesis that university autonomy has decreased since India gained independence. "I could not have chosen a more appropriate subject . . . than university autonomy in India, in view of the several attacks on university autonomy made by a number of State Governments in our country during the two decades since independence. . . . In India, the British traditions of autonomy were imported with the establishment of universities on the British model, but they have not yet had time to take root in the Indian soil. Unfortunately, the advent of political freedom in the country, instead of strengthening university autonomy, has tended to weaken it. . . ." The author makes special reference to the conflict between Osmania University and the state government of Andhra Pradesh. Legislation was introduced to give the government final say on educational policy and grant to the governor authority to remove the university's chief executive officer at any time. Although Osmania was able to secure some modification of the legislation, its autonomy has been substantially reduced.

The cause of autonomy was also argued forcefully by Amrik Singh in his article "Universities and Government"[64] published in an Indian journal *Quest*. That issue of *Quest*, March 1967, was devoted to a symposium on higher education in India.

The role of political parties and universities in Singapore was discussed in an article by Roland Puccetti in *Minerva*.[65] The author concludes that "the boundaries between the university, the ruling party and the government have become fainter as the university has increasingly become an instrument of the government, not by the usual functions of producing trained persons for government posts or by doing research useful for society, but rather by the more direct political activities of affirming the policies of the PAP (the controlling party) within the university and on the outside and building up the prestige of the party, even to the point of blurring the differences between the party and the university."

Few attempts have been made at comparative analyses of the politics of higher education. Often such studies merely contain separate chapters describing the situation in a particular country. An exception is an article by Minir Bashshur in *Comparative Education Review* that compares universities in Syria and Lebanon in regard to government interference.[66] Syria has had excessive interference, and the Syrian University has become a center of political friction and a training ground for future political leaders. Its focus has become political, not educational. In Lebanon, both the French and American universities have contributed significantly to the nation's political development, but without the overt government control seen in Syria.

In a new book, *Higher Education from Autonomy to Systems,* James A. Perkins stresses that there must be more coordination between institutions in each country, and the institutions collectively must be viewed as a system.[67] "Coordination and consolidation are the order of the day for most countries, while decentralization and increased autonomy are the course for others. These two tendencies will meet somewhere in the middle between autonomy and political authority." A large portion of the book is devoted to developments in the United States, but in addition, there are chapters on twelve other countries or world regions.

Much has been written about student politics around the world. Symposia on the subject were published in *Daedalus* in 1968[68] and in the *Comparative Education Review* in 1966.[69] Both are useful references on the relationships between students, universities, and governments in various countries.

Sir Eric Ashby has brought together information on the development of *Universities: British, Indian, African: A Study in the Ecology of Higher Education*.[70] The book is well documented and is a valuable resource work. It devotes a great deal of space to the question of autonomy and government relations.

Resources for Further Analysis. The resources for international and comparative studies on the politics of higher education are somewhat limited. As might be expected from the number of citations mentioned, the British journal *Minerva* (a review of science, learning and policy) is a source of relevant articles. The new Elsevier (The Netherlands) journal *Higher Education* (an international journal of higher education and educational planning) may also develop into a useful resource. A source for information and data (but not journal articles) is the *Bulletin* of the International Association of Universities. The *Bulletin*, published with financial resources from UNESCO, includes, in its May 1972 issue, a list of journals and similar publications around the world.

The World Book of Education, 1971-72 is devoted to *Higher Education in a Changing World*.[71] It includes a series of articles on developments in various countries. One interesting section is devoted to "Factors Influencing Policy in Higher Education." Its bibliography contains a rather complete list of bibliographies. There is also a list of centers for the study of higher education around the world.

For methodological and other issues on international policy studies, the conference papers *International Studies: Present Status and Future Prospects* is a good source.[72] It is not, however, aimed directly at higher education.

Other Directions in the Study of Higher Education Policy. The possibilities for policy analysis in higher education (however defined) are many. One can look at the partisan political relations, as we did here, between institutions of higher education and their governments. Or one can look at the type of training given and its effect on the political culture of a country. Does the training reinforce the existing culture, or is higher education a force for change? In this connection, is higher education strictly elitist oriented, or does it aim at the masses? Both questions involve policy analysis. Another question worthy of further inquiry is the locational pattern of individual institutions in a country, and its effect on migration patterns within the country. In some countries, these locational decisions seem to encourage movement to urban areas; in other countries the opposite seems to be true. Another policy issue which has been given some attention is the question of students as a distinct political force in a particular country, and how the governmental decision makers react to this. Still another policy question that has also been given some attention is the role of universities in developing countries. Sir Eric Ashby, who is mentioned earlier, has been interested in this question in regard to Africa. Others have been concerned with the same policy question in other parts of the world.

Notes

1. *American Political Science Review* 53 (1959):1032-51.

2. *Journal of Educational Administration* (Australia) 8 (1970): 53-88. For a similar set of judgments see Michael W. Kirst and Edith K. Mosher, "Politics of Education," *Review of Educational Research*, 39 (1969): 623-40.

3. (Lexington, Mass.: Lexington Books, D.C. Heath and Co., 1972).

4. "Introductory Essay—Political Science: The Long View and the Short," in Michael Kirst (ed.), *State, School, and Politics: Research Directions* (Lexington, Mass.: Lexington Books, D.C. Heath and Co., 1972), pp. 1-10.

5. Ibid. pp. 238-44.

6. *Journal of Higher Education* 39 (1968):182. An updating of that bibliography is Samuel K. Gove and Carol Everly Floyd in the *Public Administration Review* (January 1975).

7. *Journal of Politics* 31 (1968): 289-310.

8. (New York: McGraw-Hill, 1970).

9. These papers were published in the *AAUP Bulletin* (Autumn 1973) plus a paper by Joseph Tucker on the politics of higher education in Ohio.

10. (New York: McGraw-Hill, 1971).

11. (New York: McGraw-Hill, 1971).

12. For elaboration, see Frederick M. Wirt and Michael W. Kirst, *The Political Web of American Schools* (Boston: Little Brown, 1972), Ch. 1 and Part 3.

13. For tabulation and analysis of these reports over a decade, see Ibid., 136-44.

14. See a popular graduate textbook, Edgar L. Morphet, Roe L. Johns, and Theodore L. Reller, *Educational Organization and Administration: Concepts, Practices, and Issues* (Englewood Cliffs, N.J.: Prentice-Hall, 1967), 2d ed.

15. For details of the groups mentioned in this paragraph, see Wirt and Kirst, op. cit., Chs. 3, 7.

16. For a conceptualization of this subject, see Laurence Iannaccone, *Politics in Education* (New York: Center for Applied Research in Education, 1967). For empirical studies, see Nicholas Masters et al., *State Politics and Public Schools* (New York: Knopf, 1964) and Harmon Zeigler and Michael Baer, *Lobbying* (Belmont, Calif.: Wadsworth, 1969).

17. For a conference report including many members of this group, see Michael W. Kirst, ed., *State, School, and Politics: Research Directions* (Lexington, Mass.; Heath, 1972).

18. P.E. Jones, "Comparative Method and Educational Policy Making," doctoral dissertation, University of New England, 1972.

19. P.E. Jones, *Comparative Education: Purpose and Method* (St. Lucia: University of Queensland Press, 1971).

20. W.G. Walker, Caroline Steele, and J. Mumford, *Education in Five English Speaking Countries: A Glossary of Terms* (St. Lucia: University of Queensland Press, 1972).

21. W.G. Walker, "Educational Administration," Chapter IX in R.W.T. Cowan, *Education for Australians* (Melbourne: Cheshire, 1964), pp. 193-217.

22. W.G. Walker, *Centralization and Decentralization: An International Viewpoint on an American Dilemma* (Eugene, Oregon: Center for the Advanced Study of Educational Administration, University of Oregon, 1972). (A Special CASEA Report).

W.G. Walker, "Centralization or Decentralization: The Key Issue in Catholic Education," paper read to the First National Conference on the Administration of Catholic Education, Armidale, University of New England, 1972.

W.G. Walker, "Administrative Structure: Centralization or Decentralization?" paper read to the Special Seminar Series on Designing an

Education Authority, Canberra, Australian National University Research School of Social Sciences, 1972.

23. P.E. Jones, op. cit., p. 26.

24. Quoted by Ladislav Cerych, *Problems of Aid to Education in Developing Countries* (New York: Praeger for the Atlantic Institute, 1965), p. 92.

25. K. Eide, "Educational Developments and Economic Growth in OECD Member Countries," Chapter V in E.A.G. Robinson and J.E. Vaizey (eds.), *The Economics of Education* (London and New York: Macmillan and St. Martin's Press, 1966), p. 196.

26. C. Flexa Ribiera, "Reconciling Planning and Education," UNESCO News, 1969, 20, pp. 6-8.

27. P.H. Coombs, *The World Educational Crisis: A System Analysis* (New York: Oxford University Press, 1968).

28. Clearly the process of planning, like policy making, will always consist partly of art and partly of science.

29. Torsten Husen, in "Final Reports of the Conference Working Groups," International Conference on the World Crisis in Education. Williamsburg, Virginia, October 5-9, 1967, p. 1, Mimeo.

See also J.E. Vaizey, "Economics of Higher Education," Armidale Conference on Planning in Higher Education, University of New England, August 1969.

30. C.A. Anderson, *The Social Context of Educational Planning* (Paris: UNESCO: IIEP, 1967), p. 34.

31. R.F. Campbell, "The Administrator and Educational Planning," address delivered to the Australian National Advisory Committee for UNESCO National Seminar on Educational Planning, Canberra, September, 1968.

32. H.L. Elvin, "Educational Planning and National Development," address delivered to Australian National Advisory Committee for UNESCO National Seminar on Educational Planning, Canberra, September, 1968, pp. 11-12.

33. T.W. Schultz, "Returns on the Investment," in J.W. Hanson, and C.S. Brembeck (eds.), *Education and the Development of Nations* (New York: Holt, Rinehart and Winston, 1966), p. 128.

34. Frederick Harbison, "Strategies for Investing in People." in J.W. Hanson, and C.S. Brembeck (eds.), *Education and the Development of Nations* (New York: Holt, Rinehart and Winston, 1966), p. 149.

35. Philip Foster, *Education and Social Change in Ghana* (Chicago: University of Chicago Press, 1965), p. 294.

36. Talcott Parsons, "Some Ingredients of a General Theory of Formal

Organizations," Chapter III in A.W. Halpin, (ed.), *Administrative Theory in Education* (Chicago: Midwest Administration Center, University of Chicago, 1958), p. 47.

37. C.E. Lindblom, *The Policy-Making Process* (Englewood Cliffs, N.J.: Prentice-Hall, 1968), p. 1.

38. D.W. Miller and M.K. Starr, *The Structure of Human Decisions* (Englewood Cliffs, N.J.: Prentice-Hall, 1967), p. 99.

39. B.N. Cardozo, *The Nature of the Judicial Process* (New Haven: Yale University Press, 1921).

40. OECD, *Educational Policy and Planning: Netherlands* (Paris: Directorate for Scientific Affairs, OECD, No date), p. 37.

41. N.S. Glasman, "A Structural Change Proposal in the Israeli Schools: Conflict and Conquest," *Journal of Educational Administration* 8 (1970): 88-108.

42. Leila Berg, *Risinghill: The Death of a Comprehensive School* (Harmondsworth, Middlesex: Penguin Books Ltd., 1960).

43. See, for example, Mark Blaug, "The Rate of Return on Investment in Education in Great Britain," *Manchester School of Economic and Social Studies* 33 (1965): 205-51.

44. See, for example, Hector Correa, *Quantitative Methods of Educational Planning* (Scranton, Pa.: International Textbook, 1969).

45. J. Tinbergen and H.C. Bos, "An Appraisal of the Model and the Results of its Application," in Tinbergen et al., *Economic Models of Education: Some Applications* (Paris: OECD, CIRCA 1965).

46. John O. Andes, Roe L. Johns, and Ralph B. Kimbrough, *Changes in Organizational Structures of Large School Systems with Special Reference to Problems of Teacher Militancy and Organizational Conflict* (Gainesville, Florida: University of Florida, 1971).

47. Edgar L. Morphet, et al. (eds.), *Designing Education for the Future: An Eight State Project* 7 vols. (Denver: 1966-1969).

48. Walter G. Hack et al., *Educational Futurism 1985: Challenges for Schools and Their Administrators* (Berkeley, California: McCutchan, 1971).

49. K. Nozhko, et al., *Educational Planning in the U.S.S.R.* (Paris: UNESCO-IIEP, 1968), p. 287.

50. OECD, *Educational Policy and Planning, Sweden* (Paris: Directorate for Scientific Affairs, 1967), pp. 33-34.

51. *The Journal of Educational Administration*, University of New England, Armidale, N.S.W. Australia 2351. Twice yearly. Subscription US $3.50.

52. G.S. Harman, *The Politics of Education: A Bibliographical Guide* (St. Lucia: University of Queensland Press, 1972.)

53. Frederick M. Wirt, "Theory and Research Needs in the Study of Educational Politics," *Journal of Educational Administration* 8 (1970): 53-87.

54. One problem in looking at higher education in other countries is the great variation in the meaning of the term "higher education." In countries under British influence, higher education means universities with a strong "educational" or liberal arts influence. In countries under French "Faculty" influence, higher education means professional or technical training. In this essay we will use the term "higher education" to mean post-secondary education.

55. (Ottawa, Ont.: University of Ottawa Press, 1970).

56. See, for example, the Robbins Report, Great Britain, Committee on Higher Education, *Higher Education* (London: HMSO, 1963).

57. "The Dilution of Academic Power in Canada: The University of Toronto Act," *Minerva* 10 (1972): 242.

58. (Berkeley and Los Angeles: University of California Press, 1950).

59. "British Universities and the Public Purse," *Minerva* 5 (1967): 520.

60. "Government, the University Grants Committee and the Universities," *Minerva* 6 (1968): 244.

61. "The Universities, the Government and the Public Accounts Committee," *Minerva* 6 (1967):28.

62. "The Growth of Federal Power in the West German University System," *Minerva* 9 (1971): 510.

63. (Bombay: Lalvani Publishing House, 1967).

64. *Quest*, Special Number (March 1967), p. 40.

65. "Authoritarian Government and Academic Subservience: The University of Singapore," *Minerva* 10 (1972): 223.

66. "Higher Education and Political Development in Syria and Lebanon," *Comparative Education Review* 10 (1966): 451.

67. (New York: International Council for Educational Development, 1972).

68. *Daedalus,* Journal of the American Academy of Arts and Sciences, 97 (1968).

69. *Comparative Education Review*, the Official Organ of the Comparative Education Society, 10 (1966).

70. (Cambridge, Mass.: Harvard University Press, 1966).

71. Brian Holms and David G. Scanlon, eds. (New York: Harcourt Brace Jovanovich, Inc., 1971).

72. Fred W. Riggs, ed. (Philadelphia: The American Academy of Political and Social Science, 1971).

13

Poverty And Welfare Policy

Theodore Marmor
and
Hugh Heclo

I. Some Preliminary Observations

This subject, like others, grows or contracts with the meaning given to its two principal elements: poverty and welfare. There are among scholars widely different meanings in use, ones that crudely fall into what I will call without pejorative intent the "narrow" and the "broad" views, of both poverty and the governmental policies to ameliorate it.

On the narrow view, poverty is the condition of those at the bottom of the income distribution, with resources that barely if at all provide subsistence. The measure dividing those "in" and "out" of poverty is some level of income, adjusted by family size, below which subsistence is a serious problem. Operationally, researchers employ either the widely advertised poverty line of the Social Security Administration (now just under $4000/year for a family of four) or the level of assistance which local public assistance officials provide eligible families without other income.

"Welfare" policy, on this view, are those government actions which are directed toward relieving the circumstances of poor persons. Those policies are symbolized by public assistance programs, income maintenance measures for the aged, blind, disabled, and fatherless among the poor, and in some states, general assistance relief for those who fall outside these restrictive categories. In addition, a wide variety of other programs redistribute income (either in cash or in kind) to the poor: veterans' programs, social security, medicaid, public housing and home ownership or rent supplement subsidies, etc.

A number of research issues have arisen since the early 1960's for the field so defined. Counting the poor has become the special province of HEW and the Social Security Administration, with OEO and the Census the providers of continuing information on the number, composition, and over-time characteristics of the low-income population. The origins of federal interest in overall policies toward the poor has been well described in at least four scholarly studies: Marris and Rein, *Dilemmas of Social Reform* (Aldine-Atherton, 1968); J. Kershaw, *The War on Poverty* (Mark-

---

Sections I and II of this chapter were authored by Theodore Marmor. Section III was authored by Hugh Heclo.

ham, 1971); G. Steiner, *Social Insecurity: The Polities of Welfare* (Rand McNally, 1966); and Robert Levine's, *The Poor* (MIT Press, 1970).

All of these efforts have concentrated on the government's efforts (or failures) to improve the income position of our poorest citizens. All have documented the fact that programs *for the poor* reach a minority *of the poor*, the result of categorical programs which make the reason for one's poverty—age, disability or the loss of a breadwinner—an additional condition for the receipt of public assistance. This line of research was thoroughly extended by the nearest we have come since the Committee on Economic Security to a Royal Commission on Poverty. The President's Commission on Income Maintenance Programs, initiated in 1968 and reporting in 1970, produced three volumes of substantial interest to scholars concerned about the nature of poverty, the programs that set out to deal with it, and the nature of the choices among new policy alternatives. Its three volumes include one which summarizes the circumstances of the poor and justified a reform through a national negative income tax; the second volume has a comprehensive review of government programs that primarily or importantly redistribute income to the poor; the third has a series of technical papers, including one by Robert Rafuse that analyzes the historical relationship between state and local finance characteristics and public assistance expenditures for the poor.

The Income Maintenance commission summarized the variety of policy dilemmas that confront efforts to make income transfer programs more adequate, more equitable, more humane, and less financially burdensome to the states and localities. The compendium edited by this writer, *Poverty Policy* (Aldine-Atherton, 1971), brings together a dozen of the major policy alternatives—in substantial detail—and attempts to clarify the trade-offs among the competing objectives that in fact bedevil welfare reform.

The fate of welfare reform has been the focus of a number of other studies, some emphasizing the weaknesses of a constituency that is lacking in both resources and sympathy, others dwelling upon the seemingly atypical processes by which the Nixon Family Assistance Plan was authored and blocked in the politics of the congressional finance committees. A number of studies are under way; some, like Gil Steiner's *The State of Welfare* (Brookings, 1971) are finished. A particularly interesting effort by Daniel Patrick Moynihan is now under way arguing that the Nixon welfare reform represented Tory Democracy, the effort to implement liberal goals by conservative politicians, but frustrated by liberal Democrats asking for more than the Congress would give and conservatives of both parties attacking what was offered as too much.

Two other substantial bodies of political science literature have focused on the poor and welfare policy as described above. There is what might be called the "determinants" literature, work which measures welfare policy by expenditures for widely known public assistance policies and seeks to explain the variations in those "policies" by a variety of economic or political factors. A vigorous debate has ensued over whether political differences among the states really make much difference in the level of support for the poor, and the issue is still very much unsettled. A second area of concern has viewed the poor as we have here, but widened the definition of what improves or harms their welfare. Scholars here have concerned themselves with the poor's relation to the political system more widely, the use of protest means to further the interests of low-income people, the limits on those means, and the day-to-day patterns of interaction of the poor with the "street-corner bureaucracy". Sometimes, this interest has emerged from studies of particular policy arenas, like Lawrence Friedman's study of government and slum housing, or Michael Lipsky's study of tenant protest in New York City and San Francisco, or Peter Eisinger's study of poverty agencies as they operated in New York City.

All of these efforts have focused on the circumstances of low-income Americans and how they are helped or hindered by policies promulgated in the name of aiding them. Another wider definition of poverty (and social welfare policy) calls attention to the relations between the destitute and the circumstances of those who conventionally would not be considered poor. Relative poverty, on this view, occurs when income is very unequally distributed, and leads to an interest in income redistribution, greater equity in the tax system, and the search for means of reducing inequality which do not selectively mark out the poor as the recipients of government subsidy.

It will not be possible here to discuss this conception of the policy arena, but it clearly does lead to an emphasis on the variety of ways the government effects the primary distribution of income: through subsidy, regional development efforts, and tax incentives and disincentives. Moreover, it puts at the center of welfare policy the government's role in the redistribution of desired positions, benefits, and power. Welfare, in this view, is well-being, and policy to further it may arise from unfortunate occurrences (social insurance), weakness in the labor market, or an unequal share of national income. The result is a field of inquiry that does not select out particular policies as its subject matter, but aspects of all government policies. The various activities of government—allocating resources, redistributing income, stabilizing economic life—become part of social welfare policy insofar as they change the distribution of income. More on that later.

The fate of welfare programs and the understanding of the causes, and effects of the abortive 1969-72 reform efforts has attracted considerable scholarly attention. The Moynihan study (cited above, Random House, 1973, *The Politics of a Guaranteed Income*) has been complemented in 1974 by two well-researched books on the origins and fate of the Family Assistance Plan.

Nixon's Good Deed (Columbia University Press), by Vincent Burke and Vee Burke, resembles Moynihan's effort to provide an insider's account of why FAP arose and collapsed. But the insiders they relied on differ markedly. Moynihan's is the extensive account of a high official who participated himself in selling welfare reform to Nixon and Congress, backed up by documentary research that concentrated on 1969-70 and paid modest attention to the events of 1972. The Burkes attempted a fuller portrait: The origins of welfare ideas, the bureaucrats and professorial reformers who sustained guaranteed income ideas in the 1960s, and the fate of FAP up to the election of 1972. They have tried to present fairly the diverse views on that happening, but their most distinctive contribution is the fuller presentation of the "insider" federal bureaucrats who nurtured negative income tax ideas in the 1960s and—by stealth as well as analysis—pressed their favorite notions on the new HEW, Labor, and White House officials of 1969. The names of this saga are largely unknown—Bateman, Lyday, Harris of Democratic vintage; Patricelli, Joe, Rosow, Venneman of Republican sub-cabinet position—but their role in the rise of FAP was crucial and the Burkes explain it.

The response of Congress to this unexpected Republican Presidential initiative is the central focus of another new work: Kenneth Bowler's, *The Nixon Guaranteed Income Proposal: Substance and Process in Policy Change* (Ballinger, 1974). Bowler, who as a congressional fellow worked for Ribicoff of Senate Finance and Corman of Ways and Means, has provided a rich, authoritative account of the process by which Ways and Means (and the House) twice passed FAP and the Senate Finance Committee twice did not. Both the Bowler and Burke books add enormously to our knowledge of this issue area; FAP may rival the Cuban Missile Crisis as case study material. See also, on this subject, the work by Joel Handler, the extensive analyses of the special joint Economic Sub-Committee on welfare 1972-74, the writings on welfare reform, and negative income taxation by Walter Williams of the University of Washington and the Rein-Marmor essay on FAP in Sindler (ed.), *Politics and Policy in America* (Little-Brown, 1973), Ch. 1. The revival of interest in welfare reform, sparked both by economic recession and the extraordinary growth of the Food Stamp Program, is illustrated in 1974-75 by a transformed HEW proposal; see Barth, Palmer, et al., *Toward An Effective Income Support System: Problems, Prospects, and Choices* (Poverty Institute, Wisconsin, 1974) for a discussion of the broad features of the suggested 1975 initiative.

II. Basic Facilities and Institutions

There are few facilities that exclusively link political science to the poverty and welfare field.

The committee on Health Politics publishes the *Quarterly Bulletin on Health Politics* under the direction of Professor Ralph Straetz (NYU, 547 LaGuardia Place, NY., N.Y. 10003), a digest of on-going research, a listing of political scientists working on health, and a review of the funding sources in health. This effort is supported by the National Center for Health Services Research and Development through Harris S. Cohen, the acting chief of the Political and Legal Analysis Branch, the section of most interest to political scientists. For regular review of developments in health and health policy politics, see the *Medical Care Review,* published by the School of Public Health at the University of Michigan. This review presents abstracts of articles and testimony elsewhere. Readers might, for international comparison purposes, want to consult the *International Journal of Health Services* out of Johns Hopkins and, for domestic issues, *Medical Care.*

The American Public Health Association regularly has panels devoted to health planning and politics and there are active specialty groups in medical sociology and medical economics that have expanded considerably in recent years. A recent foundation development has thrown up the Johnson Foundation (Princeton, N.J.) as perhaps the major source of research funding outside the federal government. The Johnson Foundation is now one of the three largest foundations in the country and has made medical care and public medical policy its chief focus. The *Social Security Bulletin* and *Welfare in Review* (both HEW) remain the central statistical reporters for the two largest government health programs, Medicare and Medicaid. Readers should also know of three research institutions that have substantial and regular health research under their auspices: The Center for Health Administration Studies, the University of Chicago; The Institute for Interdisciplinary Studies, 124 E. Grant St., Minneapolis, Minn. 55401; and the Rand Corporation, Santa Monica, the site of a newly initiated, long-term experiment with alternate national health insurance models, funded by OEO.

The largest research center for poverty issues is the Institute for Research on Poverty, the University of Wisconsin. The institute has concentrated on economic research and on supervising large-scale experiments with negative income tax plans in rural and urban areas. But it also funds sociological, legal and political analyses at Wisconsin—with some short-term fellows as well—and has a very extensive set of discussion papers and reprints available upon request. The Wisconsin group, the Urban Institute and Brookings Institution in Washington have been over the past half-decade the site of the most extensive work in welfare programs, welfare reforms, and poverty research. Government research support is most concentrated at OEO, the Department of Labor, and the Social and Rehabilitation Services division of HEW. The Metro section of the National

Institute of Mental Health—headed by Elliott Liebow—is interested in somewhat broader aspects of poverty and has an active research funding program.

A number of professional journals have greatly expanded their publication of poverty-related articles, but the *Journal of Human Resources* (Wisconsin: Robert Lampman, editor) has made health, education, and welfare-poverty its central focus for some time. Northwestern Law School, through its *Clearinghouse Review,* monitors developments in the courts, public interest law firms, and OEO legal research backup centers that bear on the treatment of impoverished or welfare citizens in re welfare, housing, consumer problems, employment, legal aid, criminal prosecution and family matters. The most recent case book in the field is Levy, Lewis, and Martin, *Social Welfare and the Individual* (The Foundation Press, 1971), an invaluable text for problems in the administration of current income support and social service programs.

For those interested in Western Europe: the Ford Foundation has recently funded the Council on European Studies (Steve Blank, Director, University of Pittsburgh); the council will through its newsletter and grant assistance efforts try to assist scholars in the poverty and welfare field, graduate students seeking language training, and has offices abroad to assist in the conduct of research.

III. Comparative Poverty and Welfare Policy

Americans who travel to developed nations and inquire about issues of welfare and poverty policy are likely to be perplexed. Other nations affluent enough to worry about poverty are not likely to feel particularly absorbed by questions of "the poor," poverty income lines, and welfare rolls. Interest is likely to center on broader conceptions of income inequality, more general questions of social servicing, and steadier attention to the "at risk" or potentially eligible population for social provision. In short, important research and debate abroad encompasses poverty/welfare policy within a larger view of social policy. Here we can only highlight a small amount of the immense work underway.

A. *Income Inequality*

Undoubtedly the most thorough and rigorous empirical investigation of social inequality in any nation is the work of the recently disbanded Swedish Low Income Commission (Laginkomstutredningen). Taking a broad conception on income, the investigation conducted and commissioned a mass of research—ranging from time-series studies on the postwar distribution of disposable income among different age-group cohorts, to surveys of the differences in the population's living standards, to a study of inequality in the distribution of political resources. During the last five years, the Commission's results have gradually emerged in a series of government publications; one of the recent core volumes reports the results of a survey into the national distribution of purchasing power in 1967 and serves as a useful introduction (*Den Svenska Kopkraftsfordelningen*, Staten Offentlige Utredningar, 1971: 39). Unfortunately, only very brief English summaries of all these studies are available at the present time.

The implications of this work are, of course, considerable. The Commission emerged from dissidents' efforts within the Social Democratic Party and Trade Union Congress (LO) and has expressed as well as helped mold the movements' campaign for "increased equality." Termination of the Commission's life in 1971, as well as a rash of Swedish strikes (as LO has tried to follow the necessary implications of the campaign and narrow wage differentials) suggest the controversial and important issues being raised. Important follow-up studies on the distribution of welfare are underway at the Central Statistical Office and Social Research Institute at Stockholm University.

Most research in Sweden, as elsewhere, has dealt with the impact of government programs by inference, showing persisting social inequities despite the host of welfare state interventions. In every country, the operating environment of social policy is essentially a mystery surrounded by profound and abiding ignorance about the human beings who are allegedly to benefit: What are their serious problems? How do individuals try to solve them? How well do they succeed? How far are existing state agencies actually contributing to successful solutions? Recent research from the Danish Social Research Institute offers some of the first systematic evidence on these questions. (Socialforskningsinstituttet, *Socialreform Undersogelserne*, 3 volumes, Copenhagen: Teknisk Forlag, 1971). The Danish research is based on a sample of the population which was interviewed and re-interviewed at intervals over almost two years and drawn from the national pool of persons hit by income loss ("social accidents") due to sickness, unemployment, breadwinner's death, divorce, separation, or pregnancy outside marriage. The results show in unprecedented depth how the social policy process constitutes a sorting mechanism which secures certain persons direct access to public help and confronts others with the requirement of self-help under unrealistic conditions.

B. *Social Insurance*

Important questions of welfare policy can be discovered to be continually under study in every nation's social security (or as it is more commonly labelled abroad, social insurance) network. Descriptive facts can be garnered from the US Social Security Administration's periodic publication, *Social Security Throughout the World,* or from reports of the Research Section of the International Social Security Association in Geneva. For substantial detail and an introduction to actual practice, however, there is no substitute for the deeper studies which national government's occasionally undertake. One of the most interesting in recent years is the 1972 *Report of the New Zealand Royal Commission of Inquiry on Social Security.* Unlike many nations, New Zealand (and Australia) have traditionally relied heavily on means-and income-tested income maintenance programs financed out of general tax revenue. The Report of the Royal Commission summarizes evidence on how this "non-contributory" system is adapting and consolidating its selective approach to the changes wrought by postwar affluence.

Comparisons do not come ready-made, but national monographic research can provide useful raw materials. Norway, with its immense contributory social insurance machine, stands at something of the opposite extreme to Australia and New Zealand. Located at Oslo University, the Norwegian Institutt for Anvendt Socialvitenskapelig Forskning has undertaken an extensive program of research into changing social-economic conditions in Norway. National records from the family allowances program, for example, have proved an important point of departure for gathering hitherto unknown information about the use of Norwegian welfare state programs.

C. Social Policy Analysis

Although most such research constitutes little more than a descriptive mapping of people, programs, and occasionally their interaction, it is an essential first step in any comparative analysis of social policy which aspires to do more than repeat the slogans which every ministry's public relations office prepares for foreigners. Moreover, even these descriptions usually address questions with profound practical meaning in national societies, questions apart from which formalistic policy comparisons may be fanciful and irrelevant. Swedish research, for example, directly addresses the matter of where and how to draw boundaries in a conception of poverty which aims to go beyond absolute subsistance minima but stop short of complete uniformity. Danish research implicates the entire substance of state responsibility for offering opportunities and choices on self-help that are realistic possibilities rather than administrative dodges.

New Zealand discussion, by proposing consolidated benefits for a variety of family types, reraises issues about the justification for differential treatment of widowed, unmarried, divorced, separated mothers—and possibly fathers. The report of the British Committee on One-Parent Families (Cmnd. 5629, Department of Health and Social Security), as well reports to the 12th Conference of European Ministers responsible for Family Affairs (Stockholm, 1971), are analyses concerned with how far equity consists in treating single parent families as special and how far in treating all families the same. Similarly, the many divorce and marital law commissions which have been and are meeting in numerous nations elaborate the tensions between strict sexual equality and family responsibility.

Great Britain has again emerged as a particularly fertile ground for social policy analysis. In 1972 the Conservative Heath Government brought forward plans for the world's first national system of negative income taxation (called tax credit in Britain). Those whose tax credit exceeds their tax liability would receive a positive cash payment from the state. While, unlike the US, there are few pretensions that the tax credit scheme will eliminate the need for public relief (Supplementary Benefit) or somehow solve poverty, the plan has activated public debate and academic research into general problems of national income maintenance. The changes being worked out in Britain are rightly labelled as the most important policy innovations since Beveridge.

Possibilities for more continuous social policy analysis and a forum for interchange between academic and official research and thinking have been improved in Britain by the founding at the end of 1971 of the Centre for Studies in Social Policy. Funded by the Rowntree Trust, the Centre is an independent body with close ties to government and academic institutions. Where or how it will develop its studies of social policies remains to be seen, but with the strong influence of ex-civil servants, the Centre's relation to policy praxis is likely to be prominent.

Few strictly academic studies can match the analysis of reflective participants who have left the heat of battle; even more informative is the ex-civil servant who is willing to discuss the politics as well as substance of social policy. Such works are rare, but a recent volume by Sir John Wally, a retired Deputy Secretary with over forty years direct policy involvement, fills the bill admirably. (*Social Security; Another British Failure?* London: Knight and Sons, 1972). It, along with Bentley Gilbert's volumes (*The Evolution of National Insurance,* London: Michael Joseph, 1966; and *British Social Policy, 1914-1939,* London: Batsford, 1970) are essential for understanding the background of British social policy during this century. More important, Wally identifies both the inescapable policy issues in any system of income maintenance and the peculiar constraints which a nation's social policy inheritance imposes. Programs and mechanisms are not exportable from the home of the "Welfare State"; good sense in drawing lessons from the experience of social policy may, however, teach by example.

Indexes

Index of Names

Aaron, Henry, 33, 34
Abel-Smith, Brian, 59
Abrams, Mark, 60, 149
Adelman, Irma, 26, 34
Adorno, Theodore W., 136
Albertini M., 44, 45
Aldous, Tony, 56
Alexander, Herbert, 122, 131
Alexander, James R., 74
Alford, Robert, 128
Allardt, Erik, 128, 130
Allison, Graham T., 73
Almond, Gabriel, 67, 135, 139
Ambler, John, 74
Andenaes, J., 169
Anderson, C. A., 186, 195
Anderson, James E., xii, 109-118
Andes, John O., 196
Andrews, Wililliam, 119, 131
Angell, Norman, 156
Angell, Robert C., 151
Antonovsky, Aaron, 144
Aquina, Herman, 45
Arian, Alan, 129, 144
Arrow, Kenneth J., 38, 46
Ashby, Sir Eric, 190, 192, 193
Ashford, Douglas, 32
Atkinson, Tom, 140
Aubert, Vilhelm, 169
Ault, Gary, 34
Ayres, Richard E., 131

Baer, Michael, 194
Bain, Joe S., 87
Bain, Richard, 123, 132
Baldini, Nullo, 42
Banks, Arthur, 34
Banta, John S., 99
Banton, M., 60
Barber, James David, 153
Barnes, Samuel, 129
Barton, Allen H., 148
Bashshur, Minir, 191
Bateman, Worth, 40, 202
Bauer, Raymond A., 140, 149
Baumol, William, 39
Bay, Christian, 101
Bazelon, Judge D., 104
Beal, George M., 133
Becherman, Wilfred, 56
Beck, Carl, 127, 145
Becker, Theodore, 19, 31

Beer, Samuel, 124
Bell, Wendell, 148
Beloff, Max, 189
Benstock, Marcy, 86
Bentham, Jeremy, 3
Berdahl, Robert O., 189
Berelson, Bernard, 134
Berg, Leila, 187, 196
Bergson, Abram, 26, 34
Berkman, Paul L., 144
Bernstein, Marver, 118
Best, James J., 135
Bish, Robert L., 46
Black, Duncan, 38, 46
Blank, Blanche, 76
Blank, Steve, 204
Blaug, Mark, 187, 196
Blucher, Viggo Graf, 144
Blumler, Jay G., 60
Bobbio, N., 41, 46
Bobrow, Davis B., 140
Bode, Kenneth, 124
Bogart, Leo, 140
Bonilla, Frank, 149
Booms, Bernard, 30
Booth, Charles, 58
Bos, H. C., 187, 196
Bosanquet, Nicholas, 56
Bottomore, T. B., 146
Bowden, Lord, 190
Bowen, Frank M., 178
Bowen, William G., 131
Bower, B. T., 97
Brady, Linda P., 35
Brand, J. A., 60
Bratholm, 169
Braybrooke, David, 61, 66
Brembeck, C. S., 195
Brewer, Thomas L., 151
Brody, Richard A., 151
Brooks, Ralph M., 133
Bruner, Jerome S., 136
Buchanan, James M., 37, 38, 39, 42, 46
Buchanan, William, 139
Bullitt, William C., 152
Burgess, Philip M., 133
Burke, Vee, 202
Burke, Vincent, 201
Burnham, Walter Dean, 120
Burton, Ian, 88
Burton, John W., 153
Butler, David, 129

Butwell, Richard, 132
Byung-kyu-Woo, 148

Cairns, Paul, 106
Caldwell, Lynton, 84, 87, 97, 99
Campbell, Angus, 131
Campbell, Donald T., 30, 38, 46
Campbell, R. F., 186, 193
Canon, Bradley C., 116
Cantril, Hadley, 135, 139, 140
Cape, Jonathan, 16
Cardozo, Benjamin N., 187, 196
Casey, Ralph D., 139
Cater, Douglass, 87
Cattaneo, Carlo, 42
Cerych, Ladislav, 195
Chambers, M. M., 183
Chapman, Brian, 66
Charlot, Jean, 143
Chittick, William O., 136, 149
Chong Lim Kim, 148
Christie, 169
Christoph, James B., 78
Clark, Ramsey, 119
Clarke, James W., 17, 29, 170
Cleary, Edward J., 86
Clegg, H. A., 60
Coase, R. H., 39, 40
Cohen, Bernard C., 135, 150
Cohen, Steven, 76
Cole, Allan B., 144
Coleman, James, 23, 39, 107
Congalton, A. A., 145
Connery, Robert H., 118
Conrad, John, 161-174
Converse, Philip, 129, 131
Cook, Thomas J., xi, 17-24, 30, 31, 32
Cooley, Richard, 85, 87
Coombs, P. H., 186, 195
Coons, John, 103, 107
Cornish, 170
Correa, Hector, 187, 196
Cottrell, Leonard S., Jr., 140
Crecine, John P., 40
Crenson, Matthew A., 87
Crewe, Ivor, 146
Crick, B., 56
Cristiansen, Bjorn, 136
Crossman, Richard, 16
Crotty, William, 119-132
Crozier, Michel, 43, 46, 65, 67
Cutright, Phillips, 33

Daadler, Hans, 129
Dahl, Robert A., 67
Dante, 156
Darby, John, 60

David, Paul, 123, 132
Davies, J. Clarence, 84
Davies, R., 60
Davis, Bruce E., 140
Davis, David Howard, 118
Davis, Kenneth C., 107, 117
Davis, Otto, 40
Dawson, Richard, 17, 29
De Jouvenel, Bertrand, 44
Delorme, Henene, 143
Denitch, Bogdan, 148
de Rivera, Joseph, 137
Derivry, Daniel, 78
Derthick, Martha, 72
de Sola Pool, Ithiel, 140, 147, 149, 150, 151
Deutsch, Karl, 107, 149, 150, 156
Devine, Donald J., 140
Dexter, Lewis Anthony, 140, 148, 149
Diamant, Alfred, 41, 44, 46, 69-80
Dickson, Paul, 15
Diez-Hochleitner, 186
Dobgerkery, S. R., 191
Dogan, Mattei, 78, 128
Dolbeare, Kenneth, 31
Donnison, David, 59
Doob, Leonard W., 153
Downs, Anthony, 38, 46
Dror, Yehezkel, 3-16
Duchene, F., 59
Dulles, John Foster, 150
Dunn, William L., 15
Dunphy, Dexter C., 151
Duverger, Maurice, 130
Dye, Thomas, 3, 17, 18, 29, 30, 32

Easton, David, xii, 17, 128, 175, 176
Eberhart, Sylvia, 140
Eckhardt, William, 137, 155
Eckstein, Otto, 33
Edinger, Lewis J., 74, 147, 148, 149, 152, 153
Eide, K., 186, 195
Eisinger, Peter, 201
Eliot, Thomas, 175
Elvander, Nils, 45
Elvin, H. L., 186, 195
Englebert, Ernest, 86
Epstein, Leon, 177
Erikson, Robert S., 140
Esposito, John C., 87
Etzioni, Amitai, 32
Eulau, Heinz, 29, 176, 177
Everts, Philip P., 157
Eyestone, Robert, 29

Fagen, Richard R., 150
Fairweather, George W., 46
Falk, Richard A., 87

Fallows, James J., 87
Farah, Barbra, 129
Fegiz, Pierpaolo Luzzatto, 143
Feierabend, Ivo, 101, 124, 132
Feierabend, R. L., 132
Fenton, John H., 29
Fesler, James W., 71
Finlay, David J., 150
Fisk, Donald H., 30
Flanagan, Scott, 67, 101
Floyd, Carol Everly, 177, 193
Fogelman, E., 101
Foss, Philip, 85
Foster, Philip, 187, 195
Fowler, Edmund, 29
Fraser, 123
Frederickson, H. George, 69-80
Free, Lloyd A., 140, 148
Freeman, Myrick, 84
Frenkel-Brunswik, Else, 136
Freud, Sigmund, 152
Frey, Frederick W., 28, 35, 147
Fried, Robert C., 33
Friedman, Lawrence, 201
Friedman, S., 99
Friedrich, Hannes, 15
Frisch, Helmut, 44
Frolich, Norman, 33, 40
Fry, Bryan R., 29, 33
Fuller, Edgar, 179

Gallpu, George, 138, 139
Galnoor, Itzhak, 16
Galtung, Johan, 137, 157
Gardiner, John A., xi, 161-174
George, Alexander L., 150, 153
George, Juliette L., 153
Giddens, Anthony, 146
Gilbert, Bentley, 207
Gilmour, Robert S., 118
Glad, Betty, 153
Glasman, N. S., 187, 196
Glass, Gene V., 30
Goldman, Ralph M., 123, 132
Gorden, Morton, 149
Gordon, Robert J., 41
Gouldner, Alvan, 170
Gove, Samuel, xii, 175-198
Graber, Doris A., 136
Green, Mark J., 118
Green, Philip, 32, 157
Greenfield, K. R., 42, 46
Gregg, Phillip, xii
Grigg, 101, 106
Gross, Betram, 76
Grossman, David, 176
Groth, Alexander J., 25, 63

Gurin, 107
Gurr, Ted, 101, 106

Haas, Ernst B., 156
Habermas, Jurgen, 135, 141
Hack, Walter G., 196
Haefele, Edwin, 84
Haveman, Robert, 84
Hagevik, George H., 87
Hagstrom, Warren, 106
Halberstam, David, 146
Halloran, James D., 60
Hallstein, W., 44, 46
Halpin, A. W., 196
Hamilton, Hamish, 16
Hanson, J. W., 195
Harbison, Frederick, 186, 195
Harman, G. S., 188, 197
Harris, Joseph, 119, 131, 202
Harris, Louis, 126
Hart, Henry, 86
Haskell, Elizabeth, 85
Hayek, F. A., 47
Hayes, Samuel P., 88
Head, Kendra, 137
Heady, Bruce, 78
Heard, Alexander, 122, 131
Heclo, Hugh, 16, 199-208
Heidenheimer, Arnold J., 33, 34, 74
Henderson, J. M., 30
Henderson, Keith M., 76
Hennessy, Bernard C., 135
Henning, D. H., 97
Hermann, Charles F., 34, 35, 151, 152
Hermann, Margaret G., 35
Hero, Alfred O., Jr., 140
Hersberg, Donald, 119
Hilton, Gordon, 151
Himmelstrand, 130
Hinich, Melvin J., 46
Hirsch, Werner, 40
Hitler, Adolf, 155
Hochman, Harold, 40
Hodder-Williams, Richard, 143
Hofferbert, Richard I., 17, 29, 30
Hofstetter, Richard, 128
Hogan, James B., 33
Hoggan, Daniel, 85
Hoggard, Gary, 33
Holden, Matthew, 84
Hollenhorst, Jerry, 34
Holler, Frederick, 133
Holms, Brian, 198
Holsti, Ole R., 150, 151
Holt, Robert, 33, 35
Hoogerwerf, Andries, 45
Hosoya, Chihiro, 150

Hu, Teh-Wei, 30
Hudson, Michael, 35
Huitt, Ralph, 115
Humphrey, Hubert, 126
Hunter, Robert E., 160
Hurtubise, Rene, 189
Husen, Torsten, 186, 195
Hyman, Herbert, 30, 106

Iannaccone, Laurence, 194
Ilchman, Warren F., 87
Inglehard, Ronald, 129
Inkeles, Alex, 144
Irwin, Frances, 90
Isard, Walter, 140
Isserlis, A. S., 60

Jacob, Herbert, 17, 19, 29, 31, 32
Jaeggi, Urs, 146
James, Dorothy, xi
Janda, Kenneth, 125, 128, 130, 132
Janne, Henri, 44
Janowitz, Morris, 134
Jennings, Kent, 129
Jensen, Lloyd, 107, 149
Jewell, Malcolm, 29
Joe, 202
Johns, Roe L., 194, 196
Johnson, Harry, 41
Johnson, Lyndon B., 119
Johnson, Ralph W., 99
Jones, Charles O., 91
Jones, P. E., 185, 194, 195
Jones, Susan D., 133
Jones, W. H. Morris, 59
Jouvenel, B., 47

Kadushin, Charles, 148
Kammerer, Gladys, 177
Kant, Immanuel, 156
Katona, George, 32
Katz, 107
Kaufman, Herbert, 85, 163
Keller, Suzanne, 146
Kelley, Stanley, Jr., 119, 131
Kelly, D. R., 98
Kelman, Herbert C., 137, 154
Kennedy, John F., 119, 124
Kennedy, Robert, 124, 125
Kennet, Lord, 44
Kershaw, J., 199
Kessler, Allan, 151
Kessler, Marie-Christine, 78
Key, V. O. Jr., 29, 123, 134
Kim, O., 129
Kimbrough, Ralph B., 196
King, Martin Luther, 124

Kirkham, J., 132
Kirst, Michael W., 176, 193, 194
Kirton, M. J., 145
Klonglan, Gerald E., 133
Kloss, G., 190, 191
Kneese, Allen, 39, 84, 97
Knight, Frank, 39
Knutson, Jeanne N., 153
Konz, Peider, 172
Koolman, Jan, 45
Kracauer, Siegfried, 144
Krislov, Samuel, 101-108
Kronhausen, Edward, 106
Kronhausen, Phyllis, 106
Krutilla, John V., 39
Kurth, James R., 41

Lall, Betty G., 160
Lampman, Robert, 204
Landecker, Manfred, 136
Landis, James M., 109
Lane, Robert E., 134, 137
Langer, Walter C., 153
LaPalombara, Joseph, 33, 41, 47, 76, 80
Lasswell, Harold, 6, 13, 14, 37, 41, 47, 136, 139, 146, 147, 150, 151, 152
Laulicht, Jerome, 141, 149
Lautman, Jacques, 78
Lawton, Raymond W., 133
Lazarsfeld, Paul, 30
Lebrun, Achille, 143
Lee, Eugene, 178
Legg, Keith R., 34
Leiden, Carl, 124, 132
Leites, Nathan, 150
Lemelin, Claude, 141
Lentz, F., 137
Leon, P., 47
Leoni, B., 41, 43, 44, 47
Lepawsky, Albert, 86
Lerner, Daniel, 41, 47, 147, 149
Lescohier, Mary Amend, 40
Levin, Martin A., 31
Levine, J. P., 106
Levine, Robert, 200
Levinson, Daniel J., 136
Levy, S., 132, 204
Lewis, 204
Liebow, Elliott, 204
Lijphart, Arend, 45
Lindblom, Charles, 33, 47, 61, 66, 72, 187, 196
Lineberry, Robert, xii, 29
Linz, Juan, 128
Lippmann, Walter, 134
Lipset, Seymour, 101, 128, 130
Lipsky, Michael, 32, 201

Little, Alan, 60
Lockard, Duane, 29
Lodge, Milton C., 151
Lodge, Thomas, 170
Lompe, Klaus, 15
Lowenthal, David, 88
Lowi, Theodore J., 41, 44, 47, 71, 107
Luhman, Niklas, 135, 141
Lundqvist, Lennart, 45, 83-100
Luttbeg, Norman R., 136, 140
Lyday, 202
Lyden, Fremont J., 72

Maass, Arthur, 86
Masse, Pierre, 76
MacAvoy, Paul, 115
Mack, Raymond, 101, 106
MacRae, Duncan, 40
Macridis, Roy C., 33, 149
Mancke, Richard B., 118
Mann, Dean, 83-100
Mann, Lawrence, 185
Margolis, Julius, 40
Marini, Frank, 71, 73
Marion, Jean-Claude, 141
Markel, Lester, 135
Marmor, Theodore, 199-208
Marris, 199
Marshall, Hubert, 86
Marshall, T. H., 56
Martin, Roscoe, 86, 204
Masotti, Louis, xii
Masters, Nicholas, 194
Mathiesen, 169
Matthews, Donald R., 147
Mayer, Martin, 107
Mazlish, Bruce, 153
McClelland, Charles, 33
McClosky, Herbert, 101, 106
McGee, Gale 121
McGovern, George, 123
McGowan, Patrick J., 142
McKean, Roland, 40
McKechnie, J. Thomas, 145
McKibbin, C. R., 177
McKinley, Charles, 86
Meehan, Eugene J., 47
Meehl, Paul, 104, 107
Mekeirle, J. O., 99
Mendel, Douglas H., Jr., 144
Merritt, Anna J., 142
Merritt, Richard, xi, 35, 133-159
Meyhew, Lewis B., 183
Michelat, Guy, 143
Michelena, Jose A. Silva, 149
Michels, R., 41, 43, 47
Miller, D. W., 187, 196

Miller, Ernest G., 72
Miller, Warren, 107, 128, 129, 131
Milliman, Jerome W., 40
Mills, C. Wright, 146
Mitchell, Joyce, 33
Mitchell, William, 33
Modelski, George, 149
Mondale, Walter, 180
Montemartini, G., 43, 47
Moos, Malcolm, 123, 132
Morgan, Robert, 85
Morganstern, Oskar, 35
Morphet, Edgar L., 194, 196
Morris, Cynthia Taft, 26, 34
Mosca, Gaetano, 41, 42, 43, 44, 47, 146
Mosher, Edith K., 193
Mosher, Frederick C., 70
Moskos, Charles C., Jr., 140
Moulin, Leo, 78
Moynihan, Daniel Patrick, 200, 202
Mueller, Dennis C., 40
Mueller, John E., 141
Mulkey, Michael, xi
Mundt, Robert, 67
Murphy, Walter, 106
Myrdal, Gunnar, 102

Nadel, Mark, 118
Nader, Ralph, 86
Nagel, Stuart S., xi, 20, 23, 31
Nakanishi, Naomichi, 144
Namenwirth, J. Zvi, 151
Nash, Roderick, 88
Neale, A. D., 118
Nesvold, Betty, 101
Neumann, Erich Peter, 142
Newland, Chester, 116
Niskanen, William A., 38, 48
Nixon, Richard, 112, 126, 200, 202
Noelle, Elisabeth, 142
Nordlinger, Eric A., 26, 34
North, Robert C., 147, 151
Nottage, Raymond, 59
Nozhko, K., 196

Ogden, Daniel M., 87
Ogilvie, Daniel M., 151
Olson, Mancur, 37, 39, 42, 48
Oppenheimer, Joseph A., 40
Orcutt, Alice G., 32
Orcutt, Guy H., 32
Ordeshook, Peter, 46
Orvik, Nils, 143
Osculati, F., 43, 48
Osgood, Charles E., 157
Ostrogorski, 41

Ostrom, Elinor, 32, 40, 48
Ostrom, Vincent, xii, 37-50, 84

Pantaleoni, M., 42, 43, 48
Pareto, Vilfredo, 3, 38, 42, 43, 48, 146
Parris, Henry, 60
Parsons, Talcott, 187, 195
Patricelli, 202
Patterson, Samuel C., 31, 128
Paul, John, 141, 149
Peacock, Alan, 59
Pearson, Jim B., 179
Perez, Rita, 44, 48
Perkins, James A., 192
Peters, B. Guy, 33, 34
Peterson, Robert L., 149
Phillipart, Andre, 99
Piekalkiewicz, Jaroslaw A., 144
Pierce, Milo C., 183
Pierce, Roy, 129
Pinder, J., 60
Plowden, William, 15
Pollitt, Christopher, 16
Posner, Richard A., 40, 118
Presthus, Robert, 146
Prezzolini, G., 48
Pride, Cletis, 184
Prothro, James, 101, 106
Pryor, Frederic, 25
Puccetti, Roland, 191
Puchala, Donald J., 136, 141
Putnam, Robert, 45, 77
Pye, Lucian W., 46

Quinley, Harold, 177
Quinn, Frank, 88

Radzinowicz, Sir Leon, 171
Rafuse, Robert, 100
Rakoff, Stuart H., 15
Randall, R. S., 106
Ranney, Austin, 32, 84, 123, 124
Rapoport, Anatol, 157
Raser, John R., 146
Rauta, I., 143
Rawls, John, 38, 48
Reagan, Michael, 69-80
Rein, 199
Reller, Theodore L., 194
Ribiera, C. Flexa, 186, 195
Richardson, Lewis Frye, 156
Ridley, F. F., 79, 80
Riemer, Reynold A., 74
Riggs, Fred W., 76, 198
Riker, William, 38, 39, 48
Rimlinger, Gaston V., 33
Roberts, Marc, 84

Robgy, 107
Robinson, E. A. G., 195
Robinson, James, 17, 29
Robinson, John P., 137, 140
Robson, W. A., 56
Rogow, Arnold A., 153
Rokkan, Stein, 35, 63, 67, 128, 130, 141
Romagnosi, Giandomenico, 42
Rooney, John, 116
Roosevelt, Theodore, 153
Rose, Richard, 41, 45, 48, 51-67
Rosenau, James N., 33, 135, 137, 146, 149
Rosenbaum, Alan, 177
Rosenblum, Victor, 177
Rosow, 202
Ross, H. Lawrence, 30
Ross, Murray, 189
Rossi, Peter, 23
Rossolillo, F., 44, 45, 48
Rothwell, C. Easton, 146
Rourke, Francis E., 73, 107
Rowat, Donald C., 189
Ruckmann, Kurt, 141
Rusk, Jerrold G., 129, 137
Russett, Bruce, 26, 34

Saarinen, Tom, 88
Sabetti, Philip, 37-50
Salmore, Barbara, 17, 24-35
Salmore, Stephen, 17, 24-35
Sand, Peter H., 98
Sanford, R. Nevitt, 136
Sarlvik, Bo. 129
Sartori, G., 41, 48, 130
Sax, Joseph, 86
Scanlon, David G., 198
Schaefer, Guenther F., 15
Scheuch, Erwin K., 35
Schiff, Ashley, 85
Schiller, Herbert I., 157
Scioli, Frank, xi
Schmidtchen, Gerhard, 142
Schueller, George K., 147
Schmiedeskamp, Jay, 32
Schultz, Theodore, 39, 186, 195
Schwartz, Mildred A., 141
Schweigler, Gebhard, 143
Scioli, Frank P., Jr., 17-24, 30, 31, 32
Scott, Robert E., 184
Scott, William A., 140
Scoville, Herbert, Jr., 160
Searing, Donald D., 148
Sears, David O., 134
Seidman, David, 31
Seidman, Harold, 73
Seligman, Lester G., 148
Selvin, Hanan C., 101, 106

Sereno, Renzo, 146, 147
Sewell, W. R. Derrick, 88
Shannon, Jasper, 122, 131
Sharkansky, Ira, 3, 15, 17, 18, 29, 30, 62, 66
Shaver, Phillip R., 137
Shaw, Stella, 58, 67
Sheatsley, Paul, 106
Shils, 107
Shonfield, Andrew, 58, 59, 67
Simon, Frances, 170
Simon, Herbert, 39, 72
Simon, Rita James, 140
Singer, J. David, 133, 151, 156
Singh, Amrik, 191
Siwek-Pouydesseau, Jeanne, 78
Small, Melvin, 156
Smith, Adam, 37
Smith, Bruce Lannes, 139
Smith, Chitra M., 139
Smith, M. Brewster, 136
Smith, Marshall S., 151
Smithburg, Donald, 72
Solomon, Barbara Whiteside, 177
Spiegel, John, 152
Spreafico, A., 43, 49
Springer, Beverly J., 74
Sprout, Harold, 87
Sprout, Margaret, 87
Stanworth, Philip, 146
Starr, M. K., 187, 196
Stauffer, 101
Stein, Harold, 70
Steiner, Gilbert, 72, 200
Stewart, William H., 86
Stigler, George S., 39
Stogdill, Ralph M., 147
Stokes, Donald, 129, 131
Stone, I., 152
Stone, Philip J., 151
Stoppino, Mario, 47
Strunk, 139
Suchman, Edward A., 30, 49
Suleiman, Ezra, 74
Sullivan, John D., 151
Szass, Thomas, 104, 107

Tanenhaus, Joseph, 106
Tavernier, Yves, 143
Taylor, Charles L., 35
Textor, Robert, 34
Thoenig, Jean-Claude, 78
Thomas, Jean-Pierre Hubert, 143
Thomas, Norman C., 118
Thompson, Victor, 72
Tillett, 123, 132
Tinbergen, J., 187, 196
Titmuss, Richard, 59

Tocqueville, A., de., 41, 43, 49
Tollison, Robert D., 40
Townsend, A., 60
Townsend, Peter, 56
Treves, R., 41, 49
Tsantis, Andreas C., 26, 34
Tsuru, S., 98
Tucker, Joseph, 177, 193
Tufte, Edward, xi
Tullock, Gordon, 37, 38, 39, 40, 46, 49
Turner, John, 33, 35
Turot, P., 43, 49

Utton, Albert, 97

Vaizey, J. E., 195
Venneman, 202
Von Bertalanffy, Ludwig, 18, 30
Von Stein, 3
Vroom, Victor H., 147

Wagner, Richard E., 49
Waldo, Dwight, 71, 73, 76
Walker, Jack, 18, 39
Walker, Nigel, 171
Walker, William, 175-198
Wally, Sir John, 207
Wandesforde-Smith, Geoffrey, 83-100
Wasby, Stephen L., 19, 31
Watts, William, 140
Weber, Max, 38
Wedge, Bryant, 153
Wengert, Norman, 83, 86
Wexler, Anne, 120
Whitaker, Urban, 140
White, Gilbert, 88
White, Michael J., 14
White, Robert W., 136
Wilcox, Allen R., 140
Wilcox, Leslie D., 133
Wildavsky, Aaron, 16, 40
Wildenmann, Rudolf, 147, 148
Wilkie, James M., 33
Wilkinfeld, Jonathan, 34
Willett, Thomas D., 40, 41
Williams, Alan, 59
Williamson, Oliver E., 49
Wilson, James Q., 162
Wilson, Thomas Woodrow, 152
Winters, Richard, 29, 33
Wirt, Frederick, xii, 175-198
Wiseman, Jack, 59
Wishner, 106
Withey, Stephen B., 140
Wolfenstein, E. Victor, 153
Wolpert, Julian, 140
Worswick, G. D. N., 59

Wright, Charles, 30
Wright, Deil S., 73
Wright, Quincy, 156

Yetton, Philip Y., 147
Young, Oren, 40

Zaninovich, M. George, 151
Zeigler, Harmon, 194
Zinnes, Dina A., 151
Zonis, Marvin, 148
Zwick, David, 86

Index of Subjects

Academic perspectives on comparative policy studies, 57-59
Administering public policy, 69-80
    Bureaucracy and administration in Western Europe, 73-75
    Controversial issues, 70-73
    Methodology, 75-76
    Periodicals, 79-80
    Planning, 76-77
    Political role of elite administrators, 77-79
    Relations between policy and administration, 69-70
    Research sources, 73
Administrative Conference of the United States, 116-117
Administrators of public policy, 69-70, 73-75, 77-79
Africa, 193
Agriculture and Consumer Protection Act, 114
Agriculture, economic regulation of, 114
Air pollution, 87, 96
American Bar Association, 163, 168
American Bar Foundation, 105
American Civil Liberties Union, 105
American Political Science Association, xii, xiii, 58, 127
American Sociological Association, xiii
Amish education, 103
Antitrust Division, 112, 116
Antitrust, economic regulation, 111-112
Applied Policy Studies Directory, xiii
Arab oil boycott, 113
Arms Control and Disarmament Agency, 27
Assassination, 124-125
Attitudes toward public policy, 134-145
Australia, 206

Backgrounds, social, and foreign policy, 147-148
Behavior, foreign policy leaders, 152-153
Brazil, 9
Britain, 9, 11, 12, 13, 26, 42, 52, 53, 54, 55, 57, 58, 60, 189, 207
    Centre for Studies in Social Policy, 207
    Research on crime control, 170-171
    Resources for policy studies, 54-61
    Welfare policies, 207
Bureaucracy, 37, 38, 43, 70, 73-75, 77, 200
Burger Court, 103

Canada, 8, 26, 141, 189

Carnegie Commission, 178
Case approach to policy study, 70
Catholic Church, 52
Causes of government policies, xi
Celler Antimerger Act, 112
Censorship of media, 102
Center for Political Studies, 128
Center for Constitutional Rights, 105
Challenge of policy science, 4-6
Citizen participation, 4, 71
Civil Aeronautics Board, 110
Civil liberties policy, xi, 101-107
Civil rights movement, xii
Coleman Report, 102
Commissions, regulatory, 109-110
Common Cause, 120
Community tolerance for free speech, 101
Comparative public policy, 12-13, 24-25, 51-67
    Administering public policy, 69-80
    Concepts for comparison, 61-66
        The policy process model, 61-66
    Criminal justice policy, 168-173
    Cross-cultural policy studies, 12-13
    Cross-national policy studies, problems in research, 28-29
    Educational policy, 184-188
    Electoral policy, 128-131
    Elites, 145-147
    Environmental policy, 93-97
    Foreign policy, 27, 139-145
    Poverty and welfare, 204-208
    Resources for policy studies in Britain, 54-61
        Academic perspectives and programs, 57-59
        Publications, 55-57
        Research Institutes and funding, 59-61
        Specific policy fields, 54-55
    Usefulness of comparative studies, 51-54
Conflict resolution, 153-154
Congress, 85, 120, 121
Conservation Foundation, 96
Consumer Products Safety Commission, 110
Consumer protection, 110-111
Consumer Protection Agency, 111
Content analysis, 150-152
Controversial issues in administering public policy, 70-73
Council for European Studies, 95
Council of Social Sciences Data Archives, 127

219

Crime and criminal justice policy, xi, 161-173
　European perspectives on crime control, 168-173
　　International collaboration under the United Nations, 171-172
　　International problem-solving, 172-173
　　Norwegian studies of social control, 169-170
　　United Kingdom research, 170-171
　Policy issues in the United States, 161-168
　Questionnaire surveys, foreign policy, 148-150
　Resources for crime policy studies, 163-168
　　Grant sources, 165
　　Information sources, 166-167
　　Interest groups, 168
　　Journals, 164
　　Nonacademic research institutes, 166
　　Statistical data sources, 167
　　University programs, 165-166
Crime control, European perspectives on, 168-173
Cross-cultural policy studies. *See* comparative public policy
Cross-national policy studies, *See* comparative public policy

Decentralization, 71
Decision theory
　Incremental theory, 72
　Rational model, 72
Delegation selection procedures, state level, 123-124
Democratic National Committee, 123-124
Democratic National Convention, 122
Demographic analysis, 129-130
Denmark, social policy research, 205, 206
De-regulation, 110
Dunn v. Blumstein, 120

Eastern Europe, 144, 172
Economic regulation policy, xi, 109-118
　Basic facilities and institutions, 114-117
　Recent issues, 109-114
　　Agriculture, 114
　　Antitrust, 111-112
　　Consumer protection, 110-111
　　Economic stability, 112-113
　　Energy, 113-114
　　Industrial safety, 111
　　Regulatory commissions, 109-110
Economic stability, 112-113
Economic Stabilization Act, 112
Educational policy, 175-198
　Amish children, 103
　Basic issues and references, 175
　Comparative educational policy, 184-188
　　Elementary and secondary education, 184-188
　　Higher education policy, 118-193
　Equality of educational opportunity, 102-103
　Higher education policy, 182-184
　　Grant sources, 184
　　Journals, 182-183
　　University programs, 183-184
　Politics of elementary and secondary education, 175-176
　Politics of higher education, 176-178
　Resources for the study of education policy, 178-184, 192
　　Data sources, 179-180
　　Elementary and secondary education, 178-182
　　Grant sources, 180-181
　　Interest groups, 181-182
　　Journals, 178-179
　　University programs, 181
Economic Stabilization Act, 112
Effects of government policies, xi
Electoral policy, 119-132
　Basic facilities and institutions, 125-128
　Basic issues and references, 119-125
　　Delegation selection procedures, state level, 123-124
　　Nominating conventions, 123
　　Political assassination, 124-125
　　Political parties, 122-123
　　Role of money in politics, 121-122
　　Voter registration, 119-120
　　Voting research, 121
　Comparative electoral policy, 128-131
　　Demographic analysis, 129-130
　　Electoral surveys, 126, 128-129
　　Parties research, 130-131
Elementary education, 175-176, 178-182, 184-188
Elementary and Secondary Education Act, 175
Elites, 101
　As administrators, 77-79
　Foreign policy leaders, 145-147
Empirical research methods. *See* Research methods
Employment Act of 1946, 112
Energy crisis, 113, 117
Energy policy, 113-114
Environmental perception
　Policy implications, 96
　Social response to hazards, 96
Environmental policy, xi, 87-99
　Basic facilities and institutions, 89-93
　　Journals and periodicals, 90-93

University programs, 89-90
Basic issues and references, 83-89
Bibliographical sources for comparative study of, 97
Comparative research, 93-97
Completed research efforts, 94
Legislative studies, 94
New field of research, 93-94
Ongoing and planned research, 94-95
Research resources: institutions and information, 97
Social and political change in different countries, 94
Equality of educational opportunity, 102-103
Equality revolution, 103-104
Europe
   Bureaucracy and administration, 73-75
   Contributions to theory, 41-45
   Foreign policy data, 139-145
   Perspectives on crime control, 168-173

Federal Mine Health and Safety Act, 111
Federal Trade Commission, 110
Feedback, 65, 66
Finland, 53, 169
First Amendment, 101
Food policy, 114
Foreign policy, xi, 133-160
   Data and analyses of individual countries, 139-145
   Canada, 141
   Cross-national studies, 139
   Eastern Europe, 144
   France, 143
   Germany, 141-143
   Great Britain, 143
   Israel, 143-144
   Italy, 143
   Japan, 144-145
   United States, 139-141
   West Europe, 141
Foreign policy leadership, 145-154
   Behavior, 152-153
   Comparative study of elites, 145-147
   Conflict resolution, 153-154
   Motivations of foreign policy, 152-153
   Peace research, 154-160
     Developmental trends, 155-157
     Literature on peace research, 157-160
   Perspectives of foreign policy leaders, 148-152
     Content analysis, 150-152
     Questionnaire surveys, 148-150
   Public opinion and foreign policy, 134-145
     Nature of public opinion, 134, 135
     Public opinion data on foreign policy, 137-139
     Role of public opinion, 135-136
     Sources of foreign policy attitudes, 136-137
   Social background and foreign policy, 147-148
France, 26, 42, 53, 143
Free speech and civil liberties policy, 101-107
   Basic facilities and institutions, 104-105
   Equality of educational opportunity, 102-103
   Media consequences, 101-102
   Presupposition of tolerant community, 101
   Security publicity, 102
   The equality revolution, 103-104

Germany, 8, 9, 11, 13, 141-143
Grant sources
   Criminal justice policy studies, 165
   Education policy, 180-181, 184
Great Britain, 143

Headstart Program, 18
Health, Education, and Welfare, 27, 199
Higher education policy, 182-184, 188-193
   Politics of, 176-178

Impact evaluation, 65
Income inequality, 204-205
Independent regulatory commissions, 109-110
   Dissatisfaction with, 110
   Life cycle theory of, 109
   New commissions, 110
Industrial safety, 111
Inoyue-Udall Universal Voter Enrollment Act, 121
Institutional growth of policy science, 6-7
Interest groups
   Criminal justice, 168
   Education, 181-182
Institute for Research on Poverty, 203
Intergovernmental Grants in Aid, 72
International collaboration under the United Nations, 171-172
International Consortium for Political Research, 23, 27, 121, 129
International Political Science Association
   Environmental policy panel, 1973, 94
   Specialists on environmental policy, 97
International problem-solving, 172-173
International Sociological Association, 130
Interstate Commerce Commission, 110
Ireland, 52, 53
Inter-University Case Program, Syracuse University, 70
Israel, 143-144

Issues in public policy
   Administering public policy, 70-73
   Criminal justice policy, 161-168
   Economic regulation, 109-114
   Educational policy, 175-198
   Electoral policy, 119-125
   Environmental policy, 83-93
   Peace research, 155-160
   Poverty and welfare policy, 199-208
   Theory, 37-49
Italy, 42, 43, 143

Jail sentences, 112
Japan, 8, 9, 93, 144-145

Land-use policy
   Comparative study, 96
Law Enforcement Assistance Administration, 105, 161, 162, 163
Leadership, foreign policy, 145-154
League of Women Voters, 120
London School of Economics, 59

McGovern-Fraser Commission, 123
Media, consequences of free speech, 101-102
Mental institutions, 104
Methodology. *See* Research methods
Midwest Political Science Association, 177
MIRACODE System, 125
Money in politics, 121-122
Motivation of foreign policy leaders, 152-153

National Crime Commission, 161, 163
National Environmental Protection Act, 111
National Institute for Mental Health, 22, 105
National Municipal League, 120
Negative income taxation, 202, 207
Netherlands, The, 11
New Public Administration, 71
New Zealand, studies in social insurance, 206, 207
Nixon Administration, 112
Nixon Family Assistance Plan, 200
Nominating conventions, 123
Nonacademic research institutes, criminal justice policy, 166
Norway, 169-170
   Studies in social policy, 206

Occupational Health and Safety Act, 111
OECD, 11, 26, 94, 95, 96, 187
Office of Economic Opportunity, 199

Participatory democracy, 101
Peace research, 154-160
Pentagon Papers, 102

Periodicals relevant to policy studies
   Administering public policy, 73, 79-80
   Criminal justice policy, 163-168
   Economic regulation, 114-117
   Educational policy, 175, 178-184, 192
   Electoral policy, 119-128, 130-131
   Environmental policy, 83-97
   Foreign policy, 139-145
   Free speech and civil liberties, 101-107
   Peace research, 155-160
   Policy studies in Britain, 55-57
   Poverty and welfare, 199-208
Planning
   Administering public policy, 76-77
   International problem-solving, 172-173
Policy impact analysis, 19, 20
Policy science, 3-16. *See also* Public Policy
   Challenge, 4-6
   Developments outside U. S., 12-13
   Institutional growth, 6-12
Policy Studies Directory, xiii
Policy Studies Journal, xiii, 23
Policy Studies Organization, xi, xii, xiii
Political assassination, 124-125
Political parties, 122-123
   Research, 130-131
Political role of elite administrators, 77-79
Political science, xi, xii, 177
Politics-policy distinction, 12-13
Politics, role of money in, 121-122
Politics of elementary and secondary education, 175-176
Politics of higher education, 176-178
Pollution, air, 87, 96
Pornography, effects of, 102
Post-behavioral movement, xii
Poverty and welfare policy, xi, 199-208
   Basic facilities and institutions, 202-204
   Comparative poverty and welfare policy, 204-208
      Income inequality, 204-205
      Social insurance, 205-206
      Social policy analysis, 206-208
Prescriptive approach, 3, 4, 5
Price and wage controls, 112-113
Prison reform, 103, 167, 169-170
Problems in cross-national policy research, 28-29
Program-Planning-Budgeting Systems, 72
Public administration, 69-70, 71
Public Choice Society, 39
Public law, 19, 20
Public opinion, 101, 126
   Foreign policy, 134-145
      In regions and countries, 139-145
      Nature of, 134-135

On foreign policy, 136-139
Role in foreign policy, 135-136
Public policy
  Administration of, 69-80
  Challenge, 4-6
  Comparative, 12-13, 24-25, 28-29, 51-67, 69-80, 93-97, 123-131, 139-147, 168-173, 184-188, 204-208
  Crime and criminal justice policy, 161-173
  Economic regulation, 109-118
  Educational policy, 175-198
  Electoral policy, 119-132
  Environmental policy, 87-99
  Foreign policy, 133-160
  Free speech and civil liberties, 102-107
  Institutional growth of, 6-7
  Poverty and welfare, 199-208
  Theory, 37-49
  Publications, policy studies, 10-12, 22-23, 37-39, 55-57, 73, 79-80, 83-97, 109-118, 119-128, 130-131, 139-145, 155-160, 163-168, 175, 178-184, 192, 199-208
Publicity, security, 102

Racial prejudice, 102
Railroad rate regulation, 110
RAND, 7, 8, 12 .
RANN, 23
Recreation, 87
Registration, voter, 119-120
Regulation, economic, 109-118
Regulatory commissions, 109-110
Relations between policy and administrators, 69-70
Research institutes for policy studies, 7-8, 9-10, 21-22, 89-90, 97, 165-166, 181, 183-184
Research methods, xi, xii, 17-35
  Administering public policy, 75-76
  Comparative study of public policy, 12-13, 24-25
    Comparative process model, 61-66
  Content analysis, 150-152
  Electoral surveys, 128-129
  Environmental research, 93-97
  Foreign policy, 139-145
  Political parties, 130-131
  Poverty and welfare, 202-208
  Questionnaire surveys, foreign policy, 148-150
  Resources for public policy analysis, 21-24, 54-61
    Data sources, 23-24, 27-28
    Funding, 23
    Periodicals, 22-23
    Research centers, 7-8, 21-22

  Substantive policy research areas, 25-27
  Trends and issues in empirical research, 17-21
  Types of cross-national analysis, 27-29
Research in public policy, 114-117
Research sources
  Administering public policy, 73, 79-80
  Crime and criminal justice policy, 163-168
  Economic regulation, 114-117
  Educational policy, 175, 178-184, 192
  Electoral policy, 119-128, 130-131
  Environmental policy, 83-97
  Foreign policy, 139-145
  Free speech and civil liberties, 101-107
  Peace research, 155-160
  Policy studies in Britain, 54-61
  Poverty and welfare, 202-204
Resources for the Future, 41
Role of money in politics, 121-122
Role of public opinion in foreign policy, 135-136
Russell Sage Foundation, 105

Safety, industrial, 111
Scandinavia, 52
Secondary education, 175-176, 178-182, 184-188
Secrecy, 12
Security publicity, 102
Social background and foreign policy, 147-148
Social change, 101
Social control, 62, 169-170
Social experimentation, 5
Social insurance, 205-206
Social policy analysis, 25, 26, 206-208
  Meaning, 204
Social Security Administration, 199
Society for the Study of Social Problems, xiii
Sources of foreign policy attitudes, 136-137
Soviet Union, 188
Stability, economic, 112, 113
Stagflation, 113
State delegation selection procedures, 123-124
State Department, 27
Statistical data sources, criminal justice policy, 167
Substantive policy research areas, 25-27, 37-49, 69-80, 87-99, 102-107, 109-132, 139-145, 161-173, 175-198
Supreme Court, 19, 103, 120
Survey Research Center, 121, 127
Surveys, electoral, 128-129

Sweden, studies in income inequality, 204-205, 206

Task Force on Assassination and Political Violence, 124
Theory of public policy, 37-49
  Basic facilities and institutions, 39-41
  Basic issues and references, 37-39
  European contributions, 41-45
Tolerance of community for free speech, 101

UNESCO
  MAB Project, 13, 96
United Kingdom, 54-61, 170-71
Uniform Crime Reports, 161
United Nations, 27, 28, 171-172
  Comparative study on environmental policy, 94
University programs
  Criminal justice studies, 165-166
Education policy, 181, 183-184
Environmental policy, 89-90, 97
General policy science, 9-10
Urban Institute, 22, 41
Usefulness of comparative studies, 51-54

Venezuela, 9
Vietnam War, xii, 114
Violence, 101, 102
Voter registration, 119-120
Voting research, 121
Voting Rights Act, 120

Warren Court, 103
Water quality management
  Comparison of techniques, 96
Welfare policy, 199-208
Western Europe, 41-45, 73-75, 139-145, 168-173

Yearbooks in Politics and Public Policy, xiii

About the Contributors

James E. Anderson is a professor and chairman of the department of political science at the University of Houston. His publications include *Politics and the Economy* (1966); *Texas Politics: An Introduction* (1971); *The Emergence of the Modern Regulatory State* (1962); and *Political and Economic Policy Making* (1970). He is an editor for the *Policy Studies Journal* and the *Social Science Quarterly*.

John Conrad is a Senior Fellow of the Academy for Contemporary Problems and Adjunct Professor of Sociology at the Ohio State University. From 1969 to 1972 he was Chief of the Center for Crime Prevention and Rehabilitation in the National Institute of Law Enforcement and Criminal Justice. His international survey of correctional practice, *Crime and Its Correction,* was published by the University of California Press in 1965.

Thomas J. Cook is an associate professor of political science at the University of Illinois at Chicago Circle. He was Principal Investigator on an NSF grant evaluating volunteer programs, and has served as a consultant on program evaluation to federal, state, and local governments. He serves on the editorial boards of *The Experimental Study of Politics* and the *Policy Studies Journal*.

William J. Crotty is a professor of political science at Northwestern University. He is the author of *Party Reform* (Basic Books, forthcoming) and *Political Reform* (Intext, forthcoming) and the author, coauthor and editor of a number of other books and articles. He has held the American Political Science Association Fellowship and he served as Co-Director of the Task Force on Assassinations of the National Commission on the Causes and Prevention of Violence.

Alfred Diamant is a professor of political science and chairperson of the West European Studies Program at Indiana University. He has contributed chapters to several volumes of the Comparative Administration Group and has published articles dealing with various aspects of the French higher bureaucracy in quarterly journals in the U.S. and Great Britain. He is engaged in a study of the policy-making role of the West German *Ministerialburokratie,* with special emphasis on social and welfare policies.

Yehezkel Dror is a professor of political science and Director of Public Administration Programs at the Hebrew University of Jerusalem. This year he is on a sabbatical with the London School of Economics and Political Science. He has been a Fellow at the Center of Advanced Study in the Behavioral Sciences, Palo Alto; a senior staff member of the RAND Corporation, Santa Monica and of the New York-Rand Institute; and a consultant on policymaking and policy research to various institutions, governments and international organizations. His main books include *Public Policymaking Reexamined, Design for Policy Sciences, Ventures in Policy Sciences* and *Crazy States*. He is also working on a text in policy analysis and a study on top-level governmental decisionmaking.

H. George Frederickson is Dean of the College of Public and Community Services, University of Missouri-Columbia. He is editor of *SAGE Professional Papers in Administrative and Policy Studies* and editor of the Research and Reports section of the *Public Administration Review*. His writings have appeared in the *International Review of Administrative Sciences, Administrative Science Quarterly, Western Political Science Quarterly, National Civic Review, Public Management*, and the *Public Administration Review*.

John A. Gardiner is head of the Department of Political Science of the University of Illinois at Chicago Circle. He served as Assistant Director of the National Institute of Law Enforcement and Criminal Justice. He is the author of *Traffic and the Police* and *The Politics of Corruption*, and coeditor of *Theft of the City: Readings on Corruption in Urban America*, and *Crime and Criminal Justice: Issues in Public Policy Analysis*.

Samuel K. Gove is Director of the Institute of Government and Public Affairs and a professor of political science at the University of Illinois, Urbana-Champaign. His most recent relevant article is entitled "Research on Higher Education Administration and Policy: An Uneven Report" and was published in the January/February 1975 *Public Administration Review*. He has written several other articles on the topic of the politics of higher education.

Hugh Heclo is a staff member of the Brookings Institution and is directing a project on the 'Political Control of Bureaucracy' in Washington. He has taught in British and American universities. In 1969-70 he was on the staff of the Vice President and in 1971 served as a consultant to the British Department of Health and Social Security. His recent books are *The Private Government of Public Money and Modern Social Politics in Britain and Sweden*.

Samuel Krislov is professor of political science and professor of law,

University of Minnesota. He is the author of *The Supreme Court and Political Freedom,* a volume in the Free Press Series on the Supreme Court in American Life which he edited. He has served as editor of the *Law and Society Review* and is currently President of the Law and Society Association and President-elect of the Midwest Political Science Association.

Lennart J. Lundqvist is an assistant professor at the Department of Political Science of Uppsala University. Since 1974 he has served as a Special Consultant to *AMBIO–The Royal Swedish Academy of Sciences Journal of the Environmental Research and Management.* His publications include *Miljovardsforvaltning och politisk struktur* (Lund: Prisma 1971); "Swedens National Physical Planning for Resources Management," Environmental Affairs (1972); "Environmental Quality and Politics: Some Notes on Political Development in 'Developed' Countries," *Social Science Information* XII:2 (1973); as well as several others, some of which are mentioned in his contribution to this volume.

Dean E. Mann is a professor of political science at the University of California, Santa Barbara. He is an author of books and articles on water policy, environmental policy, with particular reference to the arid Southwestern United States. In 1970-71, he was chief of the Social and Behavioral Sciences Division of the National Water Commission. He is the principal investigator of the Lake Powell Research Project.

Theodore Marmor, the author of *Politics of Medicare,* is an associate professor of American Politics at the University of Chicago. He has written about health and welfare politics generally and is a consultant to several governmental agencies. Professor Marmor is doing research on the politics of national health insurance at the University of Chicago's Center for Health Administration Studies.

Richard L. Merritt is a professor of political science and communications at the University of Illinois at Urbana-Champaign. His work has been in the fields of international communications, quantitative cross-national research, and political integration, with special reference to Berlin and Germany. He has authored or edited several books, including *Symbols of American Community, Comparing Nations, Communication in International Politics,* and *France, Germany and the Western Alliance.* He is coeditor of *SAGE Professional Papers in Comparative Politics.*

Vincent Ostrom is a professor of political science associated with the Workshop in Political Theory and Policy Analysis at Indiana University,

Bloomington. His most recent publications include *Understanding Urban Government: Metropolitan Reform Reconsidered* (with Robert Bish); *The Intellectual Crisis in American Public Administration*; and *The Political Theory of a Compound Republic*.

Michael D. Reagan is a professor of political science and Dean of Social Sciences at the University of California, Riverside. He is the author of *The New Federalism, Science and the Federal Patron,* and *The Managed Economy,* and is the editor of *The Administration of Public Policy*. Applications of the social sciences to social policy research are his present focus of interest.

Richard Rose is a professor of politics at the University of Strathclyde, Glasgow, since 1966. He is the author or editor of more than a dozen books in the field of comparative politics. He is Secretary to the Committee on Political Sociology, International Political Science Association & International Sociological Association, and head of a CPS Work Group on Comparative Public Policy, whose publications include *The Management of Urban Change in Britain & Germany*, (1974, Urban Affairs Book Club choice), and *The Dynamics of Public Policy* (forthcoming).

Philip Sabetti is an assistant professor of political science at McGill University. His work is concerned with political theory and its application to public policy analysis.

Barbara G. Salmore is an assistant professor of political science at Drew University, where she teaches undergraduate and graduate courses in Comparative Public Policy. Her other publications relevant to policy studies include coauthorship of *Creon: A Foreign Events Data Set,* (1973), *Alternative Explanations of Foreign Policy Behavior,* (1975), and "Politics, Economics, and Social Security Programs: A Cross-National Analysis," in *New Dimensions in Comparative Politics* (forthcoming).

Stephen A. Salmore is an associate professor of political science at Rutgers University. For the past four years he has been the Director of the New Jersey Poll, conducted by the Eagleton Institute at Rutgers University. The Poll is primarily oriented toward the study of public attitudes toward state politics and policy in New Jersey. He is also a Principal Investigator in the Comparative Research on the Events of Nations (CREON) Project, which is concerned with developing multi-causal explanations of the foreign policy behavior of nations.

Frank P. Scioli, Jr. is an associate professor of political science at the

University of Illinois at Chicago Circle and Director of the Ph.D. program in Public Policy Analysis. He is co-principal investigator of a National Science Foundation (RANN Division) project evaluating volunteer programs and also research associate on a project studying tall buildings. He is coeditor of the *Journal for Experimental Study of Politics* and of the *Policy Studies Journal*. He has served as a consultant to federal, state, and local agencies.

William G. Walker is a professor of education, Head of the Centre for Administrative Studies and Dean of the Faculty of Education at the University of New England, Armidale, New South Wales, Australia. He is editor of the *Journal of Educational Administration,* general editor of the University of Queensland Press *Series in Education Administration and Organization* and is President of the international Commonwealth Council for Educational Administration. Dr. Walker is the author, coauthor, or editor of a dozen books concerned with educational administration and governance. The *Walker Lecture,* an annual lecture sponsored by the South-East England Group of the British Educational Administration Society, is named in his honour.

Geoffrey Wandesforde-Smith is an assistant professor and Vice-Chairman in the Department of Political Science and the Division of Environmental Studies, University of California, Davis. He is coeditor of and contributor to *Congress and the Environment* and is the author of articles in *Policy Studies Journal, Public Administration Review, Stanford Law Review,* and other journals. He is also a member of the Tahoe Research Group at Davis and a member of the Science Advisory Panel created by the National Science Foundation to review research on environmental problems in the Lake Tahoe Basin.

Frederick M. Wirt is Director of the Policy Sciences Graduate Program at the University of Maryland at Baltimore. The policy studies he has authored include: *Politics of Southern Equality,* and *Power In the City*; he has coauthored *The Political Web of American Schools* and *On the City's Rim*. He is editor of *The Polity in the School* (forthcoming).

About the Editor

Stuart S. Nagel is a professor of political science at the University of Illinois. He is the coordinator of the *Policy Studies Journal* and the secretary-treasurer of the Policy Studies Organization. He is the author or editor of *Policy Studies and the Social Sciences* (Heath, Lexington Books, 1975), *Improving the Legal Process: Effects of Alternatives* (Heath, Lexington Books, 1975), *Environmental Politics* (Praeger, 1974), *The Rights of the Accused: In Law and Action* (Sage, 1972), and *The Legal Process from a Behavioral Perspective* (Dorsey, 1969). Dr. Nagel has held fellowships from the LEAA National Institute, Yale Law and Social Science Program, National Science Foundation, Center for Advanced Study in the Behavioral Sciences, Social Science Research Council, and the East-West Center. He has been an attorney to the U. S. Senate Subcommittee on Administrative Practice and Procedure, Office of Economic Opportunity, Lawyer's Constitutional Defense Committee in Mississippi, and the National Labor Relations Board.